Love, Abe

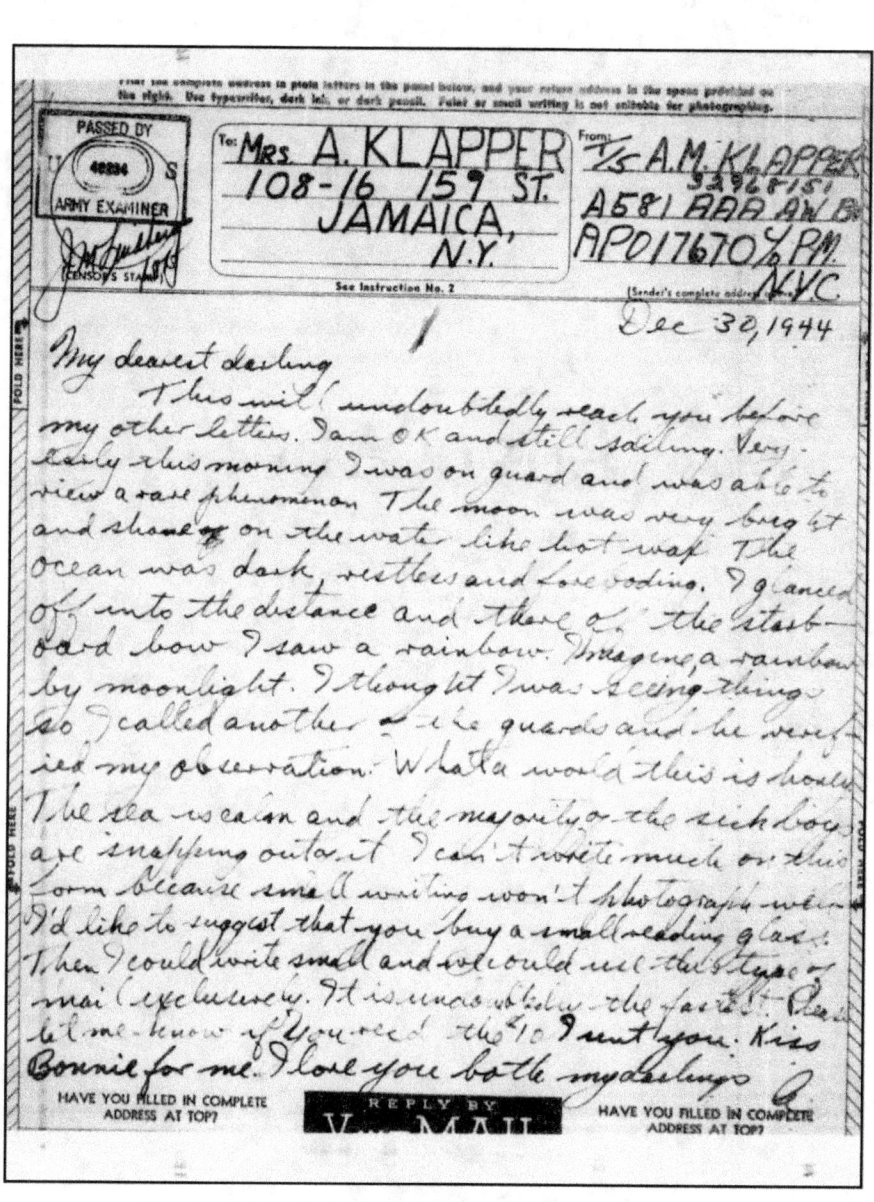

First V-mail my father mailed to my mother while onboard
the transport ship to Europe, December 1944.

Love, Abe

A JEWISH GI'S WORLD WAR II LETTERS HOME

BONNIE KLAPPER GOLDENBERG

Sunset Hills Press

Thousand Oaks, California

Copyright © 2022 by Bonnie K. Goldenberg

All rights reserved. No part of this book may be reproduced in any form on or by an electronic or mechanical means, including information storage and retrieval systems, without the prior written permission of the copyright owner, except for the use of brief quotations in a book review.

Published by Sunset Hills Press in the United States of America.
Sunset Hills Press and associated logos are trademarks of Sunset Hills Press.

To request permissions, contact the publisher at:
Sunset Hills Press
2626 Lavery Ct., Suite 307
Newbury Park, CA 91320
www.bonniegoldenberg.com

First edition

Project Management by Markman Editorial Services, www.marlamarkman.com
Editing by Tammy Ditmore, eDitmore Editorial Services, https://editmore.com
Book Design by Glen Edelstein, Hudson Valley Book Design, www.hudsonvalleybookdesign.com

Cover Photo: Lillian and Abraham Klapper hold firstborn daughter, Bonnie, in March 1944. Abraham was visiting his family in New York while on a much-appreciated furlough from training at Camp Stewart, Georgia.

Publisher's Cataloging-in-Publication Data

Names: Goldenberg, Bonnie Klapper, author.
Title: Love, Abe: a Jewish GI's World War II letters home / Bonnie Klapper Goldenberg.
Description: Includes bibliographical references and index. | Thousand Oaks, CA: Sunset Hills Press, 2022.
Identifiers: LCCN: 2021917186 | ISBN: 978-1-7377379-0-2 (paperback) | 978-1-7377379-1-9 (ebook)
Subjects: LCSH Klapper, Abraham M., 1915-2004. | Klapper, Lillian S., 1920-2006. | United States. Army. Anti-Aircraft Artillery Battalion, 581st--Biography. | World War, 1939-1945--Personal narratives, Jewish. | World War, 1939-1945--Personal narratives, American. | World War, 1939-1945--Participation, Jewish. | Jewish soldiers--United States--Biography. | World War, 1939-1945--Campaigns & battles--Germany. | BISAC HISTORY / Military / World War II | BIOGRAPHY & AUTOBIOGRAPHY / Military | BIOGRAPHY & AUTOBIOGRAPHY / Jewish
Classification: LCC D769.343 581st 2022 | DDC 940.54/1273092--dc23

Printed in the United States of America

To My Parents

Abraham Martin Klapper (1915–2004)
T5, 581st AAA AW Battalion, A Battery,
49th AAA Brigade, First Army

Lillian Schein Klapper (1920–2006), RN

and

To the memory of those who served so honorably with my father
in the 581st, the "Rock of Remagen"

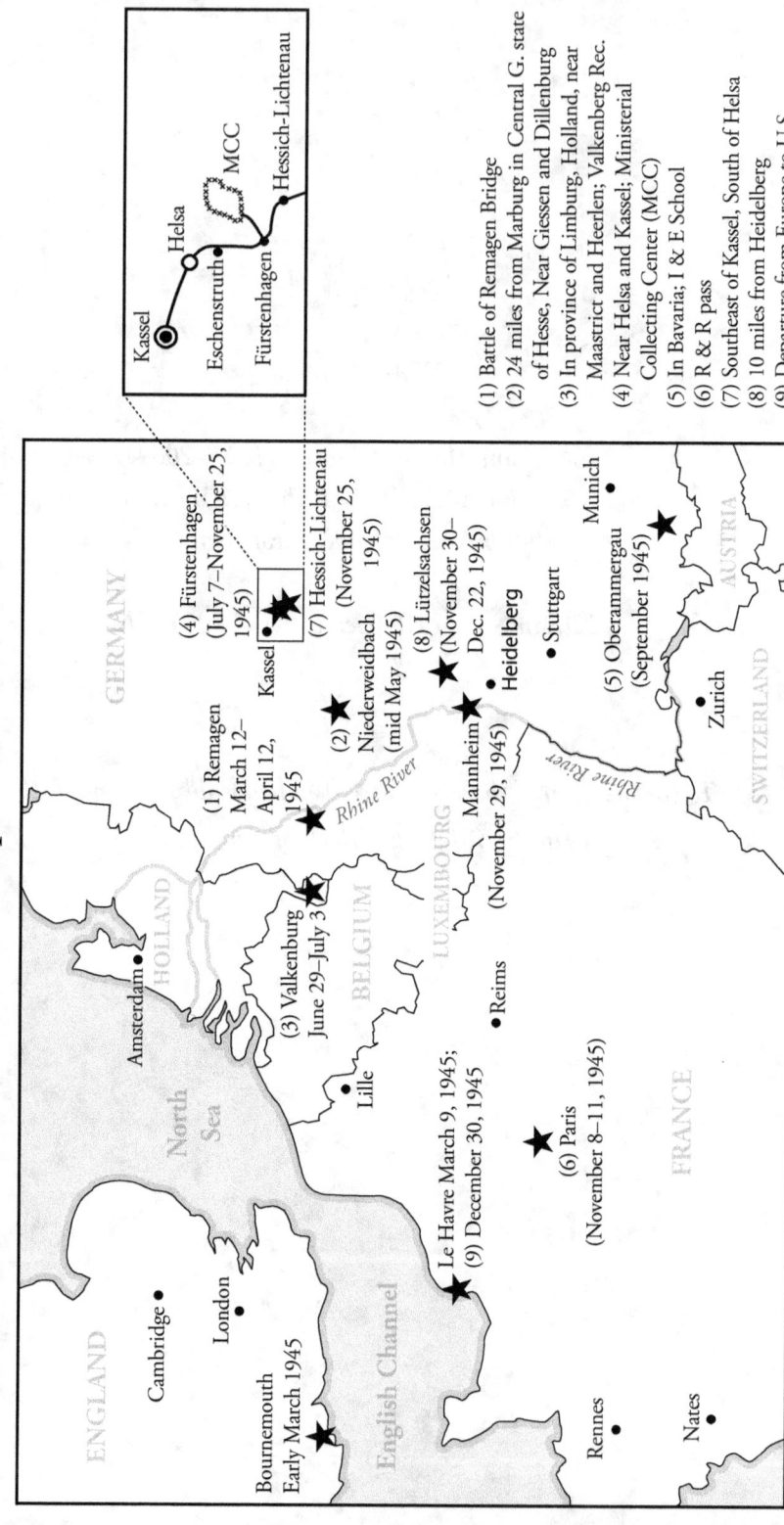

Abe Klapper's Army Service in Continental Europe, March–December 1945

CONTENTS

Preface		1
1	A Wartime Courtship	5
2	Camp Upton, New York, to Fort Eustis, Virginia	13
3	Camp Stewart, Georgia	41
4	Cherokee Homes, Port Wentworth, Georgia	55
5	Furlough, Return to Camp Stewart, D-Day!	63
6	Awaiting Overseas Deployment	75
7	On a Transport Ship—Destination Unknown	87
8	The "British Isles"	95
9	France, the Remagen Front, a Passover Seder in Germany	105
10	Death of Roosevelt, Moving Through the Countryside	121
11	V-E Day in Occupied Germany	129
12	Occupied Germany, Visit to Holland	145
13	Guarding the MCC Near Helsa	165
14	Hiroshima, Nagasaki, Victory Over Japan	193
15	Waiting It Out at Fifty-Eight Points	215
16	Oberammergau, I & E School	223
17	"Till the End of Time," October 1945	231
18	Pass to Paris, Farewell 581st, November 1945	247
19	"Processing," in Limbo, Death of Patton, December 1945	265
20	Emergency Furlough, Home!	277
Epilogue		283
Notes		301
Appendix: "D-Day, 60th Anniversary, Thousand Oaks, CA"		323
Selected Bibliography		327
Acknowledgments		331
Index		335
About the Author		345

Love, Abe

PREFACE

I KNEW MY FATHER WAS a WWII veteran, and that he had been mostly away from our family until I was about two and a half years old. Over the years, an occasional story about his war experience and discharge popped up in family conversations, but I had no more than a general interest in that war and no real knowledge about the role my father had played in it. Then, in 2003, my mother handed me several tattered shopping bags full of letters my father had written her while he served in the U.S. Army during World War II. With a secretive smile, Mom told me she had removed her letters from the cache. My siblings and I had never heard my parents mention their wartime correspondence, and none of us had any idea these letters existed. I found the prospect of sorting and reading the pile of letters daunting, so I did not even start until early 2005, about six months after my father died.

Contrary to what Mom had told me, I did find several months' worth of her letters mixed in with Dad's, but my sisters and I never found any more that she had written, even while clearing out her condo after her death in 2006. Perhaps Dad was not able to save more of Mom's letters because he did not have room to store them, especially from the time he sailed to Europe with his battalion and during his service there, which stretched from the end of December 1944 until he returned to the U.S. in January 1946.

In retrospect, I regret that I did not read all of the letters while my parents were still alive, because they raised so many questions that cannot be answered now. Maybe I was unable to read them until after Dad died because I thought it would be an invasion of my parents' privacy. Although much of my parents' correspondence was intensely personal, I feel—and I assume my mother must have also felt—that a good part of their experience belongs to the history of World War II and so deserves to be shared with the public.

Many books based on letters from World War II have been written, but this collection is unique in several ways: the large volume of letters; the viewpoint of the author, a first-generation Jewish-American; and the detailed description of daily life of U.S. soldiers and others living in Germany in the months immediately following the Allied occupation. In addition, Dad could communicate in German, so he often acted as his unit's interpreter, which gave him insights into the lives of the German civilians he met.

Dad wrote to Mom almost daily for two and a half years, sometimes more than once a day. The only exceptions were when he was in combat or when they were together stateside. As a result, the shopping bags my mom handed me held 835 letters, including a few months of Mom's letters to Dad.

In addition to the letters they wrote during Dad's service, the collection also contains letters from their courtship and dozens of letters and cards from Dad's sisters, other relatives, and friends. Dad also clipped and sent home several articles, letters to the editor, and cartoons from *Yank*, the popular GI weekly newsmagazine published by the Army during the war and early occupation of Germany and Japan, until the end of December 1945.

To supplement the material Mom handed me, my sister Jonni gave me access to memorabilia she rescued from my parents' garage in Florida, including many photos from Dad's service. Two wooden boxes made for Dad by a German civilian worker held a fascinating assortment of military documents and souvenirs, including a pair of wooden shoes he had found in Germany. When my siblings and I were children, he had explained to us that these were not from Holland, but that some civilians in Germany had worn wooden shoes during the war because leather was reserved for the soldiers.

Dad was a first-generation Jewish-American whose parents had emigrated from Russia, and his letters reflect the experiences of a

Jewish soldier fighting in Nazi Germany. While contending with the vicious anti-Semitism of the Nazi regime, he also faced prejudice on the home front, as well.

Dad's letters cover the end of the war in Europe through the end of December 1945, including his service in occupied Germany, months that have not been as thoroughly portrayed in popular history books and movies. My father provides an eyewitness account to everyday life just after the occupation by U.S. forces in Germany, an account made richer because his fluency in German (ironically made easier because of his knowledge of Yiddish) allowed him to communicate with the civilian population and POWs. He also wrote about postwar France and Holland, which he visited when he was on a pass or short leaves from duty.

This book took a long time to complete, partly due to its emotional toll. When I began to read the letters in 2005, I was still deeply grieving Dad's death and often felt torn between wanting to hear his voice again and being too overcome to continue reading. After Mom died in October 2006, it became even more painful. Sometimes, I felt like just leaving the collection in those shopping bags. However, I realized I could not pass this task to anyone else. The responsibility for chronicling my parents' wartime experiences had fallen on me, and I did not want to disappoint. So, after too many years, here is their story, one that was unique to Abraham and Lillian Klapper but also shared by millions of those who served in World War II and their families at home.

CHAPTER 1

A Wartime Courtship

ABRAHAM KLAPPER WAS TWENTY-SIX when he met twenty-one-year-old Lillian Schein in the summer of 1941. His family was visiting Far Rockaway, New York, a beach town on the western end of Long Island that was popular with working-class families trying to escape the summer heat of New York City. They went to the beach to swim, sit on the sand, or just breathe the clean ocean air. The ones who could afford it would rent bungalows or rooms in private homes and boarding houses near the beach.

Relatives of Dad's married sister, Sylvia, were renting rooms in Mom's parents' house for the summer, and Dad, his parents, and his kid sister, Shirley, had come to visit them. Everyone was sitting on the front porch while Dad was out on the street with Shirley teaching her to ride a bike on a hill near the front of the house. He was holding on to the seat while she tried to balance herself when he saw a young woman in a pretty dress come out to the porch. Their eyes met, and Dad told Shirley she would have to figure it out herself as he hurried over to introduce himself.

They were a classic example of "opposites attract." Dad had blue eyes, light brown hair, and a strong athletic build. He loved to work out on gymnastics equipment at the 92nd Street YMHA (Young Men's Hebrew Association) in Manhattan, swim in the pool at the St. George Hotel in Brooklyn, and play handball in city parks. Although he had been forced to drop out of high school to help support his family, he had earned his diploma by attending George Washington Evening High School while working during the day.

In the summer of 1941, Dad was a mail clerk at the post office, a job he had earned by outscoring many "college boys" on a civil service exam. He was self-educated, an avid reader, and loved all kinds of music, including classical and the big bands that were popular then. A good dancer, he and Shirley liked jitterbugging together. He was also artistic and was attending drafting courses at night.

Mom was petite, with silky black hair and big brown eyes. Dad would open his early letters to her by writing, "Hello, Brown Eyes." She had attended Queens College of the City University of New York for about a year and was completing her registered nurse's training at Cumberland Hospital's School of Nursing in Brooklyn.

In their later letters, it became clear that in addition to their strong physical attraction, they also admired each other's intelligence. Mom loved that Dad was so well-read and articulate. Dad respected Mom's educational achievement and ambition. Mom also liked his generous spirit, having rejected an earlier "college boy" suitor for being "cheap."

Both were the children of Jewish immigrants from eastern Europe. Mom's father, Marcus, worked as an insurance agent for the Metropolitan Insurance Company. Her mother, Sophie, raised her children, rented out rooms in the house, and sometimes worked as a department store salesclerk or as a cook in hotel kitchens in the Catskill Mountains in the summer. When I was growing up in Far Rockaway, Sophie worked at the candy counter of a local movie theater, and generations of children learned she would sometimes slip free candy to kids who had no money to pay for it. As a *Galitzianer* (the term for Jews from her part of eastern Europe), she lived up to their reputation for always seeming to earn money, even under the most adverse circumstances. One summer, she rented several rooms in a big house on the beach, squeezed her family into a single room, and sublet the other rooms, earning enough of a profit to make a down payment on her own house that fall.

Dad's father, Louis, ran a small "malt and hops" shop, where customers could purchase ingredients to make their own alcoholic beverages during Prohibition. Unfortunately, his store was located too close to a church, so the authorities eventually shut it down. But he never made much of a profit anyway, partly because he was always taking cash out of the till to give to the local synagogue or other causes. Because he was an observant Jew, he refused to keep the shop open on Saturdays, which was typically the busiest day for such a business. After he was forced to close the shop, he worked as a sewing machine operator in a dress factory doing piecework for an owner who had agreed to let him take off Saturdays and work on Sundays instead. The work paid very poorly.

Dad's mother, Miriam, called by her Yiddish name Mierke, had been apprenticed as a child in Belorussia (now known as Belarus) to become a seamstress, and she continued that work in New York. She was so talented that customers would take her to fancy stores to point out garments they liked so that she could make them an exact copy. As was the custom, she stopped working when she married and began to have children, even though it meant the family struggled financially, sometimes finding it hard to scrape up rent money when the landlord came calling. They expected their children to help support them, so both Dad and Shirley had dropped out of high school as soon as they were old enough.

By the time Mom and Dad met, the world was already at war, and it overshadowed everything. Dad had been granted a deferment because he was supporting his family. Mom was contemplating joining the Red Cross, Army, or Navy when she completed her nurse's training. As their relationship deepened, so did the opposition from both sets of parents. Mom's parents were hoping she would marry a doctor—or at least a college-educated professional man—and were unhappy that she would settle for a man with only a high school education who came from a poor, uneducated, and apparently unambitious family.

Dad's parents were afraid they would lose his financial support, and that he would lose his draft deferment if he married. As the only son, he felt a strong obligation to his family, and my parents actually broke up over the issue. In disgust, Mom told him, "Go back to your mother." However, he could not stay away for very long and asked to see her again after a couple of months.

Facing so much opposition from both families, Abraham and Lillian decided to elope. At the end of October 1942, they took their premarital blood tests. Mom was living in a nurses' residence on East 77th Street in Manhattan, and Dad listed his parents' address on West 99th Street. They were married on November 5, 1942, by a rabbi in the Bronx, with the rabbi's wife and another stranger as their only witnesses. Before they broke the news, Mom wore a Band-Aid over her wedding ring at work. At first, they shared an apartment in Greenwich Village with Dad's married cousin Marty Ellman. According to my dad's sister Shirley, my parents just "disappeared," and their families did not know where they were for a couple of weeks.

Before too long, they rented an apartment in the Village on Sullivan Street. Dad's sister Sylvia sent a telegram to that address on November 18, 1942, offering congratulations. On a postcard dated a week later, Dad's paternal aunt Ceil wrote that she had spoken to his father and "things seem to be much smoother and brighter" than before. She said she was doing her best to help.

My parents knew their marriage would end Dad's deferment, which had been based on his financial support for his mother and Shirley. After his marriage, the Army would not consider him part of his original family unit, so rather than wait to be drafted, Dad decided to enlist. Although Mom protested his decision, Dad felt he had more options this way. In a letter he wrote to her after he entered the service, Dad explained that if he had waited to be drafted, he could have been sent into the infantry, where the mortality figures were higher than in other more skilled units.

On May 27, 1943, just a little more than six months after my parents had been married, the Army sent Dad an "Order to Report for Induction" at his local draft board on Broadway in Manhattan at 6 a.m. on June 11, 1943. On that date, he received an order calling him to active duty at Camp Upton, New York, on June 25, 1943. That order also included instructions about military rules, possessions he could bring with him, life insurance, and "Information on Servicemen's Dependents Allowance." The last was more important than ever, because in addition to his mother, sister, and wife, Dad now had to worry about supporting a child, because Mom had become pregnant and was due in August.

My parents gave up their apartment in the Village about a month or so before Dad's induction date and moved in with Mom's parents in Far Rockaway in an attempt to save money. The move would also make it easier for Mom's parents to help her with the impending birth and childcare.

After being married for only seven months, Dad reported for induction on June 25, 1943. It was the beginning of what Mom would later describe as "two long, terrible years."

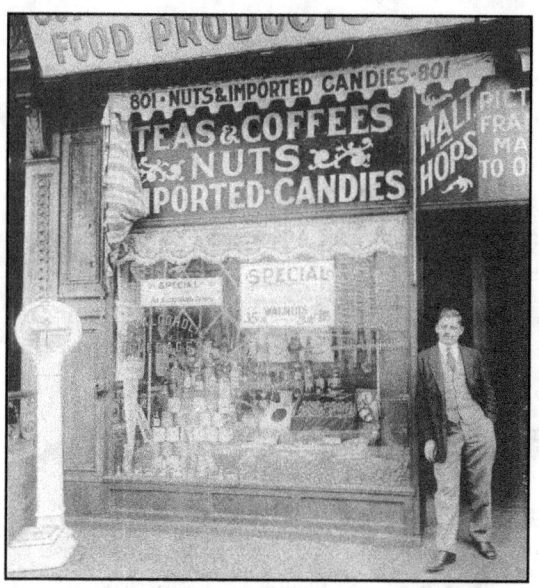

Dad (on the left) with his friends in Manhattan, age 19, 1934.

Dad's father, Louis Klapper, in front of his "malt and hops" shop during Prohibition, where Dad worked as a youngster. These ingredients were purchased by customers who wanted to make their own beer. It was eventually closed down by the police, partly because it was located near a church that had objected to its presence.

Dad enjoys a swim, probably at the St. George Hotel in Brooklyn, 1937.

Mom in her early twenties before meeting Dad.

Mom in nursing school, Cumberland Hospital, Brooklyn, New York, ca. 1941.

Mom's nursing school graduation photo, ca. February 1942. Mom had inscribed this photo to Dad "With all my love, darling. Lil."

Mom's nursing certificate from the City of New York, September 3, 1942.

Mom's RN license from the State of New York after completing her training, December 16, 1942. Although she had already married Dad, the license is in her maiden name.

Mom and Dad's marriage certificate, November 5, 1942. Note signatures of witnesses, the rabbi's wife and a stranger.

Dad's order on June 11, 1943, to report for active duty into the U.S. Army on June 25, 1943. In anticipation of the order, he and Mom had already given up their own apartment in Manhattan and moved in with Mom's parents in Far Rockaway.

CHAPTER 2

Camp Upton, New York, to Fort Eustis, Virginia

ON JUNE 25, 1943, the Long Island Railroad delivered Dad to Camp Upton on Long Island, the first stop for inducted servicemen from New York City. Upton, near Yaphank, was about a two-hour train ride and a different world from Pennsylvania Station in Manhattan. After immunizations, classification tests, and his first Army "grub," Dad wrote Mom and asked her to send along his furlough bag and white T-shirts. "Very limited facilities" would make phone calls difficult, he warned her, but Dad still promised to try.

He enclosed a document from the Red Cross that included his serial number and told her the Red Cross would be the link between them. The document advised Mom that a Red Cross home service worker was available to help with advice on allotments, allowances, budgets, and personal and family problems. The Red Cross material also relayed instructions for requesting leaves and provided tips for what the family should do in an emergency. Dad signed his first letter home, "Love, Abe," which he would later shorten to "Love, A," on his many letters to follow.

Five days later, while waiting to be sent to his training base, Dad finally had time to write a detailed letter about all the "processing" that the Army had been providing at Upton. He described the strict instructions for making and unmaking beds, explained how he had learned to call the food "chow," and mentioned the "short arm inspection," where all the men were examined for venereal diseases.

(By this time in the war, those found to be infected would still be inducted, but they would be treated before being sent to active duty.)

The most important processing task was to take classification examinations, which were used to determine assignments. The AGCT (Army General Classification Test) measured general learning, vocabulary, and arithmetic and used the "block-counting test." The higher the score, the better the chance for specialized or technical training. Since Dad had worked in the post office in civilian life, he was initially classified as a postal clerk.

Uniforms were also passed out at Upton, and Dad, who came from a poor family, was impressed. "I never wore such good shoes," he wrote. "The uniforms and field jackets and raincoat are of excellent quality."

The Army took seriously its role in instructing the men how to deal with sex while they were in the service. In WWI, thousands of servicemen per day had been lost to duty because of venereal diseases. Although awareness-raising efforts and better medical treatments had greatly reduced those numbers by mid-1944, in 1943, "a case of gonorrhea required a hospital treatment of 30 days, and curing syphilis remained a six-month ordeal," according to the WW2 US Medical Research Centre. Dad wanted Mom to know about the Army's war on venereal disease.

June 30, 1943

> Oh, yes, on Saturday we also were addressed by a chaplain on religion and abstinence from temptation by a Colonel on Army law and by a doctor on sex hygiene. You notice that I seem to stress sex, but it is nothing to the way they stress it around here. Signs all over the place.

His first K.P. assignment was to wash dishes and mop the floor. Although he hated it, he was fascinated to see how the Army fed a "tremendous amount of hungry men" and clothed a "large body of rookies." Everyone received several immunization injections; some of the men actually passed out from the pain, but most, including him, experienced only a sore arm for a few days. Dad's immunizations were for typhoid, typhus, and tetanus. Later, he received smallpox vaccines and additional typhoid and tetanus doses after being shipped to his training base.

On July 1, he sent Mom a postcard telling her he was being shipped out but did not yet know his destination. On a postcard the next day, stamped "Newport News," he wrote that after traveling for sixteen hours, he had arrived at Fort Eustis in Newport News, Virginia. On a second card sent the same day, he said he had been assigned to an antiaircraft training group, and that everyone was saying they were "slated for school." On July 5, he sent a card with an address Mom could use to send him letters and packages: "Pvt. A.M. Klapper ASN32968151, A Battery, 14 Battalion, 2 Platoon, Ft Eustis, VA."

Fort Eustis was a training center; however, the Army interviewer was puzzled about where to place Dad. His 124 IQ score had been his ticket to Fort Eustis as "only those whom the Army wants to train for some specialty are sent here," but his classification as a mail clerk could not go through because that quota had been filled. Because his IQ score was high enough to allow him to try for Officer Candidate School (OCS), the interviewer decided he should take his basic training and apply for OCS to get into the Adjutant General's Office, Postal Section. It was hard to get into the OCS, especially with poor eyesight, and Dad wore glasses. But the camp had a lot of schools, including an antiaircraft training center, and Dad was relieved to learn that this branch of the Army had the lowest mortality rate.

He was already lonely for Mom and the rest of the family, especially because he had not yet received any letters, and he asked her to write soon and often. Dad also began to inquire about passes and determine how far he was from New York. Basic training would last through October, but Dad hoped to get an emergency pass through the Red Cross when Mom gave birth in August, even though he warned her that emergency passes were very difficult to obtain.

Basic Training

Basic training began on July 5, and Dad wrote about marching several miles "along a dusty road until we reached the gun park." While attending lectures, the men could hear the firing of guns in the distance by more advanced units. They were instructed about military courtesy, sex hygiene (again), and rules concerning standing guard on post. These were "drilled into us day in and day out," he wrote.

Dad described his "air-conditioned" helmet, with a strap arrangement that allowed air to circulate between the helmet and the head. The Army wanted them to wear them during drills and hikes to prevent sunstrokes.

Because of Mom's impending delivery, Dad was comforted to learn that Army Emergency Relief had plenty of funds available, if necessary, to help with an operation or pregnancy. He was also happy to learn about a guest house at the camp that cost only a dollar a day for lodging and included two or three meals, an arrangement so popular that the men had to make reservations a month in advance. However, he did not think Mom's condition, plus the "tough accommodations" on the train, would allow for a visit until after the baby was born.

Mom began to write to Dad almost as soon as he left but had to wait to mail her letters until she knew his exact address. On July 13, 1943, she reminisced it had been two years since they had met. She was feeling low because she had not been able to accompany her mother and his sister Shirley to see him off at Penn Station, due to her advanced stage of pregnancy. She was also becoming increasingly uncomfortable in the hot, humid New York summer and found relief only by going to the beach and dipping into the ocean. But she was able to tend the Victory garden he had started and reported that the family was enjoying the vegetables very much.

Their Victory garden was part of a nationwide effort to help families supply their own food and alleviate shortages. The private gardens helped lower the commercial prices of produce, which in turn lowered the nation's costs to feed the troops, so they were considered an important way to aid the war effort. People planted gardens in their yards, window boxes, or rooftops, and by 1944, it was estimated that Victory gardens produced 40 percent of all the country's vegetables.

Since Dad had been raised in the city, he had never tended a garden before and thoroughly enjoyed the one he had planted in her parents' backyard. He often asked Mom about his garden in his early letters.

Mom, who had not yet received any of Dad's letters, was feeling lonely and frustrated that she could not just jump on a train and see him on his days off. She even fantasized about going to Virginia to have her baby in a hospital on the base. It wasn't really an option though, because getting there would have meant a ten- or eleven-hour ride on a crowded train—not a safe trip in her stage of pregnancy.

In early July, Mom wrote Dad that although she enjoyed the nursing career she had recently begun, "I would gladly trade [it] for the few months we had together before you left. Nursing could never give me what I found with you darling." Once in a while, Dad was able to call her on a Sunday, which made her feel better. However, she had very little privacy in her mother's crowded house, and she was initially so excited when she heard his voice that she was almost tongue-tied while on the phone.

Dad's letters finally began to reach Mom during the first week in July, and he received her first letters on July 10, allowing the two to communicate about actual events and people. After receiving Dad's first letters describing his arduous military training, Mom wrote that she hoped he would return with the same positive attitude he had left with. "Come back with the same grin that you had."

Intermingled with personal news, Mom's letter of July 27, 1943, refers to Italian dictator Benito Mussolini's "resignation" and a supposed pro-Ally prime minister taking his place. On July 28, she wrote that she had listened to U.S. President Franklin D. Roosevelt on the radio last night. "He said practically nothing new.... The war is still on and will continue for a long time yet ... other things don't interest me. I just want you to come home."

In early July, Dad described how exacting military inspections were and how much they were expected to learn in the thirteen weeks of basic training.

> July 9, 1943
>
> Except for sex hygiene lectures and certain drill formations, almost every lecture is different. We must learn to drill, recognize aircraft, friend or foe. We received our rifles and field equipment yesterday, and now we must know the various parts of the rifle and how to clean it. . . . We learned how to pitch tents in the field in military formation. . . . I am the only fellow from New York City here. Most of the men are from New England, and some are from Ohio and Georgia. My bed partner is 'sho nuff' from Georgia . . . . You should hear him talk. . . . Our beds are constructed like railroad berths. An upper and lower. I sleep in the lower.

Many of their early letters focused on the coming baby and when they could see each other again. In a July letter, Dad warned Mom not to try to visit him until he gave her the word because even if she made the long trip, he might not be able to see her, and she might not have a place to stay. If she tried to stay in Newport News, "which incidentally is very crowded, you would be stopped at the gates [of the base] by M.P. and not permitted to pass. And I am not allowed to leave until I receive a pass."

Contemplating giving birth without him, Mom wrote, "You won't be able to pace the floor or hold my hand, you won't know until it's all over." But since he was stationed in the South and had a southern bunkmate, she asked him to ask his friend for some "nice Southern names for boys and girls," although they had for months been calling the baby "Barry," hoping it was a boy.

She also wondered if the Army would let Dad come home for a *bris* (circumcision) if she gave birth to a boy. Because Dad's father was an Orthodox Jew, he would expect her to also observe a *Pidyon ha-Ben*, a ceremony on a firstborn son's thirty-first day that recalls the redemption of the firstborn son from his duty as a priest or official during the Temple period in Jerusalem. Maybe Dad could make it home for that ceremony if he could not get a leave for the bris, Mom speculated.

Dad wrote that he now hoped he would not need to get an emergency pass from the Red Cross, because that would mean she had become very ill, which he certainly did not want to happen. If, however, an emergency should occur, he told her that the family should go directly to the Red Cross instead of trying to contact him, because otherwise they would lose precious time.

He also explained how difficult it was to call her because he often had only a half hour free, but it could be a two-hour wait for the telephone. But after he finally was able to make his first call to her, he wrote he almost felt like he could touch her. The call cost $2.16 for eleven minutes, so Dad asked if he could reverse the charges next time. He had to make his first paycheck last through August, and he was expecting to get only six or seven dollars after the required laundry fee and a $6.90 deduction for a $10,000 life insurance policy.

Dad was looking forward to a five- to seven-day furlough at the beginning of October before being assigned a permanent base. But he was not eligible to obtain a thirty-six-hour pass until he had been in the service for at least five weeks, and he didn't expect that Mom would be able to travel to meet him since she might already be a "Momma" at that time.

Dad discovered in July that he had lost a chance to go to officers' school in North Carolina because his pupils had been too narrow when he was tested for stereoscopic vision. He guessed there would be other opportunities later, but if not, he would stay in antiaircraft, which was "not so bad." He said he would be satisfied if he became a corporal or a sergeant, so he wanted to maintain a clean record in basic to be eligible for the promotion. The Army made sure Dad had proper glasses for combat, issuing him two pairs with steel frames and shatterproof glass.

Staying "On the Ball"

In his letters, Dad described his grueling daily schedule. From 5:30 a.m. to 5 p.m., he attended lectures and participated in drills and exercises. After 5 p.m., the men had to scrub down the barracks, including the walls and floors and under their beds. That took about two and a half hours. Before they went to sleep, they had to clean their rifles and make their beds.

The schedule was even worse when the unit was sent to the gun park. To arrive there at 6 a.m., they had to get up at 4:45 a.m. and would sometimes be there until 9:30 p.m., falling into bed about 10:30 p.m., only to have to arise at 4:45 a.m. the next day. In order to keep up with his correspondence, Dad carried paper and a pen with him and wrote whenever he had the chance, such as while he was waiting in line for the eye or dental clinics.

Dad kept asking Mom and his sister to send him proper socks. They had to be long enough to fit the GI boots, because otherwise he would get blisters, and "the care of the feet is absolutely one of the most important items here" to endure the hiking and other training.

On one particularly tough day after hiking and training with their guns in the hot, humid July weather, Dad reported that about fifteen men had passed out, one had become hysterical, and some had also broken bones. They all had to be taken to the hospital. "Believe me, this is no vacation. . . . Boy, they sure kill you or cure you here. . . . Only 10 1/2 more weeks."

There was one break in his routine for him to look forward to, though. That was the chapel, where he had been told there would be Jewish food available, brought to the camp by Jewish families from neighboring towns. He attended his first chapel in late July, along with twenty-five men, five women from the Women's Army Corps (WAC), and some civilians who were members of the USO (United Service Organizations).

> July 22, 1943
>
> First time I felt like letting my hair down. After we sang some songs and had a little discussion, we went to the recreation hall and had pastrami sandwiches, sour pickles, soda, and cake. They serve different refreshments every time.

At some point, Dad expressed his belief that the grueling training was beginning to have the desired effect, saying he felt he was now more mentally alert than he had ever been. But in response to Mom's teasing that she might not recognize him when she finally saw him again, he assured her, "You'll spot me right away. I may walk a little straighter, and [hold my] head a little higher. Otherwise, I am the same in that I love you and miss you so much."

Dad's family showed their love for him by writing lots of letters, and his locker was becoming too crowded to hold them all, so he asked about sending the letters home for safekeeping. "Some day, when I am at home and wearing my slippers and Barry is asleep and you and I are alone, we can read them over again and get [a] laugh or tear from them. Tears because we will be so happy to be together again. Laughs because it will be over and just a memory."

As he had begun in his very first letters, Dad continued to teach Mom Army vernacular. "The process of changing us from civilians to soldiers is called getting us 'on the ball.' When I say I am on the ball, it means that I am doing all right, I understand, etc."

July 20, 1943

One has to be in order not to get 'ghigged' (hard 'g'). You might as well get used to this Army vernacular. Ghigged means you receive extra duty as punishment because you failed to do something that was not GI. Some of the fellows got ghigged today because they did not have their shoes shined. Some because their clothes were not hung or displayed properly. Everything must be exact. Our clothes must all hang with the right sleeve out and all buttons buttoned. If not, one can get ghigged and it might mean extra duty on Sun. when everyone else is off. So far, knock wood. That is just a small example. There are a million and a half other things one must know. You must be on your toes. I guess that is the purpose of this type of training.

Dad also provided descriptive details about training, which now included over obstacle courses, carrying first light and then heavy backpacks, in the hot southern sun.

July 26, 1943

With pack and rifle we must hurdle fences, crawl on our bellies, jump and clamber over a sheer 8-foot wall, over some more ladders and fences, then we must run up a ramp and over a wall about 12–15 feet high. Then we have to climb a steep cliff, hanging onto the ropes there. That is just a sample.

July 28, 1943

Today, we were on the range. It is so hard for me to put into words the agony of marching after spending the entire day under the blazing sun on the range. One boy passed out and was rushed to the hospital. Another boy started to lag behind, and I was detailed to look after him. He did not have any water in his canteen, so I gave him a little of mine. It was hot and salty tasting, but he loved it. I then took his rifle and we started off . . . we are now carrying heavy packs. They weigh about 40 or 50 pounds. It is tough, kid, but so far I am holding my own. One boy broke his back the other day on the obstacle course.

Despite having to wear glasses, Dad turned out to be a pretty good shot, and because of that and his record for being generally "on the ball," he was selected at the end of July to be an acting sergeant, responsible for supervising corporals and privates in his unit. There were four acting sergeants and four acting corporals in his platoon. Dad was eager to keep his new position and be in line for a possible promotion after training. And as an acting sergeant, he was allowed to avoid K.P.

Dad was particularly surprised by how well he had been able to shoot, despite his poor eyesight, lack of experience, and age. At twenty-eight, he was probably the oldest member of his battery and had expected a lot of the fellows to be better on the firing range than he was.

July 29 (I think) [*sic*], 1943

[B]ut they don't wear glasses, and they are pretty young kids. Most of them are hunters from the Georgia woods and the New England countryside. Squirrel hunters is what we call them. For a guy who has been brought up in the city all his life, I didn't do so badly.

Dad had been in very good physical condition before his induction due to his love of athletics. Considering the clothing and equipment they had to wear and carry while hiking, this turned out to be an advantage.

> July 29, 1943
>
> You cannot have an idea how that hike home is until you actually experience it. The pack is heavy, and the straps cut into your shoulder. Then your rifle and gas mask are hung on the right and left shoulder, respectively. Underneath it all is your cartridge belt from which your canteen is suspended. The heavy shoes and fatigues and helmet complete our outfit. After a whole day in the sun and then marching back under it, you know you have been through something. I hope nobody passes out today.

He pointed out how his perspiration had blurred the edges of the paper he was writing on but told Mom not to worry because he was doing well, which is why he had been chosen to be an acting sergeant. And he reminded her that the previous day he had carried the rifle of the kid who was not feeling well in addition to carrying his own load.

New Arrival at Home

Although Dad was certainly busy at Fort Eustis, both of my parents were actually more interested in what was happening on the home front during August 1943. Mom was buying baby things and putting the finishing touches on the crib and her room at her parents' house in Far Rockaway. The family could not afford a new carriage, so they purchased a used one for $35, even though it was rather shabby. Mom cleaned, painted, and reupholstered it to make it acceptable.

She was hoping Dad would be able to get an emergency pass so he could visit after the baby was born. He had received a pass earlier in August, but it was only for thirty-six hours, not long enough to get to New York and back. Both had been bitterly disappointed, and Mom was afraid she would have to wait until October to see Dad again.

She was glad to discover that Army Relief would pay her doctor's bills for the delivery and cover the hospital charges and baby visits for a year, but she was beginning to long for her own apartment since she felt her parents were interfering too much. Her father objected to Dad's weekly calls, saying they were too extravagant, and he even called the telephone company to tell them to refuse collect calls from Dad. She also felt he was taking advantage of her financially.

For months she and Dad had been referring to the baby as "Barry," hoping she would have a boy, and Mom didn't settle on a name for a girl until a few days before the birth: "Bonny Sue," later spelling it "Bonnie." I arrived on August 16, 1943, at 11 p.m., at St. Joseph's Hospital in Far Rockaway. Even though Mom had been given ether for the delivery, making her sleepy for most of the next day, she was able to write an eight-page letter to Dad describing as many of the details of the birth as she could recall. She ended her letter with, "By the way, your daughter's name is Bonnie Sue Klapper." She desperately hoped he would be able to get a pass to see her that coming weekend.

Her father sent a telegram to Dad informing him of my birth. He wrote a letter to Mom in response.

August 17, 1943

Darling,
I just heard the news. I was out at the gun park about 7 p.m. on night drill when a lieutenant approached me. He asked me my name, and I saluted.

> He returned my salute and then stuck his hand out to shake hands, saying, 'Congratulations, your wife just gave birth to a 7 1/2 lb. baby girl.' Well, you could have knocked me over with a sneeze. I am now at the telephone exchange trying to call up. I spoke to my sergeant, and he asked me how you were. He said if I told him that you didn't feel so well, he could talk to the captain. . . . If the Red Cross should call the hospital or Dr. Richman, I want them to say that I am needed. In that way, I can get an emergency pass.

Although Dad was excited and relieved, he had to remember to take care of important details. He needed the exact spelling of my name and a copy of my birth certificate as soon as possible so he could file the necessary papers for an additional allotment for a child.

Dad's officers did grant him a pass for the weekend following my birth. His pass was very short, and by August 23 he was back at camp, returning with bottles of liquor to thank the officers who had granted him the leave. But he was grateful for even the short visit, writing Mom, "After seeing you dearest I feel fortified to stand anything they dish out here. I arrived at camp at 1:30 a.m. and was able to get a few hours of sleep."

Shortly after my birth, Dad's father gave Mom a ring that had been a family heirloom and told her father to have it set for her at his expense. Mom wrote to Dad about the gift.

August 21, 1943

> Dearest, do you know what that means. The ring has become a symbol in our lives. It means that your father has finally forgiven us our deed and is lending his approval. You know, dearest, today is

really a day for us to celebrate; it's more or less a day of forgiveness. Darling, I will keep the ring till you come home again and can put it on my finger.

Mom had kept in touch with some of her friends from nursing school and in a letter told Dad that everyone seemed to be getting married or divorced, having babies, and making other big decisions rapidly, because the war affected everyone's lives.

August 29, 1943

Darling, everything seems to be done in such a rush, it seems as if everyone is in a hurry, and they are making some horrible mistakes, which they will pay for after this mad war is over. . . . Darling, it seems like we are the only sane ones in a crazy world and we are far from sane.

Dad continued his training, attending lectures, learning to identify aircraft, and preparing for gas warfare, which the U.S. was expecting Germany to use since "they are more or less on the run." They even gave the men a chance to "sniff" some of the types of gas they might encounter. Dad paid close attention and asked lots of questions, hoping to show enough initiative to be considered for promotion. It must have been noticed, because he was selected with a number of others on August 5 to fill out applications for OCS, but all were warned their chances were slim, since they would be competing against college ROTC men, who would have received higher rankings due to their educational level, and the OCS quota for their post was only four a week out of 22,000 men.

However, as an acting sergeant, Dad was able to pull guard duty as a corporal, which meant he only had to post his men every two hours, instead of walking guard duty, with six hours on and six hours off, for twenty-four hours. This gave him more time away from guard duty and thus more time away from the guard station. He explained to Mom that guard duty in the Army is an honor, although there was little responsibility during basic training. "In other fields, the lives of men depend on the guard to give the alarm in case of attack, gas attack, or fire."

At the end of August, Dad was prepped for the "infiltration" course, which he called a "dog run." When the men ran through the course, there would be "machine guns firing overhead and all sorts of simulated battle noises. It is quite thrilling. We must crawl almost the entire way, and after getting there we are just covered with mud."

The big machine guns were lined up near the water's edge on a beach of Chesapeake Bay. It was an ironically beautiful setting—dunes of pearly white sand stretching into Virginia pines. It reminded Dad of Treasure Island. The beach was less humid than at Fort Eustis, but sand got under the wheels of the guns and trucks and into the men's sleeves. He hoped it wouldn't get into their shoes, but expected it probably would, even though they were wearing leggings.

In the second week of September, Dad was able to visit Mom and me on a brief weekend pass. After the visit, Mom wrote to Dad, telling him that the longer they were married, the more she was falling in love with him. That month, she ended her letters with "Happy New Year, Darling," referring to the Jewish holiday of Rosh Hashanah. She wished they could go to "schul" (synagogue) together to celebrate the holidays and hoped next year they would be able to.

Maneuvers and Memories

In mid-September, Dad participated in his first bivouac. It lasted only two days but served as an introduction to an upcoming two-week maneuver.

September 13, 1943

> For two days we did not get out of our clothes. We slept in the ground. I mean we had to dig down about one and a half feet and then pitched our tents over that hole in the ground. During the day when it was hot, we sweated our hides off digging gun emplacements. At night when we tried to get as comfortable as possible in order to sleep, the mist would descend and in a few hours our teeth were chattering. . . . Last night it sure felt good to sleep between warm clean sheets, after a nice shower and shave.

Dad also described three "boys" of about eighteen who had gone AWOL and then been returned to his barrack by the guardhouse. The three were now accompanied by a guard with a rifle at all times. Dad could not feel any animosity toward them, he said, because they were not murderers or thieves, but only guilty of not liking the Army. He understood, though, that the treatment was necessary or "everyone who didn't like the Army would get up and go. . . . It takes discipline of the mind to make one stick it out."

While most of Mom's letters in September 1943 supplied him with details of their new baby's development, one letter described her ecstatic reaction to learning that Italy had surrendered. She had called a cousin and they both cried from joy, hoping the end of the war was now closer.

Responding to the news from Italy, Dad wrote:

September 16 (?), 1943

> The fighting in Italy is tough now. But Hitler must either fight there or permit us to go clear up to the Alp mountains. If he pours men into Italy, he must weaken himself somewhere else. That is where our

other Armies will come in, and the pressure of the Russians is nothing to sneeze at. For all we know, his resistance to us in Italy might only be of a rear guard and delaying action [i.e., that it may not be his main focus].

Despite the war news and training, Dad was always thinking about Mom, describing how he saw her in countless "memory pictures," particularly from their courtship when she was in nurse's training. He reminisced about how he would wait for her in the reception parlor of the nurses' residence in Brooklyn, watch her coming through the door, and hear the "patter of her slippers on the floor." He felt he could now see her more clearly than ever.

At the end of his eleventh week of basic, his unit was getting ready for two weeks of training in taking care of themselves in the field, including digging foxholes. As chief of his section, Dad was going to have a lot of responsibility, as the officers and noncoms were not going to tell the men what to do but only stand by and criticize. It was a test to see how much they had learned in the past eleven weeks. Tanks and planes would be trying to spot them, and "the planes will drop small flour bags to simulate bombs. We will have to sleep in tents, and it is getting pretty cold at night."

To save money, the Army had changed its procedure regarding shipping orders after furlough at the end of basic training, with men reporting directly to their new camps instead of returning to their basic camps and then moving on. The battalion that had just shipped out was going to Fort Meade in Maryland, only about three hours from New York, and Dad was hoping he would also be stationed there. The furloughs had also just been extended from five to seven days.

Dad wrote again about the men who had gone AWOL. One who had been caught and returned earlier had now tried to leave for the third time; Dad's attitude had changed from one of sympathy to anger. "We are all compelled to stay here by the virtue of belief in defending ourselves against a tyrant. We don't have to do his fighting for him. By God, that really makes me sore."

He continued to enjoy going to chapel for Jewish-style food, like chopped liver and pickled green tomatoes. He also liked the funny stories some men told in English and Yiddish and the songs they sang together. Although there had been some efforts to take the Jewish GIs to Newport News for the high holidays, they wound up not being able to leave camp for Rosh Hashanah, and Dad was too worn out from a twenty-five-mile hike to even attend services on the premises. He told Mom he "felt a little guilty about not going to chapel" but planned to tell his parents he had gone to make them happy and asked her not to mention it. He had felt compelled to attend such services at home, but Dad said that even then his "heart was not in it." He described his feelings regarding organized religion.

September 30 (?), 1943

> Religion isn't something you find in a book or a synagogue. It is locked in your heart. It is the way we treat our fellow humans. You know my attitude on the subject, dear.

However, Dad did put his name down for the convoy to Newport News for the next Saturday night, when the men would be breaking the Yom Kippur fast in Jewish homes or synagogues.

In October, Mom received confirmation from the Board of Health that they would pay her doctor and hospital bill in full. She planned to use the money to buy a winter coat or to help pay for a move if Dad were going to be stationed somewhere permanently. Her pediatrician agreed to take care of her baby for free, saying that lots of doctors were not charging servicemen's wives because "that's the least we can do." She was also happy when the Army notified her she would be getting an allotment of $80 per month while Dad was in the service.

Taking a tip from Dad, who always carried stationery and a pen to be able to write in spare moments, she often wrote to him from the post office, while I was in the carriage. Although initially disappointed to have had a daughter, she claimed she had changed her mind. In October, about a month and a half after I was born, she wrote, "I'm glad we have a daughter, darling, because when she grows older we can tell her about our love story. I don't think a boy would understand."

At family gatherings in Dad's parents' apartment in Manhattan, everyone felt his absence, making Mom miss him even more. But she was glad that the baby was bringing the family close again, considering the rocky relationship at the outset of their marriage.

Dad kept writing about fun times he and Mom had in the early days of their courtship and marriage—walking in Brooklyn in Prospect Park or around Kingston Avenue, seeing a show at the Flatbush Theatre, hanging out on the boardwalk at Coney Island. His memories helped pass the time during preparations for maneuvers and firing range practice.

On maneuvers, Dad was learning how to dig foxholes (important for protection from enemy fire during a battle), emplacements, and other installations for weapons. It was such hard work that Dad wrote he now understood why "it is an unwritten law that anyone using your foxhole, you can kill him."

Dad did get a short pass at the end of the first week in October, which left them both even more anxious for the five-day furlough they expected to come soon. He returned to face a two-day bivouac, but he marveled at the beauty of the countryside in autumn.

October 22 (?), 1943

The sun is rather warm after a cold night, the sky is clear, and there is barely a wind, which causes the tall grass and daisies and goldenrods and a million other varieties to sway gently. The trees, pines, oaks, apple, peach, maples, and a great many others are ablaze with the colors of the autumn. I never could believe the pictures or descriptions of autumn until now. Now, I can't describe it. Most of the fellows here are from the country and are more or less inured to it. But to one who has been raised in the city, it is very impressive. . . .

I am getting to be quite a woodsman. I can recognize the caw caw of the crows; I can also spot a buzzard. There is a bird that is the essence of grace in flight. They just float in the air for hours with motionless wings. You know it is against the law to kill them, as they are scavengers who eat carrion and garbage.

In his letter he enclosed a piece of a root from a sassafras tree and said one of the Georgia boys would show them how to make tea from it. Another was making a rabbit trap, because the woods were filled with small game, and the men were already pretty tired of Army "chow."

"Too bad it takes a war to wrench guys like me out of our ruts in the city to enjoy the natural glamour of Mother Nature, unmarred by the scars of stone buildings and city streets," Dad wrote. He hoped he and Mom would one day have the courage to move out of the city and into the country for the sake of themselves and their children.

During his time on maneuvers, though, he was mostly counting the days until his furlough, which was to begin shortly after he returned to Fort Eustis. They were debating where to spend it. Dad preferred to be mostly at his parents' place so they could see them as much as possible, especially because his father had difficulty traveling. It would also be easier for the two of them to enjoy outings in the city, since his parents lived in Manhattan, and he hoped they could see his extended family as well. His maternal relatives had formed a family circle group in 1938, and Dad enjoyed attending its periodic meetings.

When the men returned to Fort Eustis, the first thing they did was head to the warm showers and get out of their dirty clothes, which they had not changed in days. Then they waited for news about their furlough schedules.

AMERICAN RED CROSS

NEW YORK CHAPTER Serving **MANHATTAN & BRONX**

We congratulate you on entering the service of your country and want you to know that the Red Cross is prepared to serve you or your family at any time.

FOR YOU At every Army and Navy station or outpost there is a Field Director. See him if you are worried about personal problems or about news from home. The Field Director is in touch with Red Cross Chapters in every part of the country--and one of these is your Home Chapter.

FOR YOUR FAMILY The Home Service Department of the Red Cross is prepared to give similar service to your family. A Home Service worker stands ready to help with advice on allotments and allowance, personal and family problems, adjustments of budget. It is a medium of communications with you. The Red Cross is your friend at Home and Abroad and the link between you and your family.

EDNA J. WAKEFIELD
Director, Home Service

315 LEXINGTON AVENUE   TEL. MURRAY HILL 4-4455

American Red Cross card with instructions for serviceman and family. This was one of the first documents Dad sent Mom after induction, and he explained to her the role of the Red Cross as the communication link between the servicemen and their families.

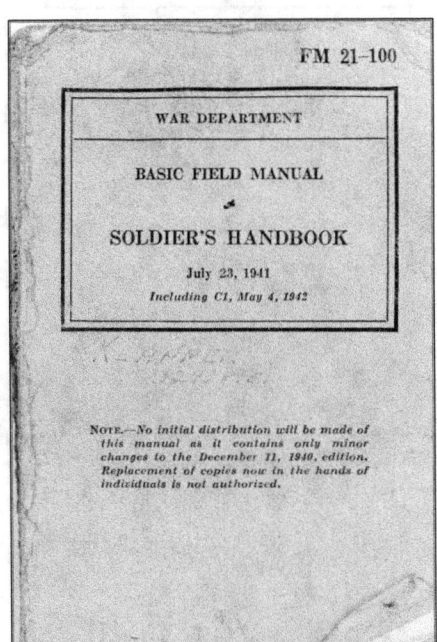

Basic Field Manual: Soldier's Handbook, July 1941. Dad probably received this upon arrival at Fort Eustis for basic training.

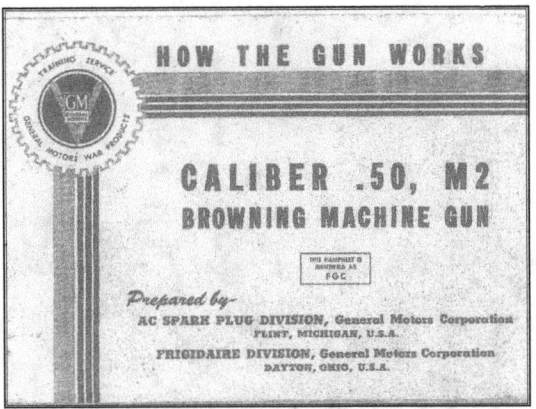

Instruction manual for using the Browning machine gun that Dad's antiaircraft unit was being trained to use. In combat, these guns were placed on half-track trucks that were used to move them into position.

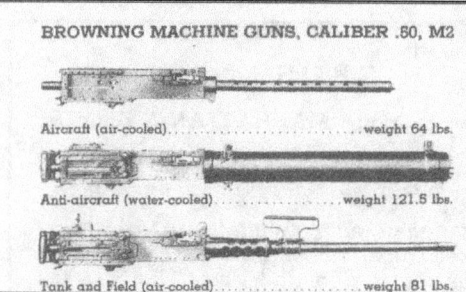

Pages from the instruction manual for using the Browning machine gun that Dad's antiaircraft unit was being trained to use.

"Victory Gardens" brochure. U.S. Department of Agriculture, 1943. Mom and Dad had planted a Victory garden in Mom's parents' backyard before he was inducted into the Army, and Dad asked about how it was doing in his letters during his first few months in the service.

One of Dad's fellow soldiers at Fort Eustis created this sketch of him, 1943.

Postcard Dad sent from Camp Upton, Long Island, 1943. A "typical company street" at Camp Upton. (Colourpicture Publication, Cambridge, MA)

Post Headquarters at Camp Upton, Long Island.

Cover of Mom's war ration book. U.S. Office of Price Administration. Many basic foods, such as meat, were rationed during the war so that the Army could provide them to the soldiers.

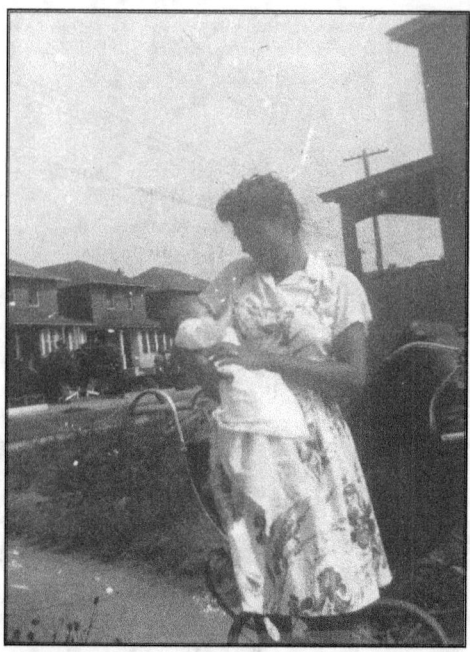

Mom holding newborn daughter Bonnie, August 1943, Far Rockaway, New York, probably near her parents' house. The carriage is a used one her family purchased for her, which she refurbished.

Dad home on emergency pass from Fort Eustis just after my birth in August 1943 in front of Mom's parents' home in Far Rockaway.

Mom, Dad (top row), and Mom's family, including her parents, Sophie (middle row right), and Marcus Schein (top left); brother Aaron (middle row left); and sister Mary (in front), taken during Dad's emergency leave home the weekend after Mom gave birth to me, August 1943. They are standing in front of Mom's parents' home in Far Rockaway.

Mom and Dad (front row) with Mom and Dad's parents, his mother Mierke ("Miriam," middle row right), and father Louis Klapper (top row right), in Far Rockaway during Dad's emergency leave in August 1943.

Dad and Mom, holding newborn daughter Bonnie, during his emergency leave, August 1943, Far Rockaway.

Dad with his sisters, Shirley on the left and Sylvia on the right, in Far Rockaway, August 1943, during his emergency leave. Dad was very close to his sisters, and their smiles show how delighted they were to see him.

Mom and Dad with Dad's younger cousin Marty, who was also soon to be inducted into the Army. Far Rockaway, August 1943, during Dad's leave just after my birth.

CHAPTER 3

Camp Stewart, Georgia

ALL MY PARENTS' PLANS FOR his furlough and hopes for his relocation close to New York were dashed when he learned he was being sent to a camp near Savannah, Georgia, without the long-anticipated break. Dad broke the news to Mom in early November 1943, and she was devastated. It didn't help that the heartbreaking news arrived near November 5, their first anniversary.

To console her, Dad pointed out that Camp Stewart was not a port of embarkation, which meant he would not be shipped overseas right away. Because she thought he would be there for a while, Mom decided to move to Georgia to be near Dad despite daunting obstacles. She asked him to find a place for her, me, and perhaps her mother to stay, and suggested that we could go to Florida if he couldn't find anything feasible near his camp. At least in Florida, we would be close enough so he could visit on passes. She also asked him to send her whatever money he could spare because she was totally broke and wanted to reserve their small amount of savings for travel expenses. Mom ended her anniversary letter with an imprint of her lipstick and scented the paper with cologne Dad had given her, declaring her love for him was stronger than it had been on the day they married.

Dad expressed similar sentiments in his letters, but he was reluctant to have Mom start planning to come to Savannah until he could find out more about accommodations. The guest house on the base was very crowded, required reservations a month in advance, and cost 50 cents a night. The men were allowed to sleep with their wives there, but a visit could not exceed five days. Dad promised to ask for help from the Jewish Welfare Board, one of the USO's constituent agencies, as soon as he could get off the base, but warned it would be hard because the city was "overrun with the military."

Dad discovered he would be training at Camp Stewart for twenty-two weeks, but the more he learned about Savannah, the more worried he became about bringing his family to the area. Soldiers in Savannah faced an 11 p.m. curfew every night, and many places were off-limits to them because of serious "race riots" that had occurred. In addition, wages were very low in the area, giving Mom only a slim chance of earning enough to support herself.

He also told Mom that Florida was out of the question because weekend passes from Camp Stewart were good only until 11 p.m. Sunday night, and it was hard to get out of camp early. That meant "Savannah or a few very small but overcrowded communities are the only ones within reach," he wrote. "And they all have that 11 p.m. curfew for soldiers because of the race riots that have occurred down here."

Dad also sadly turned down Mom's request for money because he was just as broke as she was. Part of the problem was that the Army had not yet started providing the additional allotment due after my birth, even though Dad had completed the paperwork the day after I was born, almost three months earlier.

Now that he was stationed in Georgia, the flow of mail between Mom and Dad became steady. There were actually two mail calls a day because the Army knew how important correspondence was for soldiers' morale. Dad agreed with that assessment, telling Mom that writing and reading letters helped him bear their separation more easily. He felt it was almost like seeing her.

To cheer both of them up, Dad continued to write about his memories of home, including sitting around the fireplace with friends and relatives in their apartment in Greenwich Village, and dreaming about the future.

November 10 (?), 1943

> Some day when our Sue is old enough, you and I will be sitting comfortably in our own home and we will recall these instances for her. I think she will understand and love our love story as we do.

My parents also discussed issues affecting the country and the world. Because his base was in the South, Dad frequently wrote about race relations and the situations he was witnessing. During WWII, the Army was segregated and African-American units were called "negro detachments." Dad's officers warned the men not to go near those detachments because a few months earlier, some of the soldiers had broken into the ammunition dump and killed three white MPs before the "riot" was "squelched." "The negro [*sic*] problem is extremely touchy and serious here."

Dad also responded to Mom's fears that had been stoked when she heard Churchill predict that "1944 would cost the Allies a great many more lives than the previous year," despite all the progress that had been made by the Allies.

November 11 (?), 1943

> As for Churchill's speech, don't worry your little head. I personally don't believe I will see action. If they can send a bunch of us who have finished our basic through another 4 or 5 months of another basic, it seems to me that they don't need or want us over there. I personally believe that they have all the troops they need. The plans for finishing Germany and Japan are all made out. Who knows how long we may be here. But the consoling thing is that at least I will be here.

Although Mom was desperate to be with Dad again, she admitted that she was far better equipped to take care of her new baby at home. In addition, she did not think she would be able to work in Savannah since neither of them wanted to leave me with a stranger while she worked.

Even so, on his first pass to Savannah, Dad went to the Jewish Welfare Board, hoping to get more information that could help Mom to relocate to the area. He was disappointed by what he saw: sky-high prices for low-quality housing. To save money, he had taken the convoy from camp to Savannah and back, but it had taken so long both ways that it hardly seemed worth the trip.

But he did enjoy his visit to the Jewish Welfare Board, which was located in a building with a gym where he found people singing and dancing. Dad was particularly fond of the large buffet of Jewish-style sandwiches and cake, and he told Mom about how he had asked for a piece of cake while holding a sandwich in one hand and coffee in the other. "One of the old ladies behind the table looked up and said, 'Finish your sandwich first.'" He laughed because he knew Mom and his own mother would have told him the same thing.

Since it did not look promising that Mom would be moving to Savannah any time soon, she especially looked forward to Dad's Sunday phone calls. But the calls were very expensive. One call cost $4.40 with the overtime charges, leaving Dad only $6.00 for the rest of the week to cover incidental expenses such as extra snacks, toiletries, transportation to town, haircuts, and phone calls to his parents.

In a letter written not long after Dad had been assigned to Camp Stewart, Mom asked if he had been sent so far from New York because he had run into some kind of trouble he had not told her about.

November 9 (?), 1943

> Dearest, please tell me the truth. Is it because you didn't make out well on maneuvers or didn't pass in some way that they are making you do your

basic over? I can't understand it, darling. Since I got your letter, I've been in a daze, darling. I never heard of such a thing. Why should they waste so much time? I know it will keep you here longer, but darling it is awfully confusing. Is it your own fault, please tell me . . . I'll understand. . . . [M]aybe you ought to fail the exam they give you so that would mean you'd be there 22 weeks, and maybe by then the war will be over.

Dad told her he was not in trouble, but he confessed that he had been withholding information.

November 15 (?), 1943

Honey, somehow I feel you think I am down here because I am holding something from you. Well to be frank, I am, but not what you think about failing my maneuvers or problems. The truth is that the whole battalion with the exception of a few has been sent down here to form active units. That means that the teams we make here are the ones we will go into actual battle with. There are all sorts of men here who compose our unit. Men who like myself have just completed basic, and men who have been under fire. This battalion is activated and will move out together as a unit when training has been completed. The setup at Eustis was different. There, the only men coming in were raw recruits who were in active units that broke up after training, or basic I should say, and were sent to various camps to get further training. Even our officers here move out with us. At Eustis the officers stayed and are now training a new bunch. So

> you see, honey, what I was keeping from you was the fact that this is a live outfit. I personally think the war in Europe will be over by spring or before we finish our training. It is not good to get too optimistic, but you can't stop a man from hoping. . . .
>
> Well, what do you know. I just found out that the balance of the men we left behind are now down here. I went over to check up and sure enough, there they were. So you see, your boy wasn't naughty after all.

Dad was optimistic about the war ending before he could be shipped overseas because he knew that the Russians were then only thirty-five miles from the Polish border, when only six months earlier they had been 600 or 700 miles away. He also knew the German army was not growing stronger, but the American and Russian armies were.

In one of her letters, Mom wrote that she did not think it was fair that some mothers had two or three sons who were safe at home and not in the military, while some mothers—like Dad's—with only one son had him "so far away." However, she observed that an old shack near where her father worked was displaying eight stars in the window, meaning the family had eight sons in the military.

Because people at home often had more access to the news than the soldiers did, Mom would frequently update him on the war's progress. In mid-November, she wrote about the Allies' new air attack over Berlin in the attempt to avoid a western land invasion.

November 19, 1943

> Well, since last night I know why they have been postponing and increasing your training. The Allies promised Stalin an invasion date if and when

the air attack over Berlin doesn't succeed. They have started a new air attack over Berlin. They are using 1,500–2,000 planes and the other night dropped over 350 blockbusters, so you can imagine what Berlin must look like. The Allies are trying to avoid a western invasion, so they have decided to try the bombing of Germany again. I understand that the last attempt wasn't successful, because Germany recuperates too quickly and starts all over. It seems as if the Allies want to get this over with in a hurry. You know it will soon be 2 years that America is fighting.

Moments of Gratitude

Just before Thanksgiving 1943, Mom wrote Dad that the bombings over Berlin had made such a strong impact on Germany's production that an estimated 20 percent had been cut off. Experts were projecting that if production could be cut by 30 to 40 percent, Germany would have to surrender. Americans were all hoping a land invasion would not be necessary. In her letter, Mom said that the next day was Thanksgiving, and that many people were saying they did not have much to be thankful for this year. But Mom didn't feel that way, despite the war that had separated them.

November 24, 1943

I have much to be thankful for, my darling. I have you, even though we're far apart; you've become more a part of me now than ever before. And, darling, we have a lovely baby to be thankful for; we also have a furlough to look forward to . . .

We also have to be glad that our cities haven't been bombed, and that we haven't been through the horror of air raids. We have so much, darling, so very much because we have our love and sweetness.

Mom promised to cook a big turkey with all of the trimmings if the war was over and he was home for the next Thanksgiving and told him he could invite anyone he wanted. She also said she intended to save all of their letters so that when he came home they could reread them and "tie them with ribbons and put them away till Bonnie gets old enough to enjoy them and appreciate them."

Dad was relieved that she had decided not to come to Georgia, telling her that the idea of southern hospitality seemed like "a lot of bunk" from what he had seen so far. He warned, "being a Jew doesn't make it easier. These people down here as a whole are about thirty years behind times. They are fighting a war, and I'll be damned if they know what the hell they are fighting for."

On Thanksgiving morning, Dad and his unit watched a special "training film." He wrote Mom about the film and the officer who addressed them after it was over.

November 25, 1943

I guess this is the first Thanksgiving most of you men have spent away from home. And many of you would like to know what you have to be thankful for. The name of the film is *The Battle for Russia*. After seeing what the Germans did to the cities, the women, the children, and the homes of this courageous people, and to think that this might have happened to us, we can be thankful today.

Dad was very moved by the movie and the speech, and he described its effect on the men.

> November 25, 1943
>
> It made a lot of these donkeys around here run to religious services that were held today. It was something to see the Red Army fight in the icy cold. First it showed how they were driven back by the invaders to the gates of Moscow and Stalingrad. Then it showed how they defended themselves and held and finally are driving the invaders from their soil.

Again, he warned Mom not to expect an early victory and not to believe the journalists who were predicting it would come quickly. "Better be surprised than disappointed."

Dad also referred to the husband of one of Mom's cousins, who had been sent home to recover from "shell shock." Dad admitted that he was grateful he had not yet had to face real fire and wasn't entirely sure how he would react.

> November 25, 1943
>
> How must one feel when he comes face-to-face with the enemy? A bayonet thrust out in front of him. Cold steel.... Can a civilian appreciate its portent? It is a wonder more men don't go nuts than actually do. At that moment it is determined whether you are a soldier or afraid. Do you remember all that has been taught you? That's when you find out if it paid for you to listen to these lectures and do your drills diligently.

December Train to Georgia

Despite Dad's reservations, Mom was growing increasingly impatient to join him in Savannah and by the end of November was begging him to find a place for her and me to stay. She urged him to approach the Jewish Welfare Board, local synagogues, or any other possible resource. Without waiting for a response, Mom made up her mind to travel to Savannah, along with me (then three months old), her mother, and brother Aaron, who was twelve. Mom's dad supplied the train fare for Grandma and Aaron.

Dad almost panicked when he received Mom's letter announcing she would be arriving in a couple of weeks. He had not been able to find out about housing since he could only get off base on the weekends when most of the housing resource places were closed. He repeated that he would not be able to help her much financially and thought he would be lucky to give her seven to nine dollars a month from his $14.60 paycheck, which clearly would not be enough for her needs. In addition, a flu epidemic was spreading through the camp, and he worried about her safety and comfort on a crowded train with an infant to change and feed.

Nevertheless, at the end of November, Mom wrote to tell Dad that she would be leaving New York on December 12 at 11:45 a.m. and was scheduled to arrive in Savannah at 5:30 a.m. the next day. She told him that she would first go to a hotel on a Travelers' Aid list. She was still hoping to find a place to stay near the camp but was prepared to return to New York if things did not work out. She still wanted Dad to look for lodging but told him she would look herself if he could not. She was planning to write to one of her father's friends who had a house in Ray City, near Fort Benning, and to the Chamber of Commerce. Mom knew Dad would not be happy with her insistence and asked him not to "bawl her out." She only wanted to be with him for a few months longer, she explained, "and anything is worth that."

Mom said she simply could not stand to be apart from him any longer, and her only regret was that she had not followed him sooner.

She reminded him that she was a bigger gambler than he was and how she had persuaded him to take a chance on marriage despite all the obstacles they faced.

Despite his concerns, Dad looked forward to Mom's arrival with great anticipation. He was relieved that her mother and brother were accompanying her so she would have help caring for me and finding accommodations. Plus, her mother could stay with me, allowing Mom to look for a job. Dad did not think he would be able to meet her Monday morning train, but he told her to send a telegram just before she left New York. He was hoping his officer might be able to give him a special pass if he could prove Mom was traveling.

On the second anniversary of the Pearl Harbor attack, shortly before Mom left for Savannah, she told Dad that she had been secretly proud of him for wanting to join the service, even though she had objected strenuously at the time.

December 7, 1943

> Darling, so many boys are bemoaning their fate because they were drafted . . . [but] I loved you more when I knew you wanted to join up. I cried because I knew how miserable I'd be without you, but I was proud because I knew you were the kind of person who wanted to do his own fighting. You weren't just willing to let the other fellow bring you your peace. This way, darling, the peace that follows will really mean something to us, because we've fought and suffered for it.

On that same day, Dad wrote that his first sergeant (the "top kick") had said that beginning in January, their battery would be allowed to send 7 percent of the men out on furlough at one time. The order would be based on length of service. However, Dad did not believe the news, having already been burned regarding an expected furlough. He told Mom he thought the announcement was made to discourage men from going AWOL for Christmas, because the battery commander "is rated according to the number of AWOLs in his battery."

Mom continued preparing for her trip, packing a large trunk and her nursing registration card, readying a baby bathinette, and arranging for social security cards for her and her mother and citizenship papers (since she had been born in Poland and brought here as an infant by her mother and was therefore a "naturalized citizen"). Mom would need all that paperwork if she wanted to work in Georgia and was considering a defense plant if she could not find a nursing job. Mom also called her brother's school office for his report card so he could be enrolled in school in Savannah.

On December 12, Mom sent Dad the telegram he had asked for.

PN NEWYORK NY DEC 12 1024A 1943

PVT A M KLAPPER ASN 32968151=
BTRY A 581 AAA AW SP CAMPSTEWART GA=

ARRIVING WITH BABY 6 AM SAVANNAH STATION WILL WAIT LOVE=

LIL
(952A)

Cover of booklet for the 581st AAA Battalion with names and hometowns listed by battery that Dad received when he arrived at Camp Stewart, Georgia. The men were from many different cities and states, and this booklet was one of the ways the Army used to build solidarity among them.

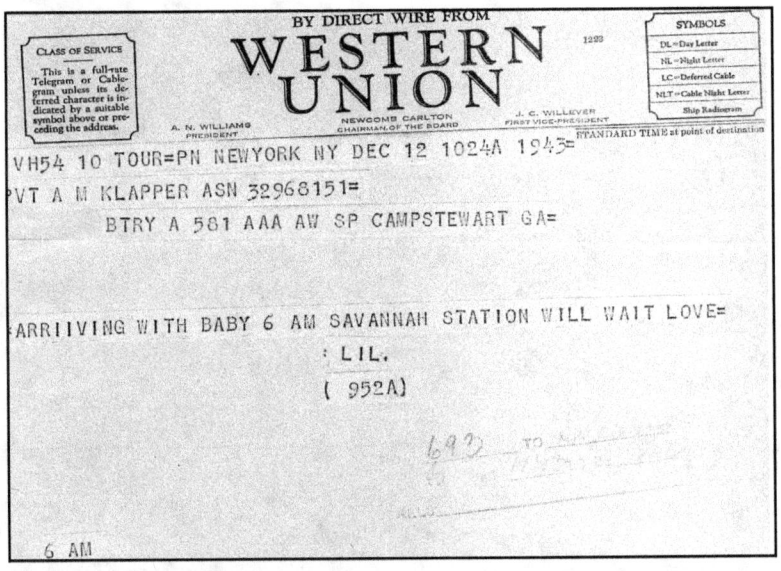

Telegram Mom sent Dad announcing her expected arrival in Savannah, Georgia, on December 13, 1943. Dad received this telegram with mixed feelings of joy at seeing Mom and his baby daughter again and trepidation about where they would be able to find lodgings in the nearby communities already overcrowded with military families.

CHAPTER 4

Cherokee Homes, Port Wentworth, Georgia

AFTER MOM AND FAMILY ARRIVED in Savannah, a girlfriend of one of Dad's sergeants told them about Cherokee Homes, 400 barrack-type apartment units about seven miles northwest of Savannah. Named for the Cherokee Indians of Port Wentworth, the temporary housing had been built for employees of the MacEvoy Shipbuilding Corporation, which was building concrete tank barges as part of the war effort. The complex, which was owned by the federal government and managed by the Housing Authority of Savannah, had been built in a mere forty-six days in 1943 when the government determined that providing affordable housing was the only way to keep enough employees to build the needed barges. Families of soldiers could also qualify to live in these rather primitive apartments about fifty-five miles from Camp Stewart, near enough for Dad to visit whenever he could get a weekend pass.

Although it was very difficult to obtain an apartment in Cherokee Homes, when my parents told the manager that Mom was a registered nurse, two families agreed to "double up" to make room for her and her family. Mom was welcome since medical care was extremely difficult to obtain, and many of the children in the complex were sick with measles and pneumonia. After she moved in, Mom set up a clinic to help take care of them.

The unit was essentially a one-room studio apartment with a small kitchen, bathroom, and two twin beds. It had a wood-burning stove for cooking and heat, as well as a portable heater. Shortly after they moved in, Mom and Grandma went to Savannah and purchased a hot plate so she would be able to heat up baby food quickly and not have to rely solely on the wood stove.

For the first time in her life, Mom had to chop wood and got many blisters on her hands from the effort. The neighbors were very friendly, though, and sometimes offered to help her. Dad said he would always recall Mom showing him how to chop wood "in the backyard of a little house in Georgia."

Soon after they arrived, a big snowstorm blanketed the area, and the neighbors teased her for being "the damn Yankee who had brought the snow to Savannah with her." Mom and Grandma settled in, taking the bus to Savannah to shop for food and other necessities not available in Port Wentworth. They also enrolled Aaron in seventh grade in a school in Savannah. Like all schools in the South at the time, it was segregated, and Aaron was the only Jewish student. The African-American school was located above a movie theater.

Dad was able to get a pass for the first weekend after Mom arrived, and they were ecstatic to be near each other again. As the snow melted, it seemed almost summerlike to Mom and Grandma, who felt lucky to have escaped the brutal New York winter.

On December 21, Dad received a promotion to technical corporal, technician fifth grade, called a "T5," approved by Lt. Col. Joseph Howe, Commanding Officer of the 581st AAA AW Battalion. At the end of that month, he also received a sharpshooter medal for accuracy on the firing range, which pleased him immensely.

Although she was enjoying the weather, Mom was extremely disappointed by Savannah, comparing it unfavorably to New York and describing it as a small town, not a big city. She perceived southern men to be gentlemen, though, because they offered her a seat on the bus and helped her carry packages but thought shopkeepers took advantage of her when they heard her northern accent.

Finding Work

At the end of December, she began to inquire about jobs but quickly became frustrated when she discovered that the defense plants and shipyards were not employing nurses because their insurance companies took care of their employees. Since Mom wasn't sure how long Dad would be stationed at Camp Stewart, she was reluctant to take a full-time job, and the private-duty nursing registry did not want a part-timer since the flu epidemic required them to give nurses two and three cases together. She was also afraid I would get sick if she accepted one of those cases. In addition, Mom was recovering from a bad cold and claimed the clammy Georgia climate made recovery take longer than up north.

Nonetheless, she was grateful to be near Dad. "I didn't expect to find it easy, but I found something else that resembles heaven, especially when you come home."

Dad was not able to get a pass on the weekend of New Year's Eve, so Mom wrote him about her wishes for the year and prayed they and their families would be able to celebrate the next New Year together.

December 31, 1943

> I'm trying to remember what we did last year. I think we both went to work New Year's Eve. Never again will I ever do such a silly thing as be separated from you on such an evening. It's not that it's such a holiday, but it's a symbol of so much, and I always want to face the coming year with you. Of course, I'll excuse this year because it's beyond our power.... Before you left, I thought I knew exactly how I'd feel when you left, but I was only fooling myself because the real pain came only after you had gone.

On January 11, 1944, Mom received official permission from the state of Georgia to practice nursing "during the war emergency period without a license from the Board of Examiners of Nurses for Georgia." However, her job search remained discouraging. The defense plants told her she could not work there because she was an Army wife, which she found ironic. The $6 per day she could receive for a private-duty shift through a registry barely seemed worth it, considering she would have to pay "district dues" each month, buy more uniforms and shoes, pay for laundering uniforms and bus fare, and make a long commute to the hospitals.

By mid-January, however, she had changed her mind and given her name to the registry, deciding to accept the $6 a day payment for lack of a better option. She bought a new pair of white shoes and a "hypo syringe and needle," sewed a black ribbon on her cap that identified her nursing school, and hired a neighbor to launder and iron her uniforms. The day before she began to work, she spent $9 to buy coal and wood.

Mom enjoyed her first private-duty cases, which were in different hospitals in Savannah, finding it much easier to care for one patient at a time than to work in a ward with responsibility for many. Although meager, she used the money she earned to pay rent, buy clothes and other necessities, and tide her over between monthly allotment checks from the Army.

In the middle of February, the doctor assigned to medical care for Cherokee Homes residents asked Mom to assist him with a case, a five-year-old girl who was very ill with bronchopneumonia. The girl was visiting her uncle, who was the head of the Port Wentworth Corporation, and Mom thought the doctor was trying to impress the community in order to advance his career. She put in a sixteen-hour shift and at one point brought the child's 105.6 degree temperature to 101 in an hour. By morning, the girl's temperature had fallen below normal, so Mom asked for some whiskey, which allowed her to bring the girl's temperature back up. Despite being sick herself with a bad cold, Mom worked a seventeen-hour shift the next night, ensuring that the girl's emergency had passed.

The doctor was very impressed by Mom's work and told her he was completely confident in her because of her wonderful training. To reciprocate, he promised to bring her whooping cough serum made by Lederle, a well-known pharmaceutical company, to give to her own child since the "crude" serum used by the Board of Health was causing bad reactions.

Anticipating Furlough and Future Moves

By the beginning of February, Mom was already looking forward to the furlough Dad was expecting in mid-March. About the same time, Dad mused about being a civilian again, "being able to see you every night. Having evenings off and all those other things I used to take for granted. Never again will I do that."

One day in early March, Dad found himself with a few other fellows from New York City, and they began to share reminiscences, which he described in a letter to Mom.

March [?], 1944

> I recalled how in order to see the city and know it, you had to live there. How there are different things to see every hour and every season. The rush hour in the morning and evening. How the trains become crowded again about 8 p.m. for the show crowd. When the baseball season is on, the crowds that get off at the Polo Grounds and the Yankee Stadium. The Palisades all lit up in the evening and the scene from Riverside Drive. The Hudson River and the traffic of the river. The museums, Coney Island, Washington Heights, Central Park. It is all jumbled up, but that's the way these memories come to my mind. I just wish I could take a subway ride.

Unlike New York City, Savannah had a dearth of young women, and Mom, a pretty, petite twenty-three-year-old brunette, personally felt the effects of that deficit. One evening, while waiting for a bus back to Port Wentworth after she had been visiting Dad, a lonely soldier approached and asked if she needed an "escort." Another time, when she was getting off a bus from Hunter Field, a crowd of Air Force boys had yelled in unison, "Do you need an escort?" She was very embarrassed but recognized that she was traveling alone in a city filled with soldiers, most of them far from their homes and families.

In mid-March Dad learned his unit was being sent to "the middle of a swamp" somewhere on the Camp Stewart reservation. He was afraid the new location, which was about twenty miles from Savannah and about four miles off the main road, would make it very difficult to pick up a "hitch" to Port Wentworth to see Mom and the family.

To complicate their lives even further, Mom feared she might be pregnant again, a prospect that depressed her since they were barely managing with one child. Dad tried to reassure her, telling her that having children was not a "crime" and advising that she disregard criticism from others about it being the wrong time. He reminded her that he was almost twenty-nine already and said he would rather have children now than later, anyway. Responding to her thoughts about "going to the doctor," Dad told Mom not to "falter and weaken in your morals and character," but to be proud of her "fertility." All his life, Dad wrote, he had done the "proper" thing—until he met Mom. Meeting her had given him the courage to do things he had never done before, and he had no regrets—just confidence in her and in the future.

Although she probably appreciated Dad's confidence, she was still relieved a few weeks later when she learned she was not pregnant. She told Dad she had probably had a miscarriage and said a pregnancy now "would have been an awkward situation, to say the least."

Mom began thinking about returning to New York around the end of February when I became ill from teething. She had been planning to travel back to New York with Dad when his furlough came through but started to think about leaving early because I was so uncomfortable in Georgia. Back home, I would have a full-sized crib, playpen, and toys, and she would have easier access to my doctors. Dad left the decision up to her. He loved having her near him, of course, but told her to do what she thought was best for us.

She decided to give up the apartment in Cherokee Homes, hoping she could find a place in Savannah if she came back after Dad's furlough. But she vowed if she did return it would be alone, without her mother and brother. "My family is really nice, darling, but not to live with. I'm determined to do everything on my own from now on, so no one will be able to aggravate me and say things to hurt me."

Mom decided to leave Savannah in mid-March, ahead of Dad, who would have to complete a two-week bivouac—a temporary military encampment—before he could leave on furlough. This experience was considered essential to simulate what the soldiers would face in actual maneuvers and combat.

Mom made plans to stay with Dad's parents in Manhattan and wait for him to arrive on his furlough. She was looking forward to spending time in the city with Dad, and she also probably needed a break from Grandma after sharing such close quarters for three months in Port Wentworth.

Dad tried to get a pass to see us once more before our departure, but he was turned down since his unit was preparing for their bivouac. A neighbor in Cherokee Homes brought us dinner a few nights before we left, and another invited us over for our last evening. Grandma had already prepared our food for that night, but she and Mom were touched by the invitation and gave the neighbor the last of our remaining "fat" wood. Exactly three months since boarding the train to Georgia—Monday, March 12, 1944—Mom, Grandma, Aaron, and I headed back to New York.

ARMY OF THE UNITED STATES

Private Abraham M Klapper is hereby appointed Technician Fifth Grade (Temporary), ARMY OF THE UNITED STATES, to rank as such from the twenty-first day of December one thousand nine hundred and forty-three. I do strictly charge and require all Noncommissioned Officers and Soldiers under his command to be obedient to his orders as Technician Fifth Grade. And he is to observe and follow such orders and directions from time to time, as he shall receive from his Superior Officers and Noncommissioned Officers set over him, according to the rules and discipline of War.

JOS. G. HOWE
Lt. Col.
581st AAA AW Bn (SP)
Commanding.

Dad's promotion order appointing him Technician Fifth Grade, December 21, 1943, by Lt. Col. Joseph G. Howe, Commander, 581st AAA AW Bn. This was Dad's first promotion from Private, which gave him some satisfaction at the time.

1st DISTRICT NURSING COUNCIL FOR WAR SERVICE

In accordance with Section 84-1013 of the Law Governing the Practice of Nursing in Georgia

"84-1013--Gratuitous or emergency nursing.--- This Chapter shall not be construed to affect or apply to gratuitous nursing of the sick by friends of the family or as an emergency aid, nor to affect a situation in the event public emergency pronounced by the State Board of Health to exist in the State at large, or any part thereof, or in the event of an emergency declared by national health authorities requiring nursing service within or without the State, in which case unlicensed persons may be permitted to nurse or care for the sick for hire during the continuance thereof. (Acts 1927, p. 254.)"

it is recognized that Lillian Schein Klapper is practicing nursing during the war emergency period without license from the Board of Examiners of Nurses for Georgia.

Signed _____, Chairman
District Nursing Council for War Service

Date Jan-11-44

I plan to be in the State of Georgia for _____ months and wish to help out in the emergency need for nurses. Should I remain in Georgia after the war emergency period, and continue the practice of nursing, I will complete requirements for state registration.

Signed Lillian Schein Klapper
Address Cherokee Homes R.F.D. #1
Date 1-11-44

Mom's certificate to practice nursing in Georgia during the war emergency period without a Georgia license, January 11, 1944. This allowed her to work as a nurse in Georgia, so she could support herself and her family, as Dad's Army allotment was not sufficient.

CHAPTER 5

Furlough, Return to Camp Stewart, D-Day!

AFTER ARRIVING IN NEW YORK, Mom settled in with Dad's parents to wait for him. Of course, she missed him terribly but was happy to have the comforts of a real apartment again. Although it was modest, it had steam heat, a gas-fired stove, and real beds. She also enjoyed having lots of family members around; relatives from both sides visited frequently, making a big fuss over me, and Dad's mother made Friday night Shabbat dinners for anyone who showed up.

Dad's furlough finally came through the last week in March. Although I have no letters from this period, it was clearly a joyous time, as he demonstrates in his first letter to Mom after he returned to camp.

> April 3, 1944
>
> When the conductor announced Savannah, it was like taking a piece of my heart out of my breast. . . . From the minute the train pulled out of Penn Station, I felt it tugging. And as each succeeding town passed, that tugging became worse, and finally Savannah was the worst.

Although he had promised to look for a place close to Camp Stewart so Mom could move back to Savannah, he found nothing suitable. He was also hearing rumors that the camp was going to be closed by the first of June or July. He speculated it would be used as a prison camp and hospital since he knew the Army would need space for both prisoners and casualties when the long-expected European invasion occurred. Units were being shipped to other camps at the end of April, so he felt it was best to wait another month to see where he would wind up.

It had become very difficult for Dad to call Mom on the camp's overloaded telephone system. Men would have to reserve a spot on a list early in the morning and then wait many hours for their call to be placed. One Sunday in early May, Dad gave up after waiting for nine hours, hoping he would try later in the week. Because she couldn't predict when the calls would come, Mom was not always home when Dad did get through, disappointing them both.

Dad sometimes wrote of his dreams for what their life would be like after the war, and he was optimistic that they would come true because he felt his hopes were reasonable. All he wanted was a house with a garage, a car, and perhaps some land for "a few chickens and maybe a cow."

By the end of May, Mom was living with her parents but becoming more and more unhappy with the situation, so she told Dad she was thinking of renting an apartment in a wartime housing project in Jamaica, Queens. A large complex completed in 1940, South Jamaica Houses, in the New York City borough of Queens, included 440 apartments in eleven three- and four-story buildings spread over nine acres. Many of the apartments were occupied by military wives and their children, but Mom was initially nervous about moving there because of the large "negro population." Dad advised her to make the move, if that was what she wanted, and not be worried about being harmed, reminding her that she had a "negro playmate" when she was young. "Besides," he wrote, "it would only be practicing a little democracy." Eventually, Mom and I did move into the complex.

Dad was still at Camp Stewart by the end of May, and he wanted Mom to come down for a short visit, leaving me behind, if necessary. But he was also worried about her making the trip because the camp was "in turmoil," with all of the transfers in and out. He wasn't certain what would happen to him each day, although he was scheduled for a two-week bivouac starting on June 10 or 11. When his unit returned, they were expected to take the AGF (Army Ground Forces) exam and then be shipped somewhere else. Dad was hoping to be sent to a camp on Long Island, where it would be possible to see Mom whenever he had free time.

The Invasion

In June, Dad was still at Camp Stewart. He was lonely without Mom and still uncertain about her traveling to see him. But news of the imminent D-Day invasion made him feel more optimistic about the progress and sooner end of the war.

June 5, 1944

> If the Russians start their offensive soon, it will catch the Germans in a giant squeeze play. It is even possible that the Nazis already know they are licked and will offer only token resistance to the Allies and fierce resistance to the Russians. That would slow up the latter and permit the former to take Berlin. The Nazis know they will get more mercy from the Allies than [from] the Russians. Soon, maybe sooner than we think, it will be over in Europe and soon we can think of going home.

His letter on June 6, the day of the invasion, expresses his excitement.

June 6, 1944

> I have waited so long to hear it that I can scarcely believe it. The ease with which the Allies have been able to establish a beachhead is also significant. It might mean that we have overestimated her strength. After all, five years of war would be bound to have its effects.

At the time, Dad was probably unaware of the large number of casualties the Allies suffered while establishing those beachheads. Although excited about the invasion, Dad wondered if it would result in a new movement of troops, which could mean his unit would get shipped to Europe. Nothing was certain, so the men in his unit were "glued to the radio" listening to the news. There was talk they might be moved out of Camp Stewart even before their two-week bivouac was over.

Dad was waiting to hear about "a big Russian move.... With the Allies pushing up in Italy and in France, the Nazis don't know where to send their available troops first." He also expected to see more landings in Europe, "around Holland and Belgium and southern France." A few days later, he predicted "a period in which the Allies will consolidate their beachheads so as to get the enormous supplies necessary on the continent required for such a vast undertaking." Dad's speculations grew not only from the radio broadcasts, but also from his avid reading of the GI newspaper, *Stars and Stripes*, and the weekly GI magazine, *Yank*. He also devoured the regular newspapers available at the USO whenever he got into town.

In spite of the invasion excitement, he could not stop thinking about Mom, reminiscing about how beautiful she had looked in her white uniform at her nursing school graduation. "You took my breath away. Like an angel you were. I love you so much my darling. And miss you so." He promised that when he came home they would take the honeymoon they didn't have after their elopement.

Dad's unit did end up on the June bivouac, but so many men ended up "prostrated" in the Georgia heat that the medics ordered the entire battalion to cease training and to rest on the fairgrounds of the nearby town of Reidsville. A local farmer told Dad's group about a swimming hole his boys had used before they went into the Army, and the men enjoyed it a few times, which helped "tremendously."

In mid-July, Mom decided to visit Dad for a short time and found temporary housing for the two of us with a family in Jesup, Georgia. Dad was delighted to have her nearby again, but the summer heat was proving to be unbearable, especially as the house had no refrigeration. Dad promised to bring salt tablets, which the men used to help overcome heat exhaustion. But Mom became ill with a serious infection and had to leave after only a brief stay.

Far Rockaway was a welcome contrast, with its cooler climate and proximity to the beach. Mom wrote in August to tell Dad how much better I felt and looked there.

At the end of the first week in August, Dad found out his unit was indeed going to Long Island for six weeks, and they would be leaving in ten to twelve days. He was thrilled at the thought of being near home again and excited to think how much easier and cheaper it would be to get home during his upcoming furlough. But he cautioned Mom not to say anything to anyone about his movements, not even to their parents. Army security warned everyone about the importance of secrecy for everyone's safety, worrying about "unfriendly ears." Even if his unit were being moved overseas, he could not have told her.

I turned one year old while Dad was still at Camp Stewart, and he wrote me a special birthday letter. He asked Mom to read it to me, even though he knew I wouldn't understand it all.

August 16, 1944

To my daughter on her first birthday,

Darling, one year has passed since you came to us.

Your mummy and I still can't realize the miracle of having you. Each day you become more precious to us, if that is possible. You have become a source of strength and inspiration to me. To your mummy you are a comfort during her lonely hours in these times when I am so far away. Keep up the good work until I come back to you. I hope that by your next birthday, I won't have to send you greetings by mail.

I don't know if the world will be any better after this war is over, but I can tell you one thing that can help you through this society of ours. Learn to distinguish between RIGHT and WRONG. Be honest with yourself first, and you won't ever be false to others. People will respect you for that and yours will be a proud niche in society.

Happy Birthday, darling, and God bless you.

He wrote to Mom on that day also.

August 16, 1944

Darling,
Today is Sue's first birthday. All day I have been walking around telling the boys about it. 'Just imagine, my baby is one year old today. And where am I? In the goddam army.'

Well! We must face the facts. We are at war and I am in the Army because I felt that was the place I could help the most. The sadness and aggravation it has caused us has been lightened by Sue's coming. Soon, I hope the war will be over and we will have our own place. Then you can fuss and bother to your heart's content.

I can't say much of anything about what we are doing. You must understand, I know. . . .

Lights out soon, darling, so good night. Happy birthday Sue darling. [Dad used my middle name here.]

I love you both, A

Birthday card Mom sent to Dad at Camp Stewart for his birthday in March 1944. Note design and caption, "To My Husband in the Service."

Mom, Dad, and me, seven months old, while Dad was home on furlough from Camp Stewart, March 1944, in front of Dad's parents' home in Manhattan.

Dad and some buddies from his unit while training in the swamps of Georgia at Camp Stewart on bivouac in June 1944. They were enjoying a swimming hole near Reidsville that a local farmer, whose own son was away in the Army, had told them about. It was a welcome break from the sweltering summer heat.

Dad and his unit in Georgia training to use an antiaircraft machine gun, ca. June 1944.

> **To my daughter on her first birthday.**
>
> Darling, one year has passed since you came to us. Your mummy and I still can't realize the miracle of having you. Each day you become more precious to us, if that is possible. You have become a source of strength and inspiration to me. To your mummy you are a comfort during her lonely hours in these times when I am so far away. Keep up the good work until I come back to you.

First page of letter Dad wrote to me from Camp Stewart on my first birthday, August 16, 1944. Unfortunately, I did not see this letter, which was buried in the collection Mom gave me, until after Dad had passed away.

CHAPTER 6

Awaiting Overseas Deployment

ALTHOUGH I HAVE NO LETTERS from September through early October 1944, I have concluded from later correspondence that Dad's unit did get sent to Long Island. I assume there are no letters from that time because he and Mom got to visit each other frequently. But in mid-October, much to Dad's chagrin, their unit was sent back to Camp Stewart. This time they were not even housed in barracks, but in tents, without their own set of showers. He conceded it was better than being in combat, but it was harder to bear since he had become accustomed to seeing Mom often and eating her wonderful cooking.

All sorts of rumors were "running around" about the unit's fate, but nothing was certain. However, he was sending Mom information about a "new allotment," presumably for overseas duty, so it seemed the Army was finally preparing the men for overseas deployment. Dad cautioned Mom not to come to Savannah because he was sure they would not be at Camp Stewart for more than a month or two.

Although Dad wrote after a week of living in tents that his unit was moving from their tents back into barracks, he could tell her little else about what was going on at camp. Only that they were moving around a lot of equipment and receiving immunizations. Many outfits would be moving out in the next few weeks, and he wondered if his would be one of them.

Sometime in October, Mom must have communicated with Dad about the fate of her maternal grandparents and aunts, who had not immigrated with the rest of the family in the 1920s. Mom's family had learned that her grandparents and aunts had been murdered when Nazis entered Lwów, Poland. One of Mom's cousins later told me that the information had probably come from other former inhabitants or possibly through the *landsleit* organization based in New York. *Landsleit* groups were immigrant benevolent organizations formed by former members of the original communities in Europe.

In the fourth week of October, Dad responded to Mom's tragic news.

October 25, 1944

> You must have been terribly shocked about the news of your grandparents and aunts. What a horrible way to die. We are lucky to be so far removed, physically, from it all. If I go to Europe, I promise to get you a few Nazi heads. Nothing would give me greater satisfaction.

The news from Poland was especially devastating to Grandma and her two surviving brothers, Sam and Herman, who were living in the States. Herman had visited their parents in Lwów in the early 1930s to try to persuade them to move to New York. They had refused because their dairy and egg business was doing well and they didn't think the United States would be "kosher" enough, meaning they would not be able to have the traditional Jewish lifestyle they were used to.

Although we were never able to determine exactly how they perished, my own research about the Jews who had lived in Lwów during the war led me to conclude they were probably murdered either by anti-Semitic Ukrainians, whom the Nazis allowed to randomly kill Jews before they began their own "official" roundups and "Aktions," or by German soldiers before they herded the remaining Jews into the ghetto or a nearby concentration camp. Alternatively, they may have perished in either the Belzec or Janowska concentration camps, the fate of many of the Jews from the Lwów ghetto.

More Training, More Rumors

Dad's training at Camp Stewart continued. The Army liked to have the men perform in a formal parade once in a while, as part of their routine, which he found extremely annoying.

> October 27, 1944
>
> This parade business, if you ask me, is just a bunch of baloney. If you can show me how it will help win the war, I'll gladly do it all day long. For the man in a peace time army who has nothing else to do, I suppose it's all right. If the Army hasn't got anything better for me to do . . . then they should discharge us and let us go home. I was under the impression that I was drafted . . . to learn how to fight, join in battle with the enemy, defeat him and come home. That fancy stuff and nonsense is not for me.

Although the war news was encouraging, Dad still expected it to take a spring and maybe summer campaign to defeat the Nazis, but he was hoping not to be living in Germany during the winter because he knew it was going to be a cold one. Assuming he was about to be deployed overseas, he devised a code to let Mom know where he had been sent. If his letters carried only an APO address, Mom could know that he was no longer in the States, and then he would utilize their code, which was to be based on how he began his letters to her: Honey—Europe; Beloved—India; Sweetheart—China; My Darling—Pacific (Philippines or Pacific Islands). He also made arrangements for her to receive by government check the $20 he had been sending her from his paycheck. Once he was overseas, the Army would send her 20 percent of his pay.

Dad predicted that November was going to be a big month, both personally and politically. Personally, because it would be their anniversary and his destination would probably be determined. Politically, it would be important because the Americans had already "smashed the Japanese navy, and the entire Pacific Ocean is practically free for us to roam without opposition."

He predicted the Japanese troops left on islands in the South Pacific "will die and shrivel up, like the leaves of a broken limb of a tree" without ammunition and medical supplies. They were also subject to the "anopheles mosquito [that] bites them and gives them malaria, the same as they would infect a white man or a native." They would also need food and other supplies, which they would not be able to obtain without a navy. He thought we would be in complete control of the Philippines by the end of November. Then he expected the next step to be either China or even Japan itself.

In addition, Dad expected the approaches to the major port of Antwerp in Belgium would soon be open "to pour in men and supplies over a tremendously shorter route than Cherbourg. Its importance is so enormous that the Nazis didn't hesitate to use almost 50,000 troops, badly needed to defend the Reich proper to prevent us from using it." He also expected the winter to further hasten the end of the Nazi regime, because he couldn't see how they could keep supplying their troops adequately to wage a large-scale war. "No coal, no houses, living in shelters, no hope, just waiting for their impending doom, which is inevitable. And they know it too."

As he continued to wait it out at Camp Stewart, he told Mom once more how important mail call was and how her letters helped him survive.

November 2, 1944

I love you very much darling. The high spot of each day for me is mail call. Knowing you love me is what keeps me going, dearest. It is what sustains me when the going gets rough. Remember that I love you, too, and forever and ever. That's why I can bear the long hours of our separation. I know that I can always count on that. Like a lighthouse in a gale. Like the "rock of ages" against the furious sea.

All he could say about camp in early November was, "things are cooking around here." He hinted he would delay trying to call because he thought in a little while he would be able to do so more easily. He even hoped to see her soon.

On their two-year anniversary, Dad reminisced about how they had eloped to get married.

November 5, 1944

Today was anniversary day for us. Two years since I came up to that room on East 77th Street, and then we went up to the Bronx. . . . Twenty-four months of life I wouldn't give one minute of for all my single existence. Yes, I mean existence. Before we married, darling, I only hoped to meet someone like you. When at last I found you, I knew it. Just to be sure, I fought against it. But when I found that it was to be only you, I was your slave. You could wind me around your finger, just to be near you. For seven months we lived together, and now only the future will tell us when we can be together again. For good. Forever. My whole life [is] you and Bonnie.

He kept writing about the life they would share when he returned. Even on a mail clerk's salary, he expected to be able to buy a little house with a playroom, a workshop, and a spotlessly clean kitchen with lots of gadgets. And he looked forward to figuring out easy ways to do hard things, like hanging curtains. He watched news of the war fronts so closely, he wrote, because "[e]very foot of ground gained brings me a second closer to build that for you and the children." He was also closely watching the presidential election and hoping Roosevelt would win again.

By this time, Mom was settling into her apartment in the public housing project in Jamaica, fixing it up as best she could on a limited budget to make it feel like a real home. Although she was lonely at first, she began to enjoy her privacy after so many months living with her parents or her in-laws. She also began to make friends with other soldiers' wives who lived nearby. If she wanted to see her parents, she could take a bus directly from the project to Far Rockaway. Although she had been angry when Mom moved out, her mother eventually began to visit us in our apartment.

In mid-November, Dad took a chance with the censor and told her his unit would be leaving shortly. He hoped to see her soon, but he was still not certain whether they would end up in California or New York.

Mom wrote about a war-related incident she had witnessed at home that she and Dad felt was comical. On Rockaway Beach, people had seen a battalion of about 900 AAA (antiaircraft artillery) men. Dad found out the identity of the outfit and speculated the Army was worried about "buzz bombs" that might be launched from submarines or planes. He felt this was an improbable scenario, considering the ocean was patrolled for quite a distance, but he envied the men deployed there.

Dad was following the trend of Russo-Japanese relations with great interest. If Russia declared war on Japan once the war with Germany was over, it would be defeated much more quickly, he predicted.

He also wrote to report that at last, he was happy with a new assignment: conducting orientation lectures for the battery, which was "a must feature in training, and even for troops finished with training." He found this very interesting and reported the men enjoyed the "little talks" he gave every day for a few minutes.

Dad warned Mom that very soon their mail would be read by a third party, a military censor, so he would not be able to say as much as before. He told her to try to "read between the lines, and I know you will be able to discern what I mean, even if I can't write the actual words."

Dreaming of the Future

Just after Thanksgiving, he managed to get a three-day pass, giving them exactly twenty-five hours together because of Dad's travel time. Although short, the time was heaven for them after being apart for so long. It also gave him a chance to see me and enjoy giving me kisses himself, not "by proxy," as he usually directed Mom in his letters.

Both wanted to have more children and were puzzling over whether to wait until Dad was home for good or begin trying sooner if he were relocated to New York. Dad was worried about whether Mom could handle a baby and a toddler alone, although he felt it would be good to have the children grow up "almost at the same time. They will go to college and get all they can out of life. Maybe we'll have some famous kids after all. Huh?"

In early December, back at Camp Stewart, Dad's unit was given a lecture on censorship letting them know that prohibited subjects included "their location, strength, materiel, or equipment . . . installations . . . transportation facilities . . . routes, ports . . . movements of ships, troops or aircraft . . . plans and forecasts or orders for future operations . . . effect of enemy operations . . . and casualties. . . ." They were also warned about any enclosures, photos, films, or postcards that might include information that would violate the rules. The censoring was done by an officer in the soldier's unit. If the letter contained a large amount of prohibited information, the whole letter would be confiscated. If it was only a small amount, the prohibited words would be cut out or blacked out with ink. Soldiers were not always told if their letters had been confiscated, and they would not get them back. Approved letters were stamped by the censor, who would either sign his full name or initial them.

In the censorship lecture, the men were warned not to try to use any sort of code to indicate their location. After hearing this, Dad told Mom it would be best not to attempt to elude the censor.

> December 6 (?), 1944
>
> First of all, if I am in a large theater, like France, India, or Australia, they let you say so anyway. Anything more explicit than that is not necessary, and if the authorities think it is secret enough not to mention it, then it is better left unsaid until it is safe to reveal it. You understand, honey. Don't you?

Starting on the fifteenth of December, they were not supposed to leave the immediate area. The rumor was they were going to go to Camp Shanks, located in Orangeburg in Rockland County, New York. Although not as close as Fort Hamilton, in New York Harbor, Camp Shanks was still near New York City, and Dad promised he would get home somehow. Of course, Mom was not to say a word about any of this to anyone, not even her mother.

On a lighter note, Dad described often going to movies on the base as a way to pass his off-duty hours. At the end of the first week in December, he saw *To Have and Have Not* with Humphrey Bogart "and a startling new discovery, Lauren Bacall. Sex Incorporated. Wow! What a woman."

About the same time, Mom told him she thought she was pregnant. When he heard the news, Dad was concerned, but he looked forward to having another child. He told Mom that he had heard a song on the radio that should be their theme song, "I'll Get By."

As the men loaded up their boxcar to leave Camp Stewart, Dad's captain told them they were not necessarily going to Fort Hamilton but that they would not be more than thirty-five miles from New York, and that they would be allowed twelve-hour passes when they arrive. On a postcard stamped December 16, Dad sent Mom his new APO address for sending him mail at the POE (Port of Embarkation) and overseas. On Sunday, December 17, he wrote this would be their last Sunday at Camp Stewart, and that they could now count their meals there on their fingers.

On December 16, 1944, the Germans launched a surprise counterattack on the western front in the Ardennes Forest in Belgium and northern France and also into Luxembourg. That attack came to be known as the Battle of the Bulge, and my parents later told me that it was because of this attack that Dad's unit was sent to Europe rather than the Pacific. But my own research has led me to believe that the decision to send Dad's unit to Europe was made even before the Battle of the Bulge because of other events occurring earlier in northwest Europe, especially the Battle of the Hürtgen Forest. That battle had begun in mid-September 1944 and raged until early December 1944.

Ironically, much of the training at Camp Stewart had been to prepare the men for the war in the Pacific as its climate and terrain were similar to what they would have faced there. However, it became clear that the Germans were not done fighting, and that more troops would need to be deployed to the European theater. So, although Dad was not allowed to write where he was headed, he and Mom correctly assumed it was to Europe and not the Pacific.

Dad arrived at his new location, which he was not permitted to disclose, around December 20. Again, he warned Mom, "Under no circumstances mention my whereabouts to anyone whatsoever [*sic*]. Not even your mom or mine." He said if she was asked by anyone, she should only reply he was safe.

Despite his warnings, Dad's next letter received the censor's scissors as he had inadvertently relayed forbidden information. In this letter, he was realizing that he might not be able to see her again before he was shipped overseas. He told her not to worry about him but to use all of her "faculties" to take care of herself and me, because if he knew she was worried, it would only cause them both harm. He concluded, "If my letter sounds odd, honey, remember that I have had to make adjustments that are new to me."

A few days before he sailed, just before Christmas, he told her again how "funny" it felt not to be able to write as freely as he used to. "I can't even date this or tell you where or what, but the chow is good." He acknowledged how she must have felt when she had received his change of address card, but he was glad she had accepted it "with reason." His letter ended, "I need your love and letters more than ever now."

In what was probably the last letter he wrote before he left, Dad said they had received a lecture on "personal affairs" and been told that those who were unsure if their wives were pregnant should make arrangements for medical care and "a year's medical attention for the baby." As a result, he said she would be receiving a lot of forms and questionnaires about this. He also informed her that, "on or about March 1," she would start to get $35 per month, instead of the usual $20, from his overseas pay.

In an attempt to cheer up both of them, he said at least one stage in their waiting was about to end because they knew he could not come home for good until he had gone overseas. Since he was now about to do that, they were thus entering the home stretch.

December (?), 1944

> Be strong and keep well. The war news isn't as black as it looks. The Nazis are shooting their bolt. You wait and see if I am not right. . . .
> So long for now my dearest love. God bless you and keep you safe. Merry Christmas and a Happy New Year. Kiss Bonnie for me.
>
> I love you both
>
> —A

Change of address postcard Dad mailed to Mom indicating his new address with APO number, which meant he was to be shipped overseas. December 1944. He had earlier alerted her that when she received this, she would know that he would be leaving Camp Stewart.

Letter Dad wrote to Mom in late December 1944 with censor's deletion of prohibited information in blanked-out area. See encircled spaces.

Dad's Soldier's Individual Pay Record showing increase in pay to $35.00 per month and increase in monthly allotment to Mom of $22.00 due to his foreign service, dated December 26, 1944, the day his ship departed, to be effective February 1, 1945.

CHAPTER 7

On a Transport Ship— Destination Unknown

ON THE DAY AFTER CHRISTMAS 1944, Dad set sail on an Army transport ship packed with other soldiers for a location somewhere in Europe. He had never been on a boat before, so being at sea was a completely new experience.

> December [?] 1944 [undated]
>
> I suppose a sailor would call this a calm ocean, but to a landlubber like myself, the waves are mountainous. The foam that forms at their crest looks like snow on a distant mountain. The weather is beautiful and the fresh air like a tonic. I haven't any idea where we are, because wherever I look, as far as the eye can see, there is nothing but water.

He was overwhelmed by the vastness of the sea and felt "humble before it."

> December [?] 1944 [undated]
>
> Yet we have people in our world who think that they are so very important. Little people, really.

Like Shakespeare put it, 'a poor player who struts and frets his hour upon the stage and then is heard no more.' Perhaps the time is coming when they will smarten up. I hope so for their own sake.

He was deeply impressed by the natural beauty of the seascape. "The ocean looks so blue and black. The white foam stands out against the inky blackness. It looks so restless." Just before the end of the month, he described an incredible phenomenon he had seen in the very early morning while on guard duty.

December 30, 1944

The moon was very bright and shone on the water like hot wax. The ocean was dark, restless, and foreboding. I glanced off into the distance and there off the starboard bow I saw a rainbow. Imagine a rainbow by moonlight. I thought I was seeing things, so I called another of the guards, and he verified my observation. What a world this is, honey.

Although it was crowded on the ship, there was still plenty of room for activities like movies and some sports. "For a fellow who has lived on subways all his life, this isn't too bad." Also, the PX had a variety of items available, like candy and cigarettes, for very low prices.

V-Mail

While sailing, Dad began to use the "V-mail" system for the first time to write to Mom. Because the writing on V-mails was reduced to a very small size, he advised her to buy a magnifying glass to more easily read his letters and urged her to use this system, too, because it was the fastest method of sending letters overseas.

The V-mail system had been devised by the British in May 1941 to alleviate the pressure of delivering a huge volume of mail between civilians and military members in the same ships, planes, and trucks needed to transport essential supplies. The U.S. began to use the system in June 1942.

Correspondents had to use a special V-mail form, which would later be folded up to become its own envelope. The sender had to write the recipient's name and address on the back of the form and in a box at the top of the letter. Processing centers in New York City, San Francisco, and, later, Chicago would receive the V-mails in the U.S. According to a 2008 article in *America in WWII*, the form would be checked by military censors and then microfilmed, reducing its size from standard U.S. copy paper to "about the size of a postage stamp. . . . One reel of microfilm was about the size of a pack of cigarettes and weighed 12 ounces. Each reel carried more than 1,600 letters, which would have weighed 48 pounds as standard mail. A bag of V-mail reels replaced . . . 65 sacks of conventional mail."

The reels were then flown overseas, reaching their destination much more quickly than standard or even regular airmail letters, which sometimes ended up on a ship anyway. Overseas, the microfilm reels would be taken to a V-mail facility and enlarged to four inches wide by five and a half inches tall. The letters would be cut apart, folded, and placed into an envelope with the address visible through a special window. "By mid-1944," according to the *America in WWII* article, "V-mail took three to five days to reach Iceland, Britain, and even Australia; five to ten days to reach North Africa; and twelve to eighteen days to get to India. Standard mail might wait more than a month to find space on a ship and then would have to make the long, slow voyage to its destination." By war's end, American GIs and civilians had sent more than a billion V-mail letters.

Although the V-mail system was much faster, users were confined to a very limited space to write and could not send enclosures of any kind. If the writer wanted to write more than one page, he or she had to send another V-mail form. When Dad sent more than one V-mail at a time, he would write a number on top of each form so Mom would be able to read them in the order that he wrote them.

Dad came to appreciate the V-mail system, for all its faults, and he also gained a new appreciation of the Red Cross during his transatlantic journey. He told Mom that the Red Cross handed out gifts and distributed a large amount of reading material. "As soon as you hit the gangplank, their special services start functioning."

An Uncertain New Year

On January 1, he wished Mom a happy New Year but admitted that "[t]his is a solemn new year, and only god [*sic*] knows what is going to be our lot for the next twelve months. And he isn't telling." Dad said he had some idea of where they were going but was not permitted to write about that.

In his letter of January 2, he mused about how it would feel for all of those on the ship to live in a land where English was not universally spoken. "It will almost be like a show with us as the spectators." The Army was distributing literature explaining that the people where they were headed liked Americans very much. "I can imagine how I'd feel if I had been under nazi rule for so long."

On January 3, Dad used regular stationery, which gave him more room to write, to describe a beautiful sunrise at sea.

January 3, 1945

My dearest baby,
This morning I saw a gorgeous sunrise. On the horizon low was a wall of grey black clouds. Above this, the sky was changing from bright silver to darker shades of grey. Gradually, as I looked I

could see the silver change to bright red. It is afternoon now, and the ocean is as calm as a lake and such a beautiful blue. Pity is that we can't enjoy these pleasures of nature together, darling. For me the days seem to pass quite rapidly. Thank god. I keep busy with writing to you, reading, and now I am also trying to brush up on my languages. Details such as guard duty also make my time pass. . . .

I guess we will land in a few days. Where we are going is still a mystery.

He had not received mail from Mom for quite a while by this point, and he looked forward to getting "a load of it" when he finally landed. In the meantime, he wrote, "I just keep on seeing you and Bonnie in my mind, and that's when I start to daydream. Day or night."
He was still at sea on January 4, anxiously waiting to land and longing for the ultimate defeat of Germany that coming summer.

January 4, 1945

How tired we are of this business. Can you imagine how the nazis must feel. They are fighting diabolically clever, as if the devil was on their general staff. I suppose we can't blame them for fighting so desperately. Our aims, as publicly stated, offer them nothing but complete annihilation. Therefore, they resist like trapped rats, which they are.

He wrote from the ship for the last time on the evening of January 5. Since he was not permitted to say anything about their activities, he told Mom how much he missed her and the solace he took in writing.

January 5, 1945

So many miles are between us, but I feel you in my heart tonight and that brings you close to me. I can't help but feel how much water has passed under the bridge since we first laid eyes upon each other.

I can just see that old gal in Bellevue [the hospital where Mom did her nurse's training] who sat at the desk just inside the entrance on 26 St. Remember how perturbed she was when I stayed a half hour past curfew. Looking back I can see how cute that really was.

This reminiscence will take up the major portion of my letters from now on. I can't write about my activities and, besides, the past is what I seem to live in most these days. I can't seem to realize that I am so far from home. We have been on this ark for so long now, I think I am able to find my way around in the dark. This may be the last letter we will be able to send out until I land.

If I could look into the future, I'd know what was to be my lot in the next six months. Maybe it is better not to be so clairvoyant. I got enough to think about for the present. . . . What I'd give to be able to see you both now. I miss you so much tonight darling. Kiss Bonnie for me.

I love you and miss you both

—A

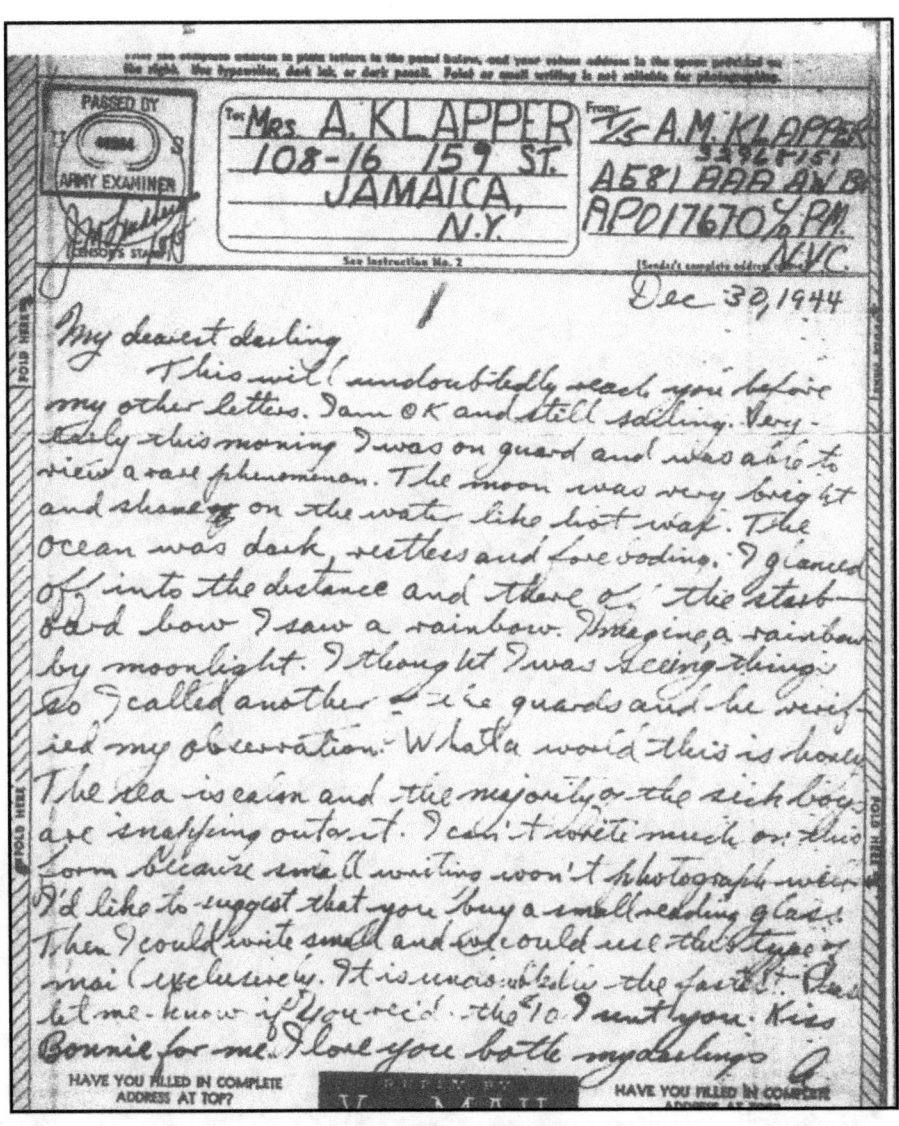

First V-mail Dad sent to Mom while onboard the transport ship taking him overseas. This was the quickest way for soldiers to send letters to their relatives and friends at home during the war and was used until the war in Europe ended. Note censor's stamp and signature on top left.

CHAPTER 8

The "British Isles"

ON JANUARY 7, 1945, Dad was finally able to inform Mom that he had landed safely, writing "England" across the top of his first letter in order to let her know his general location. After a few days, he was moved and wrote that he was stationed "somewhere in the British Isles" and that his barracks were located on the grounds of an old estate, with a large main building of "antique" architecture and many towers and chimneys and "God knows how many rooms."

Although Dad could not say exactly where he was, I know from later conversations that he was in Paisley, Scotland, at the time. In his letters, he was able to describe the general landscape, telling Mom that everything was on a much smaller scale than in the States: little neat farms, small houses, narrow roads, small autos and railroads. He said it looked like "Greenwich Village on a large-scale set in a New England background" with "very nice and polite" people. At intersections, he could imagine he saw "a toy policeman in a brightly lit uniform spring out of a box and start directing traffic with mechanical gestures. Like a musical comedy."

Army literature explained the differences between American and British cultures (they "are reserved to cover up a natural shyness") and described how much the population had suffered during five and a half years of war. During orientation lectures, Dad's unit learned how deeply the British had been affected by the heavy rationing and scarcity of goods. But they were cautioned, "they are a proud people and don't seek anyone's sympathy."

The men changed their money into British currency, and Dad was amused when he heard his buddies shooting craps saying "shoot a shilling or a sixpence." He also described how people drove on the left, took baths instead of showers, and spoke in a "quaint" manner.

ALTHOUGH HE WAS NOT ABLE to tell Mom his exact locations, he was allowed to describe his experience on his first pass. He praised the American Red Cross, because "if it wasn't for them, I'd feel lost, and that goes for most of us. They are the liaison between yourself and the natives." At their facility, he "took a hot shower and slept between clean sheets." He saw a beautiful municipal building with an interior of "solid inlaid marble, stained glass windows, and giant chandeliers suspended by great chains from the lofty ceiling."

A British woman they met at the Red Cross building invited them to a dance, and as some of the few Americans present, they thoroughly enjoyed themselves listening to a combination of American and Scottish music. They had fun "messing things up and getting in our own way" when they tried to dance the Highland fling and some reels. Dad only regretted Mom was not there to experience it too.

Mom could deduce from a letter he wrote on January 19 that he had probably helped transport wounded soldiers, although all he could tell her was he could be "a whole lot worse off than I am now." Even so, he found the war news on all fronts encouraging and was hopeful the war would be over by the summer. The Battle of the Bulge had been won, the Russians were continuing to advance in the east, and the Allies were making progress in the Pacific.

Mail from Mom was getting through only sporadically, but he did learn she was not pregnant, which was a relief in a way. He again urged her to use V-mails as those were assured of getting to him more quickly, saying that sometimes he would "rather get mail than eat."

At one point, Dad told Mom that he had wrapped her photo in cellophane because "I expect to put it up in some of the muddiest foxholes of this continent." That hint about his location made it past the censor.

Beautiful Countryside and "Decent People"

On January 21, he made it clear that he was somewhere in Scotland, describing a bus ride through countryside so beautiful it looked "like a picture postcard published by an ambitious Chamber of Commerce. The Highlands are very striking. Very little wood is used in house construction, and as a result all one sees are structures made of rock and brick."

A few days later, while on a pass, he was invited to another party. The Red Cross encouraged the men to attend these as a way of meeting the "decent people" in town. There, he impressed the local girls with his middle school knowledge of the poet Robert Burns and had fun falling over his own feet when trying to dance "those native reels."

In addition to hot showers and clean, warm sheets, Red Cross lodgings provided newspapers where the men could catch up on the war news. Everyone was excited about the "wonderful Russian offensive." He believed "if a Russian wandered into town today, he might have been mobbed. I hope they continue their drive and don't let up until the Nazis cry uncle." On another day, Dad was so exhilarated by events on the eastern front that he wrote, "God bless and speed the Russians on."

It was cold enough to snow, and the streams and ponds froze over so the children could ice-skate on them. But he was empathetic for the men fighting on the front, who were experiencing the coldest winter in years. All he could say was, "You don't know the half of it." Nonetheless, when he saw people ice-skating and sledding on a frozen pond, he remembered skating in Prospect Park in Brooklyn.

One day, Dad saw a woman with a little girl who reminded him of me. After he offered her "a few Life Savers and gum," she broke out of her shyness to speak to him. The incident made him miss us even more.

On January 29, Dad received a letter from Mom, dated January 16 indicating she still did not know where he was. It prompted him to write the following.

January 29, 1945

You know our memories give us a common source from which to nourish our lonely hours. Oh, my darling. Some day we will look back on this nightmare existence. It will probably feel unreal, just as it sometimes does now. Honestly, it sometimes is so hard to realize that all of these things are happening.

In early February, he wrote again about his admiration for the Russian forces, who had made huge advances on the eastern front, including in Poland. They had also crossed both the Vistula and Oder Rivers by the end of January, with the goal of taking Berlin.

February 1, 1945

Darling, the Russian offensive is making such news here. I am sure it is finding a similar reception in the States. How do those Russians do it? Their exploits will go down in military annals alongside the classics of Hannibal and Napoleon.

With regard to movement on the western front, he commented:

Pretty soon I reckon, the western front will come alive and perhaps put an end to this business here. I hardly dare think of how soon it may be. The dirty Nazi rats are panicky. They are being rooted out of one hole after another. Unlike rats on a sinking ship, they don't even have the sea in which to jump. East and West they are being squeezed tighter and tighter.

In the meantime, the people in Scotland made the GIs feel as welcome and comfortable as they could. He relayed an incident illustrating their courtesy and kindness. The Red Cross had given Dad and one of his buddies tickets to a performance of *Hedda Gabler* by Henrik Ibsen. On a rainy, sleety, miserable night, they boarded a tram to get from camp to the theater. When they got on the tram, they asked the motorman about the theater, and he told them to ask the fare collector to let them off on "such and such a street." They got off at the designated stop, and Dad noticed that the tram did not immediately take off again, which was odd since "Ordinarily you have to be very nimbly hopping on and off." When Dad looked around for his buddy, he saw him running down to the corner, where the motorman had left the tram and all the passengers in the middle of the street to offer walking directions to the theater!

As friendly as the townspeople were, Dad wasn't too fond of their food, finding it inferior to what was served in camp. He found the camp food even better than what he had been getting in the States because "when they take pains with that powdered food, it really tastes good." But Dad still appreciated getting a pass because he could find a good bed and shower in town.

Dad really wanted to buy Mom some souvenirs, but he discovered that everything was rationed in Scotland, even the candy bars. The men were only allowed about four bars a week, and Dad was glad he didn't smoke because cigarettes were so hard to come by. He needed coupons to buy many things, including souvenir-type items, and few Army men had them.

One day he was in a store looking longingly at a set of pretty Irish linen handkerchiefs when he met a member of the American Merchant Marine. The mariner told Dad he would be leaving soon and would not use all of his coupon allotment, so he offered a few to Dad, who was able to purchase the handkerchiefs as a gift for Mom.

In early February, Dad began to receive letters from Mom that were addressed to his new APO address, indicating she finally knew that he was still safe in Great Britain. Knowing that Mom was receiving his letters, Dad again began describing his love for her, writing that he held her "high on a pedestal, like the gods of ancient Greece and Rome were worshipped. For me to simply say that I love you is to be guilty of an understatement."

On the Move

In a V-mail dated February 15, Dad wrote "England" rather than "British Isles" at the top of the page and made a passing reference to his lack of sleep "on the train last night"—his way of telling Mom that his unit had been relocated. Dropping another hint, he said he might "run up to London" if he had time. On February 21, he wrote "Southern England" at the top of his V-mail, which indicated his unit was being moved closer to an embarkation point for France and on to Germany.

In response to Mom's concern about where he would go next, Dad was only able to say, "The less you know about the details of where I go, the better." He assured her he would be able to handle what was coming because "whatever any other human flesh can stand, I certainly will be able to stand." Their love and memories would carry him through and be his strength. "I couldn't be physically strong if the other were missing," he told her. He wrote less and less about his surroundings as February progressed, saying only that they were staying in a hotel looking over a municipal park, and that he was impressed by how the entire population, including older people, rode bicycles.

Although he was obviously anxious about what was going to happen to him, he was also concerned about Mom on the "home front." He urged her not to give up her apartment in Jamaica, even though she planned to spend the spring and summer at her parents' home in Far Rockaway. He also asked her not to leave me with her mother while she went back to work, although he objected to any thought of leaving me in a nursery with strangers. His objections were fruitless, however, as Mom needed to return to nursing to support herself and me. The Army allotment was not sufficient for her to buy clothing for the two of us, let alone any extra "luxuries." Unable to afford a sitter, and probably unable to trust one either, she often turned to Grandma to help care for me, despite Dad's misgivings.

In early March, Dad was able to get a pass to London, where he located his old friend Ike, who was stationed there with the Navy. Ike gave him a tour of the city, and they visited the Royal Academy of Arts, which was then showing an exhibition of Soviet art. Dad took photos of the art and sent them to Mom's sister Blanche, while sending Mom the catalog as a souvenir.

But he didn't want to give her the impression that he was "enjoying" himself, so Dad told her he was touring London only to keep from thinking about home. But he added, ominously, that "time is short."

Dad could not write that his unit was about to be shipped to the continent to join what would be one of the most important battles in the final months of the war in Europe.

The military handed out booklets explaining British culture to American GIs. *A Short Guide to Great Britain.* War and Navy Department, Washington, D.C., 1944.

Last page of *A Short Guide to Great Britain*, explaining to the GIs the importance of showing "Respect" and "Patience." These sections were excerpted from the British Army Bureau of Current Affairs *Bulletin*, No. 22, July 18, 1942, "Meet the Americans," and so are from the British perspective. For example, under "Patience," it advises that people ask about the foreigner's hometown to help create a real "Anglo-American understanding," which will be essential to "the real thing—the alliance which survives the peace and becomes a permanent force in the shaping of the new world."

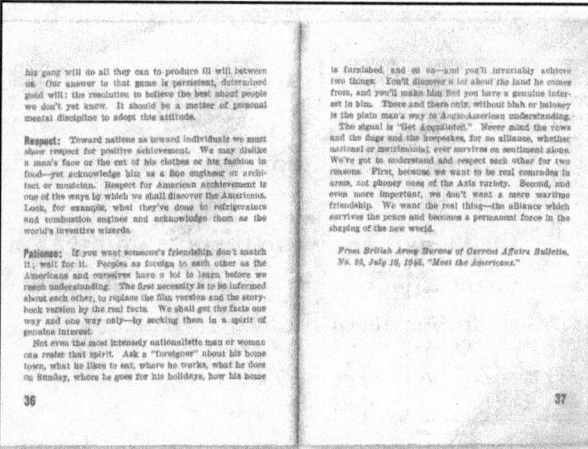

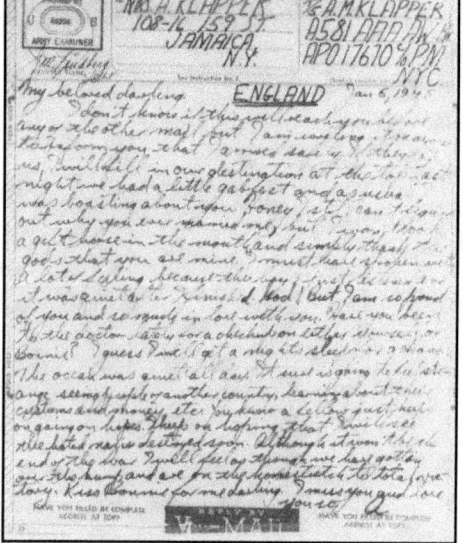

Dad's first V-mail indicating he is in England, January 5, 1945. The censor's stamp and signature on top left meant he was allowed to disclose his location.

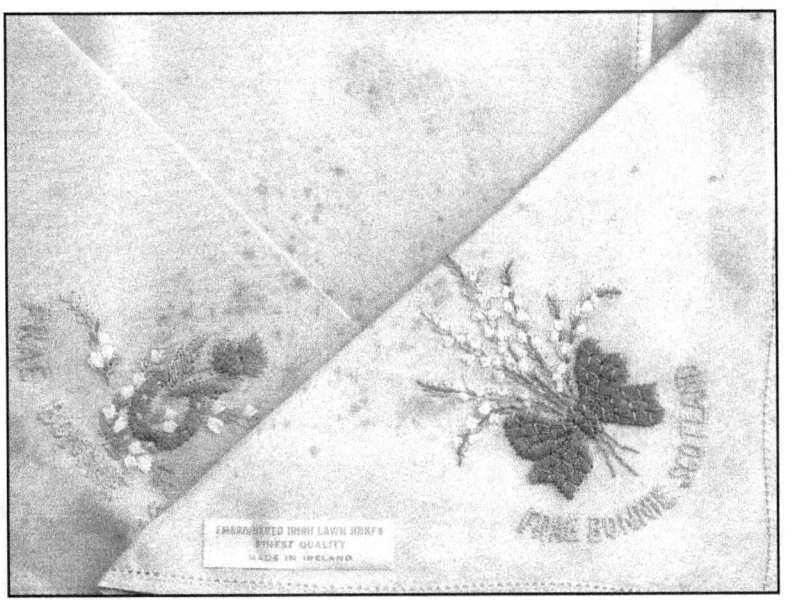

Irish linen handkerchiefs Dad bought in Scotland for Mom with ration coupons provided by a Merchant Marine seaman who was going home soon and kindly told Dad he didn't need them anymore. Practically everything in Scotland was rationed at the time, so everyone needed coupons to purchase goods.

Example of a V-mail Dad wrote from the "British Isles" with a prohibited location blacked out by a censor.

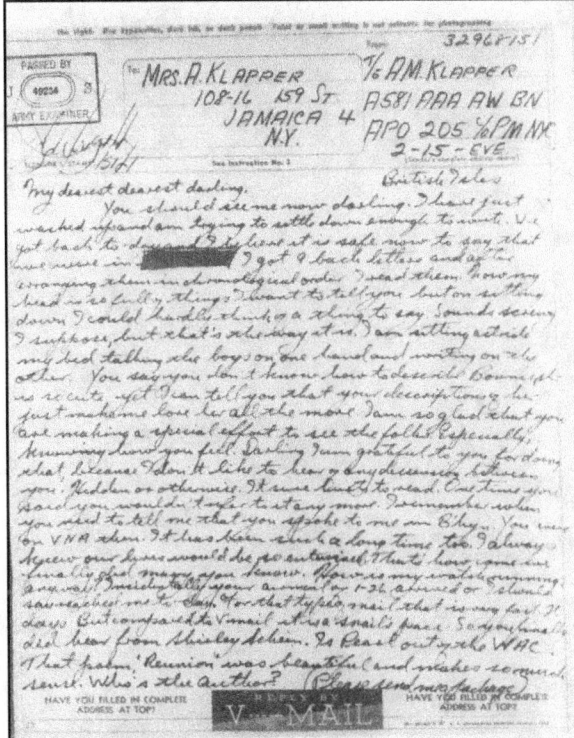

CHAPTER 9

France, the Remagen Front, a Passover Seder in Germany

DAD'S UNIT WAS SHIPPED TO France, landing at Le Havre on March 9, 1945. Just two days earlier, other units of the First Army had been amazed to find the Ludendorff Bridge still standing in the town of Remagen as German dictator Adolf Hitler had ordered all bridges over the Rhine River to be demolished. General Dwight D. Eisenhower approved the orders to take the bridge, and after his approval, several units had been able to use the bridge to cross the Rhine River to the eastern side by the time Dad's unit arrived. The Germans were furiously attempting to destroy the bridge with V-2 rockets, what was left of their air force, and explosives that were to be set by specially trained swimmers (although they did not succeed and were all captured before they could set off the explosives). The 581st antiaircraft unit was desperately needed as quickly as possible to support the frontline troops that were crossing the still intact bridge.

After the bridge had been captured, Hitler told Field Marshal Albert Kesselring that Remagen was "the really vulnerable spot on the western front . . . and that it was urgent to 'restore' the situation there." The bridge's crossing was extremely important to the morale of the American and Allied troops and the nation.

Although in rapid transit from France to the front at Remagen, Dad somehow found the time to write a V-mail on the evening of March 10.

> March 10—evening
> FRANCE
>
> My beloved darling,
> By looking at the top of this letter you will understand why I have been unable to write. So much has happened in the past week, yet I can't tell you a thing. I am feeling OK and you haven't anything to worry about. We are on the move, as you must realize, and my letters will have to be written where and when I can.

His next letter was dated March 15, 1945, and he was literally writing it from the front lines. Because Dad could say little about what he had been doing, I include a description about his unit from Brigadier General E. W. Timberlake's commendation to the battalion on May 10, 1945, just after the German surrender.

> The 581st AAA AW Battalion landed at Le Havre, France, on 9 March 1945, and on 12 March 1945, after a record nonstop motor march (except for fuel halts) was going into position in defense of the critically important Remagen bridge. The initial mission found the battalion a part of the coordinated antiaircraft defense of the then still intact Ludendorf [*sic*] Bridge and the pontoon bridges at Remagen and Kripp. [The Ludendorff Bridge had collapsed on March 17]. The battalion remained in this area until 12 April, continually shifting and expanding its defense until eventually it was providing the only automatic weapons protection for the two (2) pontoon bridges at Remagen, the pontoon bridge at Kripp and the pontoon bridge at Hohnegen [*sic*-Hönningen]. A secondary mission of protecting these all important structures against

damage from floating mines and saboteurs caused several fire units at each site to be located so as to cover the water and bank areas adjacent. Perfect coordination with engineer units was maintained to facilitate the proper functioning of this activity, and no damage was sustained by any of these bridges, in spite of concentrated air and water borne attacks.

As General Eisenhower wrote in his postwar memoir, *Crusade in Europe*, the significance of this battle was that it was the first time the U.S. Army "pierced . . . the traditional defensive barrier to the heart of Germany[.]" After this, the Allies knew that the war in Europe would be over much sooner than they had expected.

>March 15, 1945
>GERMANY

>My dearest darling,
>I hope you haven't been too worried about my not writing, but as you can see I have been rather busy. This is only going to be a short note to let you know that I am at least OK. There is so much I have seen and so much to tell, but I can't write about it. A fellow feels funny spending a night in Germany. Here we are in the place I have been reading about all these years. When I see German POWs and now German civilians, I get a strange feeling in my breast. We have seen Polish and Russian slave labor[ers] and are they glad to see us.

>I haven't had any mail for ages it seems. But we are gradually reaching the end of our quest, and when we get more or less situated, I hope the mail will start to come through again.

That's all for now my darling. Keep your spirits up for my sake and yours. Kiss Bonnie for me. I love you both so very much. Tell the folks you have heard from me, dearest.

Early Spring, Signs of Victory

He wrote again on March 20 with "I think" added after the date, because as he explained, he was losing track of time and knew little about what was happening beyond his immediate surroundings, which was devastating. He mentioned his tentative use of German, aided by his knowledge of Yiddish and Army handouts. It was a hint of how his language skill would become useful in the coming months in Germany.

March 20 (I think)

My beloved darling,
I have been so busy for the past few days. I can't tell you much of anything, as per usual. As a matter of fact, it seems that the closer one gets to the front lines, the less news one gets. I haven't heard a radio or seen the newspaper *Stars & Stripes* for several days. I am permitted to say that I saw Rouen, Le Havre, Soissons, Liege and a host of other cities. What destruction. I know now, more than I ever did before, that I am fighting here to prevent that happening to us in America.

You should hear me struggle with German. There are still a few civilians left in these towns. I can make myself understood, which is something.

Please note my new APO number. I'll have to knock off now, dearest. Please be patient about the mail. I haven't had any for so long, I damn near have forgotten the shape of your handwriting. Au revoir, my darling. I'd say Auf Weidershein [*sic*], but I don't know how to spell it.

He was actually able to write Mom the next day as well.

March 21 (Spring?)

My dearest and only heart,
I am writing this by candlelight in the front room of what was once a beautiful home. A bomb hit it some time ago and made a shambles of it. Fortunately, the weather has been nice, and that is a break. . . .

Dearest, it seems like ages since we last saw each other. Believe me, the more I see of the rest of the world, the better I like the good old USA. What in the world could ever have convinced these damn Germans to start a war of conquest. The parts of Germany I have seen are really beautiful. We must not fraternize with them in any way. We must make them remember the year 1945 as one in which they were the conquered. These civilians we come across say that they are not Nazis, but how can you believe them. Sometimes, I believe a man should do to them like they did to others when they had them down.

Good night darling.

Kiss Bonnie and God bless you both.

—A

Finally, on March 23, he received mail from home. He was irritated by some of the relatives who had written to say they were hurt because he had not answered their letters. He also described his feelings on meeting more German civilians.

> March 24 (?) [*sic*]
>
> Maybe they don't know there is a war on and that other than writing letters, I have a few other things to think about. Such as keeping a whole skin. This isn't Camp Stewart. Some people will never learn.
>
> The civilians we see here are indeed a beaten lot. The boys are pretty rough with them on occasion, and they know how their own army acted, so they are scared. We live in their homes and eat off the fat of their land. They did that to other nations.

It was now early spring in Germany, and he kept writing about the beautiful scenery, as if in wonder at its contrast with the horrors brought on by the war. Although he was always careful to avoid descriptions that would reveal his exact location, certain details in his letters were still blacked out by the censor. Thanks to Brigadier General Timberlake's narrative in his commendation, we know Dad's unit was in the Remagen area until mid-April.

> March 25, 1945
>
> The scene before me is beautiful. The trees are beginning to bud, and we can see for a great distance from our position on top of a hill. I can see the [blacked out by censor] and the [blacked out by censor] far below me and in the distance the rise of green mountains. As the mountains get farther

away, they become blue and still bluer until they fade into the mist of the horizon. The small towns are very close, and some are very badly battered. They are picturesque, but so is everything else.

One of the boys came over just this minute and showed me a German pistol he found. The boys are souvenir crazy. I personally have passed up all of that stuff. I have enough souvenirs in my mind so that I don't need anything to remind me of these years. I'll probably want to forget as much as possible.

Even so, just before Dad left Germany, he did send home some war souvenirs, including a German helmet, pistol, wooden shoes (German, not Dutch), prewar currency from Germany and other European countries, a German military pin, and a beautiful piece of embroidered beaded cloth he said came from an underground factory. He packed most of these items into a wooden box a German worker made for him after the war.

On March 26, he wrote he had heard news on the radio for the first time in a long while and was thrilled to learn of the rapid advance of our armies.

March 26, 1945

The advance of our armies is phenomenal. At this rate, darling, the war will be over soon. God! How I hope and pray for that day. To come home to the peace and quiet of our home. Just the everyday routine of living provides an exciting prospect. If only our supply lines can continue to supply our advancing troops. I'm so excited I can hardly write. It looks like we arrived here just in time for the kill.

> The retreating Nazis are so dazed, they don't know what hit them. Maybe they want us to get to Berlin before the Russians.

Although he could see that the war in Germany was going to be ending soon, he wondered whether he would be discharged or sent to the battle in the Pacific as he estimated it would take the Allies another year to defeat Japan, even when they could focus all their power on that front. Although he thought the Japanese fighters were "fanatical and crafty," he thought the Germans were better soldiers.

March 28, 1945, was the first night of Passover, which Jews traditionally commemorate at a special dinner called a seder and recount the story of our exodus from slavery in Egypt. Dad celebrated the holiday in Nazi Germany, a remarkable experience given the Nazi regime's campaign against the Jews.

March 29, 1945

> Yesterday was the first day of this Passover. Never in my wildest dreams did I ever envision myself in the heart of Hitler's land on Passover. And what's more, with the Nazis about crushed. Somewhat similar to the Pharaohs of old.

The next day, he described the impromptu seder he had attended.

March 30, 1945

> It was significant and symbolic more than anything else. We held it in an old hotel in a town which I am not able to reveal now. The ceremony, coupled with the good news, was interesting. The chaplain distributed matzos. I brought a box up to the boys, and we had it for chow.

Even the weather seemed to be cooperating in hastening the end of the war, as it had been mild and fair.

March 29, 1945

The weather is holding up nicely.... Good weather will have a direct bearing on the length of the war. Perhaps the gods are with us now. No mud to get stuck in, and maybe we'll be in Berlin before long. Maybe, (and I say with bated breath) by April. What a thought. Am I dreaming, or is that really me saying that? God, if only it would end soon.

Navigating a New Language— and the Mail System

April 1 was his first payday in Germany. While in the field, the men were paid in "Allied invasion" money, which looked like "cigar coupons" and was considered legal tender by the local commanders. It would not have been possible to use local currency in combat zones or in German areas, such as this one, where the German government had not yet surrendered.

Dad had gained access to a few German language books and planned to "brush up on some stock words and phrases. A fellow needs to know the lingo a little bit." Because he knew Yiddish, a dialect of German spoken by Jews in central and eastern Europe, he was comfortable with the sound of German and familiar with some of its vocabulary.

By April 2, he finally received mail and packages of goodies Mom and other relatives had shipped to him weeks earlier. He had requested cans of salmon, sardines, and pumpernickel bread because they were still edible on arrival, and all of the men in his unit liked them. The rule was everyone shared food from home with his immediate unit. Some of his buddies had never before eaten pumpernickel and found it to be a special treat.

To reduce the quantities of packages being shipped from the States, the Army required soldiers to request particular items in writing. The sender was expected to bring this letter to the local post office, where it would be stamped to prevent the letter from being used again. A few samples of these stamps from the Far Rockaway Post Office can be seen on some of Dad's letters, appearing near the specific requests.

Although the overseas mail and shipments created logistical headaches, the Army recognized that the packages were important for soldiers' morale, so it created a system in combination with the regular U.S. Post Office to handle the mail. Letters or packages sent through regular U.S. mail to a military location would be sorted and sent in a package with others to the New York Post Office's Postal Concentration Center. There it would be processed and separated according to the branch of the service and specific units where it was being shipped. That package of mail would then be placed in a bag and sent to the New York Port of Embarkation Army Post Office, where the Army would then take over.

Next, the package or letter would go by ship or plane to the company's overseas APO. The company mail orderly would then deliver it to the soldier. If a soldier had been transferred or was temporarily in another location—e.g., a hospital—the Army Directory Service supplied the new address and the mail would be rerouted or re-sorted for delivery to the new location.

Surprisingly, Dad was able to get a twenty-four-hour pass on April 5 to a rest camp with hot springs, where he enjoyed bathing in the sulfur spring water in "an enormous bathtub." The camp had once been a fancy resort, but now the Yanks in Germany were taking full advantage of it.

He told Mom not to worry about him, even though the letters he had received so far did not indicate she knew he was in Germany. Assuming she had by then received his letters and knew his location, he assured her that "when we first came here I had a couple of close calls, but you can tell by the news that everything is under control." The "close calls" probably referred to the time he had spent at Remagen defending the bridge, the pontoon bridges, and the surrounding area of the battle. He knew Mom was closely following the war news at home, including the coverage of the successful crossing of the Rhine, so he assumed she, too, would feel optimistic about the current stage of the war in Germany.

His unit was now camped on top of a hill and living in tents. The men kept warm by using a small stove they had picked up, and the tents kept them dry during that rainy month. But it was miserable when they had to stand guard outside or go on alert.

Despite his own situation, he nonetheless tried to comfort Mom, who was beginning to feel envious of other couples who had more nicely furnished apartments and fancier clothes than she could afford. He promised to make it up to her when he returned home, but reminded her to be grateful that they had something others envied—a beautiful child.

He was now convinced that the war with Germany would be over that month or next, based on the news he was getting. The men had only a shortwave radio for military purposes and sometimes received a civilian program, but "it was a toss-up in which language it might be." He longed to be able to listen to familiar stations and voices again. He and his sister Shirley had loved to listen to the big bands often featured on the radio. In Shirley's letters, she often mentioned which radio program she was listening to while writing to him.

One day, while "working around our position," Dad stopped someone in an American uniform who did not look like a soldier. He turned out to be a Russian boy from Odessa, who had probably been a slave laborer. Since he spoke German, Dad was able to converse with him.

April 7, 1945

One night 3 years ago he was taken from his home and before he knew what happened, he was on his way to Germany. He was 16 then and is, therefore, now 19 years old. He speaks German and that is the only reason I was able to converse with him. It seems that an American officer gave him the uniform. Just before the Americans came, he hid in the woods nearby and was able to observe a group of Germans about to bury a large amount of weapons. When the Yanks arrived, he dug it up and turned the lot over to the Americans. For that deed, he proudly wears a suit of American OD's [Olive Drab uniform, the basic U.S. Army color]. I am telling you darling there are so many interesting things that happen during a day, but I can't tell you about them. When I come home, if I can remember them and you want to hear about them, I will tell you all about it.

So long for now, darling. Till the war ends (our victory words).

Kiss Bonnie. I love you so

—A

A Defeated Population, Country

From his unit's vantage point on top of a hill, Dad could see the surrounding countryside for miles. One clear Sunday in April, he saw the local population of the nearby towns come out for a promenade and gaze curiously at the soldiers.

April 8, 1945

> I wonder what goes on in their minds. Are they subdued? Do they still like the Nazi regime better than us? I know one thing. They are damn glad that the bombers, thousands of them, pass by their town. No longer must they rush for shelters. Some of them involuntarily glance up with fear in their eyes and motions, but then they recover and carry on when they hear the sound of the bombers. It is a very fearful and ominous sound. Thank God they are ours.

Although she had probably already guessed, Dad was now able to tell Mom he was in the First Army, allowing her to determine his general location by following news of the First Army. Despite hearing that the Germans were stiffening their opposition, on April 9, Dad predicted they would only last for a short time because most of their supply sources were in Allied hands or encircled. By April 1, the Ruhr industrial region, a major source of coal, had been surrounded by the U.S. First and Ninth Armies. The city of Kassel, a major industrial and transportation center, was captured by General George S. Patton on April 4. By April 5, the U.S. Seventh Army had reached Würzburg, another transportation hub. He hoped the Russians would soon begin their offensive.

The Germans living in the countryside were excellent farmers, and Dad was impressed by what he saw there. "There is hardly a piece of ground, level or on a steep mountainside, that is not utilized. All around, we can see the people plowing and planting. Must be spring." He reminisced about how beautiful springtime was in New York, with people coming out of winter hiding and promenading in the parks. He used to love to play handball and then return home to a warm shower and a great meal. He remembered Far Rockaway, too, and asked if anyone was keeping up the Victory garden he had planted at Mom's parents' place. As a city boy, he recalled getting a "great kick" out of it, especially when he had seen the first radishes appear.

Now that it was obvious the war with Germany was almost over, he and the others in his group were obsessing about their fate. Some would stay in Germany as police MPs or other occupying forces, some would go to the "Asiatic Theater," and some would return to the States. He again told Mom not to worry about him, reminding her that he had predicted if he stayed in the "AA" (antiaircraft), he would be okay, and he had been right.

On April 11, he wrote a brief letter warning her he would not be able to write again for a while. According to Brigadier General Timberlake's commendation letter, his unit stayed in the Remagen area until April 12 and then was directed to move farther east into Germany, heading toward Berlin and the Russians, who were moving west from their positions. So, on April 11, Dad and the rest of the 581st would have been busy packing up for this move.

In addition to their antiaircraft duties, the battalion also "organized and operated a provisional trucking company hauling freight, the 86th Infantry Division from the Ruhr Pocket to Leipzig, and 13,000 German POWs on return trips from the front lines." Dad took several photos during this time of prisoners loaded into Army trucks, but he had only a cheap, poor-quality camera, so the photos have faded almost too much to decipher. A note on the back of one photo describes C-Ration cans in the foreground, and Dad wrote that "after the way they were starved in the last days of the war, they considered the rations a delicacy." Although the GIs could hardly stand to look at these rations anymore, many of the prisoners had not eaten for days before they had surrendered or been captured because the German supply lines had been so disrupted.

On the back of another photo, Dad wrote "a PW [POW] enclosure," and on a third, showing rows of "PWs" sitting on the ground "about to load on trucks for transportation to the rear."

Brigadier General Timberlake praised the 581st's performance in the Rhine and Central German campaigns.

> Their battalion's record treble[d] that of any of the fifteen similar trucking companies of the 49th AAA Brigade, and is particularly noteworthy in that the 581st AAA, AW Battalion progressively moved forward in the normal performance of its AAA missions, over 150 miles, in protection of airfields, supply dumps, and other vital FIRST ARMY installations, being, on 9 May 1945, well on the Road to Berlin, and one of the few AAA units performing purely AAA functions at the cessation of hostilities.

Its accomplishments in the Remagen campaign supplied the 581st with its nickname: "Rock of Remagen."

CHAPTER 10

Death of Roosevelt, Moving Through the Countryside

LIKE MUCH OF THE WORLD, Dad and his unit were "incredulous" to learn of President Roosevelt's death on April 12, 1945. Condolences poured in to Washington from all over the world, even from the Japanese premier, which Dad described as evidence that the Japanese were "still full of tricks." The men in the field had avidly listened to Roosevelt's speeches on the radio, drawing support and reassurance from his voice. Now, the Allies knew they were so close to the end of the war in Germany, but Roosevelt would not be there to share in the victory.

During this time, Dad was speaking to more and more German civilians, many of whom said they never wanted war.

April 16, 1945

> These people I have talked to say that they didn't want war. Everybody here isn't a nazi, they hate the nazis. And I ask them why, if everyone didn't want this damn war, am I here. I didn't want it, you can bet on that. Propaganda that was fed to them stated that the American soldier didn't have anything to eat. Now, they say we can see that it was the German soldier who didn't have anything. The

nazis had plenty, but not the ordinary soldier. So they say. Who can believe them? I can't.

In the same letter, Dad predicted the end was finally in sight.

> They are stiffening their resistance now, but it is the last thing they can do. A rat when cornered is dangerous and will fight to the bitter end. Very soon, there will be a series of linkups with the Russians, and then Germany will be cut to ribbons. The war isn't over, but the end isn't far off.

He finally received mail from Mom again on April 17 but was surprised to see that she had used his old APO address and still did not seem to know he was in Germany. Instead of mentioning Germany, Mom wrote about his family's Passover seder and how everyone had missed him and his younger cousin Marty, who was also serving in the Army. In reply, Dad wrote that he looked forward to spending next year's holiday with her and the rest of the family and hoped they would have more children to add to the "usual rumpus," because "family is my life."

Moving Through Germany

As Dad had predicted, when the Russians finally began their offensive, victories for the Allies came quickly. On April 13, the Russians captured Vienna. On the 16th, the Americans took Nuremberg, entering Leipzig the next day. When the Russians opened an offensive near Berlin, Dad estimated the war would be over in about two months.

General Eisenhower had declared Germany would have to feed itself, and Dad noted that every available plot of land was being tilled in the villages he was passing through. Although the soil was rich and black, Dad said even the large farms were "just backyards" compared to those in America, and he wondered how the country would grow enough food for people in the cities.

The Germans Dad met were mostly women and children and a few old men. When he asked people "Where are your men?" the answer was always, *"Nach Krieg!"* (at the war!). They did not look like the super race, Dad wrote, but like people who are "tired and weary of this whole business. And what's more, they are the losers."

Dad had little pity for the women, children, and old men who were doing the hard work of preparing the soil because he knew that a lot of these folks had formerly used slave labor for these tasks. One middle-aged couple complained to Dad that there was nothing to buy in town, even if you had the money. Dad offered no sympathy, telling them "whether they are personally responsible for Hitler or no, they are going to suffer for his deeds anyhow."

April 19, 1945

They heave a sigh of relief and bow their heads. No, darling, they look very far from the super duper race. They have gambled and lost. The nazi radio had told them that the Americans would cut off their hands, slit their throats, rape them, and carry off their children to some distant land. When the Americans arrived, they trembled with fear. Then they saw that we were not the barbarians that the nazis made us out to be. Now they say they were glad to see us. I wonder how they will talk in a few months.

The food supply gets more critical by the day. In other countries, the populace used to line up at the garbage cans to take what we would throw away. It's awful, honey. You can't imagine it.

German prisoners were being shipped away from the front by the truckload, jammed in standing up to fit more of them into each truck. "All you can see are heads and shoulders sticking up from the side of the body," Dad wrote. It made him angry that the Americans had to feed the prisoners when he knew the Germans had forced American prisoners to "hike hundreds of miles in all kinds of weather when they wanted to move [them] from one place to the next." He had heard that Allied prisoners were kept at starvation levels.

April 20, 1945

We're civilized. We are treating these so-and-so's like human beings. Beats me. I can't understand right from wrong anymore. If I could only get back home and see you again, I might regain some balance.

On April 21, 1945, the Russians entered Berlin, and Dad was ecstatic when he heard the news the next day.

April 22, 1945

Today is an historical day. I heard over the radio that the Russians are in Berlin. Can I fathom it? The next thing to the end of total resistance, that is the biggest news. The war in Germany is almost over, darling. That day we have so fervently been praying for can be seen on the horizon. Any moment I expect to hear that the Russian and American patrols have linked up.

He was also happy to have received two letters from Mom finally indicating she knew he was in Germany. But since his mail was still being censored, he told Mom not to ask what he was doing, where he was, or what towns he was passing through, because "it will only be blotted out." He was only allowed to tell her that he was in the First Army. He also told her not to worry because he would be okay. In one of her letters, Mom wrote that she worried their daughter's generation would have to fight a war like this one, but Dad told her, "Never again will those who have seen with their own eyes America's might think of starting another war with America."

He knew Germany's end was near even before he heard that the U.S. had rejected Heinrich Himmler's (head of the Nazi SS) April 22 offer of a conditional surrender. The U.S. would only accept an unconditional surrender. "The Russians are rolling and soon, very soon, Yank and Russky will be shaking hands smack in the heart of Germany," Dad wrote on April 24.

Although Dad did not know how much longer it would take to defeat Japan, he was already dreaming of his homecoming. He was glad that Mom had decided to keep the apartment in Jamaica because he envisioned it as a refuge when he finally got home, a place to stay until they got on their feet again. He dreamed of "homecoming, our own home, a few more children, an automobile, and a few other things." Most important, of course, was to be together again.

On April 25, American and Soviet patrols met near Torgau, and the San Francisco conference to organize the United Nations opened. Dad expected the war in Italy to end soon but wondered how long it would take to "clean up the mess in Norway," where the Nazis still had many troops deployed.

By this time, Dad was meeting French and Russian refugees who had been used as forced labor by the Germans. The French had been held for five years and the Russians for about three with very little to eat while working long hours every day. They were "constantly getting beaten for the slightest infractions, and of course receiving practically nothing as pay."

April 26, 1945

The French couldn't seem to tell us enough of how good it felt to be free again. They expanded their chests with deep breaths of fresh air, and their eyes glowed so happily. I felt so good just talking to them and for being an American soldier. I guess we just like to feel like liberators.

A "deluge of mail" finally arrived. Mom wrote in two letters about how Roosevelt's death had impacted people at home, echoing much of what Dad had written to her about the sorrow and shock he and other military men had felt.

April 28, 1945

Now you know why I don't believe there is a God. If there is, I wish he would straighten me out on his idea of values. Right and wrong. If it was right for him [Roosevelt] to die and a lot of nazi bastards to live, then I give up.

Mopping Up

At the end of April, Dad had been overseas about four months and wrote that it seemed both like an eternity and such a short period. He could now understand how a man could put in thirty-five to forty months overseas "and still retain his sanity. Somehow, the time does fly." Dad found he had to keep a careful check on the day of the week, though, "because one day is exactly like the next." The only time they knew it was Sunday was when volunteers were asked to go to church, but practically no one did.

Allied forces were now engaged in large-scale "mopping up," and Dad expected Germany would be "completely subjugated, except for spotty resistance by fanatical die-hards," by June or July. He assured Mom the greatest danger for him in the ETO (European Theater of Operations) was over. Even if he had to remain in Europe for a while as an MP, he felt they could "finally see our goal on the distant horizon. No longer is it an endless road, with its end in eternity."

On April 28, Mussolini was executed by Italian partisans, and on April 29, the German forces in northern Italy and southern Austria surrendered, although the announcement was not made until May 2. On April 30, Hitler committed suicide, which was reported on May 1. Berlin surrendered on May 2, and the next day Hamburg surrendered to British forces. That day in the Pacific, the British took the city of Rangoon in Burma (now also called Myanmar).

Dad's first letter in May is dated May 3. He explained that he could not write about the past few days, other than to say he had been very "busy." Instead, he sent a list of items he wanted Mom to include in the stream of packages she had been sending him. Pumpernickel, cheese, sardines, candy, nuts, and cookies were his favorites. Anything that had to be prepared, like chocolate pudding or noodle soup, was pretty useless, since he could not "fuss" with them.

German forces in many areas were surrendering quickly to the Americans and British to avoid being overrun by the Russians. On May 4, the day that the Nazis surrendered Denmark, the Netherlands, and northern Germany to British Field Marshal Bernard Law Montgomery, Dad wrote that he guessed things in the States must be in turmoil with everyone waiting for word of V-E Day. His kid sister Shirley had reported that all the family, especially their father, kept ears close to the radio. Dad wrote that he hoped "our victory here will be made secure back home at San Francisco," where talks were being held to set up the United Nations.

On May 5, a large German force surrendered to the U.S. Sixth Army, and Dad saw only two areas of resistance left — Norway and Czechoslovakia. But the Americans and Russians were closing in fast from both directions. As German forces surrendered all around Europe, Dad was wondering what would happen to him and his unit. He knew the Army would no longer need antiaircraft forces in Europe—in fact, they had not needed them for some time because the German air force had been "kaput" for quite a while.

 The Army was also planning how to keep the men busy, both physically and mentally, once the fighting was over. Since military training was to be minimized, the Army decided to require the men to take courses and participate in recreational sports. Dad wrote to Mom that he was thinking about choosing tennis for a sport and selecting a course in elementary gasoline engine instruction, which he expected would come in handy when he got home and bought a car. He also signed up for a refresher course on elementary math and one called "psychology in life," hoping the classes would keep his mind occupied and help him pass the time until he could return home to his family.

CHAPTER 11

V-E Day in Occupied Germany

ON MAY 6, DAD WAS camped out on top of a hill, his unit's usual location whenever they moved to another town. The hilltop locations allowed for good visibility but provided little protection from the weather. He had heard no news that day and found it ironic that the fighting on the Czech and Norwegian fronts could already be over and he wouldn't even know it.

> May 6, 1945
>
> To think that we've waited so long for this day to come, and when it does, what am I doing? Sitting on top of a hill fighting the elements. Wind, cold, and rain.

He was worried about how long it would take the "redeployment machinery to go into high gear" and anxious about how long he would have to wait before finding out about his next position. Dad hoped to be sent home, but he realized that some men would be sent to fight Japan while others would have to remain in Germany as military police. He just wanted a quick decision, and time seemed to drag while he was waiting, which Dad said was so different from his days in combat where "time didn't mean a thing." Finally, he was able to tell Mom that he was entitled to wear a battle star, but he told her at the same time that she did not have to worry about his safety now.

On May 7, the Germans surrendered unconditionally at Reims. Dad could barely believe it.

> May 7, 1945
>
> It's official now. The war in Europe is over. Can this be me writing? I can't believe it. In a short while, I will know where I stand. At least one phase of this gruesome business is over. We have had it pretty easy considering what others have had to go through to achieve this memorable day. May 7, 1945. I'll never forget this day.

Based on unofficial sources, Dad did not think he stood much of a chance for a discharge, and he was worried he would be sent to the Pacific front, where even the elements were much worse than what he faced in Europe. The weather there was "a miserable hellhole," whereas his hilltop vantage point allowed him to appreciate a beautiful countryside. He described the scenery in his May 7 letter.

> The breeze blows very lightly . . . and I can see the valley below in bloom. The ground is plowed and sown in strips, and all around I can see different colored strips, just like ribbons of various shades of green and red. Damn this war, anyhow. It could be such a nice old world if it weren't for the people in it. I mean certain people.

On May 8, the surrender of Germany was ratified in Berlin, and people all over the world celebrated.

> May 8, 1945
>
> Today is a red-letter day all over the world, but you would know that better than I. I can only hear

about what is going on in distant capitals and large cities. I'll bet it wasn't safe to walk in the streets. We tried to hear on the radio about all of the high feeling that was running through the civilized capitals of the world. . . . Thank God the war here is over. It makes a fellow delirious just thinking about it. So you see, you can't hold me responsible for anything I say today.

Listening to the radio on V-E Day made Dad miss hearing Roosevelt's voice, and he wrote about how much he regretted that the president had died "just before he was able to see it. I don't doubt that he knew it was so close, but actually seeing it is another thing."

Hope for the Future

Dad wrote that he knew what was going to happen to him and his unit but could not share the details with Mom. However, he could tell her that he would be transferred to the Ninth Army, and that she didn't need to worry any longer. "A lot of guys would give a lot to be in our shoes," he wrote, describing his upcoming assignment as "the next best thing to going home or to the States."

Mom must have felt enormously relieved when she received this news because it meant Dad would be staying in Germany and not sent to fight in the Pacific. Dad speculated about whether he might be home by Christmas but said he had no way to know if that was a possibility. He did tell Mom that he expected his unit could settle down once they reached their destination.

With the war in Europe over, he could look back and say, "All in all, though, it hasn't been too bad, and a whole lot easier to take than I thought possible." But Dad was well aware that he had been lucky to enter active service relatively late in the war and also lucky to be in an antiaircraft unit rather than the infantry.

Dad mused about how long it would be before he would be able to hold Mom in his arms again and wrote that he wished she could be next to him, walking together "through these beautiful hills and woodlands."

Dad was enjoying his new accommodations. Instead of camping in tents on top of a hill, the men were now living in a 700-year-old castle formerly owned by a baron. The castle's "halfway decent" water system made it possible to wash up, and he could finally sleep through the night since they no longer needed to be on alert at all times.

He told Mom that the local people were so used to being bossed around—first by a baron and then a burgomaster (burgermeister in German, equivalent to a mayor)—that they had "no minds of their own and can still be ordered around like a bunch of sheep. No wonder they can make war and be soldiers. Discipline is born into them."

German countrywomen, Dad wrote, were the size of two women in the States and "far from fragile." Dad responded to a story Mom had relayed about her sister Blanche becoming hysterical when she found a mouse in her apartment by describing an incident he witnessed while his group was resting near a river.

May 12, 1945

On the other side of the creek was a horse farm. Now it is very hot today and the farmer or trainer or call him what you will was trying to run the horses around. I guess for exercise or something. One of the animals got sick, started to sweat, shake, and couldn't retain his balance. He fell and kicked his feet in the air. After a few attempts by the trainer to revive him, the horse died. A short while later, in comes a team of horses hitched to a wagon to cart the carcass away. A girl about 18 years old, dressed in a boy's shirt and shorts, was in complete charge of the horses. Do you think they lifted that 900 or 1,000 lbs. by a crane as we would do in the U.S. Army? Not on your life. Plain old muscle. And what do you think our character of the fair sex was doing? Stand by and watching the men doing all the work? Nichts. First she grabbed hold of one of the legs and heaved pulled with the best of them. That didn't work so well, so she ran around to the head of the carcass and grabbed it by the muzzle and with a few mighty heaves, she shoved that big old horse onto the cart. The men secured it from falling off. Then she grabbed the reins and with a few sounds known only to her and the horses, took off down the field. All the guys were watching the performance and all sorts of remarks were passed, such as 'You couldn't get my wife within 30 ft of that dead horse,' etc. Now you know why I laughed so when I read about Blanche and a little mouse.

But his experiences in rural Germany had also affected Dad's dream to buy a farm when he returned from the war. Seeing how hard farmers had to work, with no time to rest, Dad decided that was not the life for him. Now all he wanted to do was "slip back" into his old job at the post office that was waiting for him and save enough money for a car and down payment on a house. He thought he could achieve those goals in about a year or two and was looking forward to the day when they could relax and "take things easy for the rest of our lives."

May 13, 1945

I am tired of uncertainty and having people post on a bulletin board what I must wear, must say, must eat, [when I] must get up and sleep. I want to wear some clothes that are not cut in the same pattern of all the men around me. I want to go home and become a civilian again. I am tired of all this. I like the big family idea too. We'll manage to have enough money for them.

The Point System

Just after Germany's surrender, Dad learned about the military's new point system that would be used to assign discharges. The Adjusted Service Rating would be used to help demobilize and discharge enlisted soldiers and sailors in an equitable manner: one point for each month of service, one additional point for each month overseas, five points for each battle star or decoration, and twelve points for each dependent child three and younger. When the system was announced, a soldier needed eighty-five points for discharge.

Dad calculated that he had about forty-five points, and realized that most of the men in his unit would not be discharged until the war with Japan was over, which he expected to last another year. Although disappointed, Dad understood that the U.S. had to use its full strength against Japan if it expected Russia and Great Britain to do the same. He hoped that the war in the Pacific would progress quickly, allowing the Army to relax the basis for discharge and send home the ones who were no longer needed. Although he knew Mom would be dismayed that he would not be coming home right away, Dad urged her to be grateful he was out of danger and to keep up her courage because they were now in the "home stretch."

Still, he warned Mom not to be taken in by false rumors about peace, but to wait until she heard the president announce it. He knew she and others at home had been elated on April 24 when they learned of Himmler's April 22 offer to surrender, but their hopes were crushed when the U.S. refused the "conditional" offer, which Eisenhower had probably seen as ludicrous. Himmler had proposed surrendering in the West, taking over as the new leader of Germany, and continuing to fight against the Russians with help from the Americans and British. According to an article on The History Place, the Western Allies understood this was "a crude attempt to split their alliance with the Soviets" and refused to accept anything less than a "simultaneous unconditional surrender to the four major Allied powers."

After the announcement of Hitler's death, Dad wrote that he would not believe Hitler was dead "until they find the body." Hitler had been reported dead on May 1, and remains of his body were reportedly found on May 5, but Dad (along with many others) was skeptical that he had really died. Although it seems certain now that Hitler committed suicide, and that his remains were discovered by the Russians, skepticism and conspiracy theories have persisted to this day.

Dad also hoped they would "polish off Goering and all the . . . Nazis in a big hurry. Just like the Italians did with Mussolini and his henchmen." Mussolini had been captured and executed by Italian partisans, "hung upside down and then thrown into the gutter," according to *The History Place* article.

In mid-May, Dad's unit continued to move from town to town. On May 16, he was bivouacked in the attic of a "pretty nice two-story house," which was "better than a tent."

May 16, 1945

The only drawback lies in the fact that the fellows in my immediate section are stationed elsewhere. I want to be with them very much because they are the guys I trained with and they are the guys we came to Germany with. We have slept, eaten, and have lived very closely together. In other words, they are my buddies. Their home states range from Maine to South Carolina. We get along very well.

Now that the European war was officially over, Dad could write letters home on regular stationery, not just on V-mail forms. He sometimes used both, depending on which he had access to and how long a letter he wanted to write. Censorship had also been reduced, so on May 18, Dad was able to tell Mom that he was located in a small town called Niederweidbach, about twenty-four miles from Marburg in the central German state of Hesse.

They were camped out in a farmhouse with grain in the attic, cows in the basement, and a piano in the parlor. One of his buddies, Frankie Greco from Brooklyn, was playing the piano and the men were singing together when Dad suddenly became so homesick he could not sing. Frankie felt the same and stopped playing. "For a few moments, the songs we sang brought back memories, and we stopped to meditate." But then the men "snapped out of it and mixed up some cold chocolate in the kitchen."

With more time to relax, Dad's longing to be with Mom grew even stronger. He reminisced about how beautiful she had looked the last time he had seen her, "with a red rose in your long black hair." He remembered the scent of her perfume, how her eyes had sometimes changed from black to brown, and how he loved the contrast between her black hair and white shoulders.

At home, Mom was trying to decide whether to spend the summer in Far Rockaway at her parents' place. Dad warned her against the possible "aggravation and inconvenience" she might face there. In addition to problems among family members, in the summer her mother rented out rooms to tenants from the city, further complicating the living situation. Dad was glad Mom had her own apartment in Jamaica where she could retreat for privacy and peace.

However, some of Mom's news about what was happening back home disturbed him.

May 18, 1945

Your letter was very disheartening. Here I am so far from home, finally winning the battle of democracy and trying to show the Germans that our way of life is better and what happens. Behind my back, on our home front you have hoodlums, gangsters, and Jew-baiters practicing these nazi tricks that we have fought and sacrificed so much to defeat in this, the birthplace of it all. I don't know. It kind of knocks the props out from under a fellow. Keep up your courage darling. Perhaps there are enough right thinking people in America to counter balance that fanatic fringe that makes itself felt so keenly because it is so well organized.

Keeping Busy

Although Dad's letters in early May indicated he believed he would be stationed in Germany, he was starting to doubt that assessment by the end of May. He wrote about the possibility of being sent home for a thirty-day furlough before being deployed to the Pacific. Parting from Mom had been so difficult, he wrote, that the thought of having to do it again would be "very hard to take." It might be easier for all, he said, if he were shipped directly to the Pacific.

Tensions were high as the men waited to learn where they would be stationed next, so the officers tried to keep them busy with recreational programs when they were not on guard. But athletic equipment was hard to come by because it was stored in a warehouse in Paris, and resources were devoted to transporting higher-priority material. Dad asked Mom to include a small black handball in one of her packages.

Some of the men in Dad's unit were experienced hunters and were delighted to discover that the forests in Germany were well stocked with deer. They would shoot and butcher a deer, then light a fire in their cookstove to grill deer steak. The meat was a welcome supplement to the dry rations they had lived on for so many months.

Dad had never tasted venison before, and he compared it to broiled beef liver that he had enjoyed.

Mom turned twenty-five on May 25, and Dad wrote that day on regular stationery, not a V-mail form.

> May 25, 1945
>
> I am going to fool you. Happy birthday, darling. You see, I am not so forgettable [*sic*] as you think. Maybe next birthday we will be together. I say that, sincerely believing and hoping, that it is a distinct possibility. I'll pray that we are together long before then.

He enclosed a photo of himself and asked Mom to show it to me but told her to introduce it gradually, so as not to frighten me.

Part of Dad's on-duty responsibility was to check people's papers as they passed by the guard station. Some were returning by foot to their bombed-out houses in the larger cities, walking up to 150 miles, traveling by day, and sleeping on the roadsides at night.

> May 24, 1945
>
> Some have their worldly belongings on bicycles, baby carriages, carts that they pull by hand. Some carry packs on their backs. The ages vary also. From the youngest to the oldest. I tell them all, don't blame us, blame Hitler. They shake their heads and go on their way.... Oh yes! A lot of the people are displaced persons returning home from slavery. Boy! Are they glad.

Because of his facility with German, Dad had become the interpreter for his unit. In his letter of May 25, he wrote about his conversations with some German civilian workers.

> This morning I spent interpreting. In order to get our recreational program under way, we must build our own courts and baseball diamond. Of course, these people don't know anything about the dimensions and games, and we must show them what we want done. Sooo! I've been showing them what a good old-fashioned baseball diamond or a handball court looks like.

Again, he asked Mom to send him "official" handballs by airmail, telling her they urgently needed them and did not think the Army would supply them in time.

The next day, Dad told Mom not to get "hysterical" over the fact that he had received a battle star, which he had mentioned earlier. Apparently, Dad's sister had called Mom to tell her this news.

May 26, 1945

> No kidding, it was really nothing, when you consider what the infantryman has to go through in order to get the same 5 pts [*sic*]. As a matter of fact, it's not official, but we may get another star for moving up when they were driving for the Elbe River line.

It was now almost June, but the weather in his area in Germany had remained cool, and he was glad they did not have to face a winter campaign in the region, which he knew had been so rough the previous winter. Dad was now able to tell her that during his two months in England and Scotland, he had been loading the wounded onto the *Queen Mary* and *Queen Elizabeth* ships. Some of what he saw almost made him sick, "but the boys used to joke about their wounds and consider themselves lucky that they were going home. Out of the numbing cold foxholes and onto a luxury liner." Ironically, many of them had been brought to Europe on the same ship that would be taking them home.

Dad told Mom that everyone in his area in Scotland, near Glasgow, had been so good to them and alluded to what had been going on between the sexes in Europe. "You can't even begin to imagine the stuff that goes on, on this side of the ocean" but expected a lot of the girls back home would be surprised "when their Johnnie comes marching home."

But Dad assured Mom his love for her had not faltered and told her that if he were home, he would want to take her to work with him so as not to be apart for even eight hours. He was still worried he would be shipped to the Pacific, but now Dad was hoping to get a furlough home first, even though he had previously said he would prefer to go directly.

Even before the war, Dad had not believed in God, and the suffering he had seen in Europe had hardened that view.

May 28, 1945

> Look at the rotten record of this world and tell me that there is a God. Wars, famine, disease, twisted minds. If he is an omnipotent force, then why does he allow this to go on?

Many of Dad's letters included descriptions of what the men were eating or what food they missed. He told Mom that Germany's basic food was black bread, which reminded him of Jewish rye. Few in his unit had eaten that kind of bread before, but most enjoyed it very much. They were also enjoying the hot chocolate sent by his sister Sylvia, now that they were living in a house and could prepare it. But Dad asked Mom to keep sending cheese, bread, and canned fish, because those needed no preparation or cleanup.

May 30, Memorial Day, was especially meaningful for the men this year, and Dad explained how they celebrated.

> May 30, 1945
>
> Today is Memorial Day and we are honoring our dead. Also, we are having a ceremony for a flag presentation. All this time we have not had an American flag to fly over our little post. Just a small piece of America in the heart of Germany. These tiny posts are spread all over the parts of Germany we took. It kind of makes me homesick to see it fly. If only I could see that N.Y. skyline again. By the time we would actually land and I'd come home, I'd be a nervous wreck. Only God knows when I will be able to experience that exhilerating [*sic*] thrill.

However, he was buoyed by good news from the Pacific. "It sure looks like the Air Force has taken it upon itself to eliminate Japan by itself."

> May 31, 1945
>
> I was reading the *Stars & Stripes* today and although the Okinawa campaign is almost over, it is a very costly affair. It might be a curtain raiser of what we can expect when Japan itself is invaded. Maybe the picture will change when we can throw more weight at the enemy. We have it here. Time is imperative in getting it over there.

HEADQUARTERS
49th ANTIAIRCRAFT ARTILLERY BRIGADE
APO 230

Germany
10 May 1945

SUBJECT: Commendation on Performance of Duty in the Rhine, and Central German Campaigns.

TO : Lieutenant Colonel Joseph G. Howe,
Commanding Officer, 581st AAA AW Bn,
APO 230, U. S. Army.

1. At the conclusion of our victorious campaign through Europe, I want to express my deep appreciation to you, and through you, to the officers and men of your command, for the outstanding drive, tenacity of purpose, a nd aggressiveness with which the 581st AAA AW Battalion performed all combat missions in the Rhine and Central German Campaigns.

2. Narrative.

a. The 581st AAA AW Battalion landed at Le Havre, France, on 9 March 1945, and on 12 March 1945, after a record non-stop motor march (except for 2 halts) was going into position in defense of the critically important Remagen Bridge. The initial mission found the battalion a part of the coordinated antiaircraft defense of the then still intact Ludendorf Bridge and the pontoon bridges at Remagen and Kripp. The battalion remained in this area until 12 April, continually shifting and expanding its defense until eventually it was providing the only automatic weapons protection for the two (2) pontoon bridges at Remagen, the pontoon bridge at Kripp, and the pontoon bridge at Hokingen. A secondary mission of protecting these all important structures against damage from floating mines and saboteurs caused some AAA AW units at each site to be located so as to cover the water and back areas adjacent. Perfect coordination with engineer units was maintained to facilitate the proper functioning of this activity, and no damage was sustained by any of these bridges, in spite of concentrated and sustained air and water borne attacks.

b. During portions of the above period, the battalion organized and operated a provisional trucking company of 50 2½ ton trucks, in addition to its normal functions, completed 273,757 truck miles, hauled 5204 tons of high priority freight, moved the 85th Infantry Division from the Ruhr Pocket to Leipzig, and 13,000 German P.W.'s on return trips from the front lines. This record trebles that of any of the fifteen similar trucking companies of the 49th AAA Brigade, and is particularly noteworthy in that the 581st AAA AW Battalion progressively moved forward, in the normal performance of its AAA missions, over 180 miles, in protection of airfields, supply dumps,

-1-

Commendation Dad's unit received just after V-E Day on their performance in the Rhine and Central German campaigns from Brigadier General E.W. Timberlake to the unit's commanding officer, Lieutenant Colonel Joseph G. Howe, May 10, 1945. The commendation supplied the narrative of the unit's actions in the important battle at the bridge at Remagen, which Dad had not been permitted to write to Mom about because of the military censorship.

United States Senate
COMMITTEE ON BANKING AND CURRENCY

May 28, 1945

Cpl. A. M. Klapper, 32968151
A581 AAA AW
APO 230, c/o Postmaster
New York, N. Y.

Dear Cpl. Klapper:

I received your letter dated May 5 telling me that upon your return to civil life you would like to obtain an appointment in the Railway Mail Service.

If you will get in touch with me upon your return to New York, I assure you I will be happy to give you every possible assistance.

With my kindest regards and every good wish, believe me to be,

Very sincerely yours,

Robert F. Wagner

Letter Dad received from New York Senator Robert F. Wagner promising to assist him in his effort to obtain a position in the Railway Mail Service, May 28, 1945.

Dad with a buddy from West Virginia.

Two of the men in the unit holding a deer they had just shot. Once the men discovered that the countryside was full of deer, they hunted, cooked, and ate them to supplement their Army rations.

Dad wrote on this photo, "In the barn on my left, the pigs. On the right, the cows. In the rear, the displaced family and the chickens. To the front, not visible lay the fragrant manure pile."

One of Dad's buddies sitting "at the helm of the old wagon."

"The two daughters of the owners of the house in the background where we lived. The cows lived in the barn to the right. Between them and the privy, shown, one needed a gas mask."

"The only male in the household of the [family] whose hospitality we enjoyed. Get the mama chicken with her brood. Cute?"

CHAPTER 12

Occupied Germany, Visit to Holland

As HIS DAYS IN GERMANY stretched on, Dad was finding it difficult to uphold the Army's nonfraternization policy that prohibited military members from even speaking to Germans except on official business. Near his unit's guard post was a family with a grandmother, mother, and a little red-haired daughter, who looked about the same age as me. Dad wrote that she had an irresistible smile, and he showed her a photo of me. She was afraid of his comrades, but not of him.

The encounter made him miss Mom and me even more. When he was alone in his room looking at photos of us, Dad found "uncontrolled tears came to my eyes." He sent Mom a nostalgic poem, "Nocturne," that he had clipped from a column in the *Stars and Stripes* called "Puptent Poets."

Like Dad, many U.S. military men were beginning to ignore the nonfraternization policy, but for distinctly different reasons. Because many German men had either died or been captured during the war, a lot of German women were alone, so even the threat of heavy fines and jail sentences didn't deter many American soldiers from spending time with the lonely women.

June 1, 1945

I guess you know that we have what is known as a nonfraternization policy. We must not talk to them

> except on official business. Of course you can realize how hard it is on most of the Casanovas around here. The army has even resorted to heavy fines and jail sentences if they are caught. But the women are more than willing, and the boys don't give a damn, especially when they are beautiful and the men have the CBI [China-Burma-India Theater] staring them in the face.

The Army had imposed the strict nonfraternization policy partially in response to strong negative public opinion about friendly treatment given to Goering and other high-ranking Nazi leaders. But military authorities knew the policy would be difficult to enforce once the war was over, especially as the enlisted men claimed it was enacted just to allow officers "the first crack at all the good-looking women." Because GIs were allowed to fraternize with members of the Women's Army Corps and their French equivalents, soldiers often claimed their female companions were members of one of those groups—even if the women were not in uniform and were speaking German.

The Army was also concerned about the increasing spread of venereal disease (itself a strong indication of fraternization) and feared the policy was preventing men from obtaining prophylactics or getting checked or treated. According to Earl F. Ziemke in *The U.S. Army in the Occupation of Germany*, the military announced on June 4, 1945, that contraction or treatment of a venereal disease would "not be used directly or indirectly as evidence of fraternization." The move was one of the final blows against the nonfraternization policy, which Ziemke says did not actually come to a formal end but rather "disintegrated" by the end of July 1945.

Even before the policy fell apart, the Army allowed soldiers to shop in German stores and purchase non-rationed items. Dad wrote to Mom that he was going to look for a good camera and hoped he could buy one "for a song."

"A Bloody Business"

June 6, 1945, was the one-year anniversary of the invasion of Normandy, and the Allies celebrated the day as a holiday. All duties, except for guard and "fatigue" (upkeep duties, such as barracks cleaning) were suspended for the day. Dad wondered when D-Day for Japan would occur and wrote that he expected there would need to be multiple invasions, including one against the China coast and several against Japan's home islands. Even though Dad knew he could not return home until the Japanese were defeated, he was bothered by the fire bomb raids "raising hell with their crowded cities" and dismayed by "what a destructive bloody business" war is.

He had seen a movie, *In Our Time*, that reminded him and his buddies of how terrible the Nazis had been and cautioned that they would try it again if given another chance, even though the Germans he was meeting now "were meek enough." Dad wryly commented that he would pull the Americans out of Germany and let the Russians, Poles, and others "who have felt the Nazi heel" deal with them.

German civilians were "continually surprised" when he spoke to them in German, and many of them would then proceed to tell him their troubles and claim they were not Nazis.

June 6, 1945

That's when I blow my stack and tell them off. A handful really aren't or ever were nazis. They are returning home after being released from various concentration camps. To hear some of their tales takes a strong stomach. Whenever we want to have fun with them, we tell them that soon we are leaving and then comes the Russky. They are more afraid of the Russians than they are of a plague. They keep thanking God that the Americans are here. The Russ. [*sic*] don't spare them anything and are ten

> times more strict with them than we are. If I had on my conscience what these people have, I'd fear the Russ. too. As far as I am concerned, they can give all of Germany to Russia to do with as she pleases.

Dad was able to speak enough German to communicate with the owners of the house they were occupying, and he ensured that his unit received a regular supply of fresh eggs, black bread, and butter. In exchange, he told them they would get their house back when the unit moved out of the village, and that the men would try not to "wreck the joint," which the family appreciated.

The beauty of the German countryside continued to amaze Dad, especially because it stood in stark contrast to what the Nazis had done to other people and countries.

June 7, 1945

> The wheat is ripening and tall now. As the wind moves over it, it looks like the waves of the restless ocean. Off further in the distance are dark green or black forested hilltops. The sky is beginning to cloud up, and it looks ominous and foreboding. This country is very hilly, and when it clouds up, it somehow reminds me of what a backdrop or scenery to a Wagner opera must look like. This is a rich country and a beautiful one.

But Dad found it difficult to reconcile the beautiful scenery with the "twisted minds of these people." The more he heard about the atrocities the Nazis had committed "when they were riding high," the harder it was for him to grasp. "How could something so beautiful hide something so rotten as a concentration camp?"

Because the war in Europe was over, Dad was able to write about the destruction he had seen in France, Belgium, and the larger cities and villages of Germany. He told Mom that Germans still fearfully looked up to the sky when they saw a fleet of C-47s or "pursuit ships" flying over. "I think the Air Corps accomplished more psychologically than physically, although the latter was terrific too."

He felt that everyone in Europe was sick of war and assured Mom "we'll have peace in our time yet." At the same time, he knew the U.S. would occupy Germany for a long time.

Life Under Military Rule

Several of the officers who had been in charge of Dad's unit at Camp Stewart in Georgia had shipped over with the unit. Dad was particularly contemptuous of one who had made it unnecessarily difficult for him to secure passes to see Mom when she was in Port Wentworth. Even after "that lousy top kick" was shipped home in June, Dad never forgave him for the way he had treated him stateside. He had told the officer just what he thought about him one night in England, just before they shipped over to France.

Dad had refused to become a corporal on the gun crew of the battery because he did not want to be promoted to sergeant, which would have been the next step. He hated the unnecessary discipline of the Army and the officers or noncoms who "dished it out" and did not want to join their company.

June 9, 1945

> Only on the actual front line, where your life isn't worth a plugged nickel can a man be a leader without being a rotten character. . . . After all, when the men are in the tightest spots, where you need the most discipline, all chicken disappears. Then why have it when we are relaxed and resting? I realize that you must have law and order, but some of that stuff isn't necessary.

Dad was following the latest news as best he could, and he wrote that he hoped the trials of the Nazi war criminals would begin soon, and that there would be no qualms about meting out the death penalty "the way the accused used to do." But meeting so many German civilians in small towns was making him think about "the complexity of trying to pick out the good people from the Nazis." He was beginning to think "it is probably true that a great many of these people, particularly the small village people, were forced to comply."

June 11, 1945

> The people say to resist in any shape or form meant that a person was taken from his family and never again heard from. In the beginning, the hardy ones spoke out, and they were promptly dealt with. . . . The rest realized that discretion was the better part of valor and shut up. The party men were in the minority but were strong enough to have things their way.

Because the Germans had been brought up to be so disciplined, it took only "a word" and they complied, Dad wrote. They just did not understand liberty "as we know it. Even now, when they speak of nazi terror, they glance apprehensively behind them and lower their voices." He thanked God "we are Americans."

As the nonfraternization policy continued to erode, Dad wrote that many of the healthy young guys could not resist the beautiful young German women. "You can't begin to imagine how little these people respect the morals we have been brought up on." Of course, Dad's absolute loyalty and love for Mom helped him avoid such temptation, but he wrote that he was also repelled when he thought of Buchenwald and other concentration camps. "What monsters the bellies of these beautiful women conceive."

Dad wrote that he was not sure what he was "learning or not

learning in this occupation business, but it sure makes an impression on me. Some of the stuff I'll forget, but some I'll never."

His role as "orientation man" made some of the other men seek his advice and information on matters about which he had no knowledge.

June 13, 1945

Just because I am the orientation man in our battery and somewhat better informed than the rest of the boys on international and national affairs, the boys come to me with all sincerity and ask, 'Abe, when are we going home?' I try to make them understand that if I only knew the answer to that question, I'd gladly give it to them.

Everything is in a chaotic state now, with redeployment not yet in full swing, the South Pacific battles for bases still raging, the critical score for discharge not arrived at yet. How can I, a little person in this world with no more information available to me than what I read in the paper, give them the answer they want so much to hear? Maybe they like to talk about going home, even if they realize how impossible it is. Must be like getting something off your chest, or misery loves company. I am a good listener, and generally we wind up talking about something else.

Dad was also worried about how Mom was getting along because he had read in *Stars and Stripes* that the food shortage at home was critical, especially for meat and eggs. He knew it must be tough for her right now but asked her to hang on, "especially with the end not as far off as it used to be."

Finally, on June 17, Dad learned his group was officially in the Seventh Army, the Army of Occupation of Germany. He would not be shipped to the Pacific, and he and Mom would not have to deal with a heartbreaking furlough and another goodbye.

Knowing that he wouldn't be facing another farewell, Dad was finally at liberty to describe his last few days in New York Harbor and tell Mom why he had not been able to contact her, even though he had been so close by.

June 18, 1945

> Darling, I'll never forget how things were the few days before we left the States. We had a close censorship, and our mail in Stewart was even held up. We hit Shanks [the embarkation point for troops headed to Europe, located in Orangeburg, New York] under the same secrecy wraps. It was cold and snow lay on the ground. We had a lot of last minute things to get. We were there for three days, but couldn't get out because we were alerted. Up to the last minute, we hoped for a break. Then they said, 'Pack it all up men, we're getting on board today.' That was December 24. We boarded ship, got our bunks and instructions, then [were] confined to the ship. That evening was Christmas Eve. The loud speaker system ironically was blaring away with Christmas carols, the winches on board were loading the hatches, and I, I was the glummest specimen you ever did see.
>
> In the evening, I looked out on West Street. We were still tied to the pier. I could see the traffic going up 42 St [*sic*] and on the elevated highway. Spiritually, darling, I was trying to reach out to you

to let you know how close I was. Yet, I might have been on the other side of the world for all the good it did. I'll never forget that night, darling.

Occupying Germany, Time Dragging On

June 1945 brought beautiful spring weather to Germany, and everyone was out in the fields pitching hay in the area where Dad was staying. He wrote to Mom describing how the road was full of "hayload after hayload coming into the barns." Milk cows were being used to do the work of oxen, mules, or horses, which Dad thought would have been illegal in the States.

Dad was hearing rumors that wives and children might soon be able to join the men remaining in Germany as occupation troops, and he asked Mom if she would consider trying it. He said he would love to show her the countryside and walk with her through the fields and forests. To allay her fear of becoming seasick on the way to Europe, Dad said he had not been seasick on his trip over because he had gone up on deck for fresh air, unlike the men who suffered. Also, his unit had served as MP on board, which helped to pass the time.

On a melancholy note, he sent her the words of a chorus to a German song he loved, called "Komm Zurück" ("Come Back") and asked her to translate it as he knew her skills in German were better than his own. He had tried to do it himself, but "it comes out very stilted. That's the way it is with foreign language transcriptions." He thought the song would be a big hit, if it ever reached the States.

Dad told Mom that the local population seemed meek and compliant enough, especially now that everyone was busy harvesting and hauling hay and full of aches and pains at night after the hard work. But serving guard duty sometimes meant enforcing discipline to uphold the rules.

June 20, 1945

Yesterday while on post a woman and two men who had bicycled all the way from Cologne, about 150 kilometers, were stopped by me. They only had about 9 kilometers to go, but I wouldn't let them pass. They didn't have the proper papers to travel. They try to give you a "sob story," but I told them to git [*sic*]. I also added that they were lucky I wasn't a German soldier and they Frenchmen or Pole, etc. If they didn't like it, they could thank their Adolph. Then I pointed my rifle at them and told them to take off, "Zürück, shnell."

Another time, two young girls were caught out after curfew and brought to the burgomaster, who found them a place to sleep. The next morning, the burgomaster had to fine them five marks apiece.

Dad wrote on the next day that no one in his unit had received any mail for a few days, and he speculated that pointed to an imminent relocation of the group. He had not yet received any word about a move, but a lack of mail for a few days in the past had been followed by a move.

Toward the end of June, Dad found out the British were going to permit wives to join occupation troops, so he again asked Mom if she thought it would be too difficult to make the trip overseas. Dad thought Mom's knowledge of German would be a great asset, and he speculated that homes would be divided among married families, with single men quartered in other houses. But he wondered how the Army would deal with transportation, food, and medical care issues.

Time dragged during this period. "This whole business has turned into a waiting game. When the war was on, the time flew. We moved frequently and were too tired to notice the length of the days." To keep himself occupied, Dad went to USO-sponsored traveling shows, such as *Junior Miss*, which he saw in Giessen. He mostly enjoyed seeing "real live American actresses," including one who strongly resembled Mom's sister Blanche, then a struggling young actress in New York. He also went to the movies in Dillenburg, another nearby town.

The USO brought top artists to perform for the GIs. One afternoon, Dad saw a variety show with a leading ballerina, a baritone, a soprano, and a violinist. These shows and movies were an important break for the men because the village where they were stationed was so small the railroad did not even run near it. A small combat shortwave radio was required to hear any American music or news.

Athletics was another important outlet for Dad and his buddies, and he was excited when a box from home arrived toward the end of June with those long-awaited handballs. Unfortunately, the handball court could not be completed because the cement they needed was being shipped to the big cities to rebuild bombed-out buildings.

Dad was now allowed to tell Mom that he had traveled to Europe on the *George Washington*, an Army transport ship originally owned by Germany and acquired by the U.S. after World War I. But he spent less time writing about recent past experiences than imagining what the future would look like when he arrived home again. He visualized arriving at Penn Station in Manhattan and then resting in their little apartment in Jamaica with Mom fussing in the kitchen with the radio on. He saw me sitting in my highchair, although he conceded I might already be big enough to sit at the table by the time he got back. "I can hardly envision actually being able to relax in my own home with my own family." He once again encouraged Mom to hang on, because now they had much to look forward to and live for.

Late-night guard duty could be cold, even in late June, but Dad consoled himself by remembering that "we won't have to spend winter in the field, in foxholes or snow." He estimated he would have to stay in Germany for another year to eighteen months but was happy to be there rather than fighting in the Pacific. This way, he could come home "with two arms, two legs, and my sight. . . . War is hell anywhere, but in the Pacific it is that plus."

Three Days in Holland

Passes to travel to nearby countries were becoming available, but Dad turned down a pass to Spa in Belgium because he had heard the only things to buy there were "lousy high-priced liquor and whores." He was hoping to go to Holland—where the people spoke pretty good English—or to Paris to see the sights and meet up with a friend stationed there.

At 4 a.m. on June 29, Dad was awakened and told to be ready in fifteen minutes to leave for a three-day pass at the Valkenburg Recreation Center in Holland. Dad was facing an eight-hour ride on a GI truck, but he looked forward to swimming and sports when he arrived.

The Army had created the center even before V-E Day to give GIs a place to relax and become somewhat acclimated to civilian life again, selecting Valkenburg because it already had some of the necessary facilities. Although it was a civilian town, the men were expected to wear their uniforms, obey curfew, and check their weapons with the manager of their hotel. At Valkenburg, the men could get free haircuts, shaves, and shampoos at the barbershop, enjoy free movies, make purchases at the PX, and exchange currency for free. Best of all, the men were offered three good meals a day, prepared by chefs and served by uniformed waiters at tables actually covered with tablecloths! They could go to dances or participate in swimming and boating, weather permitting. Or they could take a free tour of the town's main tourist attraction—caves that were thought to be some of the world's oldest.

Valkenburg, which before the war had been a popular honeymoon destination, had been invaded on May 10, 1940, by the Germans and liberated four years later by the U.S. Ninth Army. Now, the town's motto for the GIs was to "Enjoy the freedom for which you fought so gallantly."

The recreation center had been opened for the GIs on March 10, 1945, and was now operated by the 19th Corps after previously being under the command of the Seventh Armored Group and the

Ninth Army. By the time Dad arrived at the end of June, the complex contained twenty-two hotels, a motion picture theater, and two dance halls and could accommodate 1,150 soldiers at one time.

Although he described the food as just OK, Dad was delighted to eat off of real dishes set atop a table covered by a tablecloth. The men were served by a waiter "dressed in swallow tail black coat." What a welcome change after two years of eating out of mess kits! After dinner, Dad had a choice of shows and dances at two different hotels, but he opted to go to bed early the first night, luxuriating in the fresh linen on his hotel bed. He no longer took such basic amenities for granted. Dad also described the relief of being able to speak freely with civilians again, most of whom spoke English or German, which he understood now.

But he found the financial situation in Holland "all screwed up," because people had plenty of money but very little to buy. As a result, locals swarmed the trucks loaded with GIs, offering to buy whatever anyone was willing to sell, and prices were thus "sky-high," with a carton of cigarettes selling for $23. The situation had been caused by the Nazis, who forced the Dutch to use their resources for the benefit of the Germans, depriving their own people of food and industrial products and draining its workforce. Transportation facilities, including railcars, barges, and bridges, had been destroyed, and the Dutch people were actually close to famine by the end of the war. On his second day in Valkenburg, Dad wandered around town in search of souvenirs, but the prices were "outrageous."

Although the hotel was mostly comfortable, it had only one bath and limited toilet facilities, and Dad did not feel like standing in line for those because this was supposed to be a break from Army routine. But he was happy that he did not have to stand in line for dinner and could just walk in when it was announced. The day was too cloudy to use the big, beautiful pool, but after dinner, Dad saw a movie — *Guest in the House* — which he enjoyed. As he was about to retire, "the boys were rolling in one and two at a time" from having drunk too many beers. There was a curfew for the GIs, and they had to be in by midnight. After that, all hotel doors were locked.

On his second full day at Valkenburg, Dad heard "some kind of chanting outside" the hotel and went out to "investigate."

> Holland
> July 1, 1945
>
> I found the streets gaily bedecked with flags and orange banners. I guess that's for the royal family. Practically the entire population was parading through the streets. It was a religious festival. After that was done, one of those traveling carnivals you read about or see in the movies opened up shop. It has been standing in an open field outside our hotel for several days without opening for business. I guess today's holiday was the cue. It is the first time in 4 years that either the festival or carnival has been here. The nazis wouldn't permit it. Very popular though according to the way the townspeople are flocking to it.

Dad toured Valkenburg's famous caves on his last day there, admiring the beautiful paintings and drawings on the walls. The man-made caves are carved out of soft stone made up of pressed tiny fossil skeletons from prehistoric times, and they served as a refuge in 1794 when France invaded Holland. The tour guide told how several hundred Dutch youth had also hidden there in 1940 to avoid being forced into labor in Germany.

To give Mom a flavor of "what goes on over here," Dad told her how he had been standing outside the hotel with a fellow soldier who was wearing a short jacket made out of a GI blanket by a woman in Germany. Two Dutch women were standing near the entrance, and one of them said in broken English, "You giff me that jacket, yah." The fellow decided to tease her and asked what she would give him for it. She replied, "I giff you myself." He asked, "For how long?" She thought for a minute, "evidently measuring the value of the jacket, and said, 'From tonight 7 o'clock until tomorrow morning 7 o'clock.'" The men then shooed the women away, saying, "No dice." Dad's companion had concluded "he would probably wake up with the clap and no jacket, and probably no money either."

Preparing to Move

Dad left Holland on July 3, arriving at his base later that afternoon after a "long, tiresome trip" but grateful to have had an opportunity to get away for a while. Upon returning, he found his unit getting ready to move to another area of Germany. In preparation, the men had to turn in their big machine guns, but they were allowed to keep their "personal small arms," including rifles.

Most American soldiers were in a holding pattern until the Army figured out which battalions were to be moved where, leaving them and the Germans around them in a state of tension. According to Dad, because the American occupation forces did not behave like Nazis, some of the local people, especially the younger ones, got the idea that the GIs were "soft," which led to some dangerous encounters. Dad wrote Mom about one incident he had heard about.

July 5, 1945

> It seems that a group of young squirts got a little frisky in one area about 50 miles from here. A group of them went by a security guard post similar to ours in some sort of formation, goose-stepping and heiling. A guard on duty at the time told them to break it up. They walked right by paying

no heed. He yelled 'Halt,' but still they went on. He leveled his rifle and gave them another chance, but it was still no dice. Then he let go. Killed one and wounded another. The rest broke it up and fled. I'd like to see some of them smart bastards try that around my post. There'll be more dead nazis. Incidentally, the chap who did the deed was an Indian [Native American].

Dad was involved in a couple of less dramatic incidents because of his role as an interpreter.

July 6, 1945

I was pitching some horseshoes this afternoon also, when a couple of German women came up to one of the boys and asked for something to eat. He called me over and said, 'Hey Abe, what the hell are they jabbering about?' It seems that they are refugees from some bombed-out big city and were coming through. First, I asked them if they were German, then I told them that we never have anything to eat for Germans. I don't care if they were hungry. They can thank 'Adolf' for their misery.

Shortly afterwards, another German civilian came over and asked for some tobacco. Dad's reaction was similar.

That burned me up. What in blazes do these people think I came here for. To feed them? Well, I told him off as best I could. It evidently was enough, because he took off like a scared deer. I ought to know. I have seen enough of the poor creatures frightened. Somehow, I can't bring myself to go hunting and shoot them. They are so graceful and fragile. Very handsome animals too.

Cover of booklet, *Pocket Guide to Germany*, Dad received from the Army on entering Germany. Note warning to the GIs, "DO NOT FRATERNIZE," a policy that proved to be unenforceable after a short time the GIs were in occupied Germany.

IMPORTANT SIGNS

German	English
Halt!	Stop!
Langsam!	Go slow!
Gefahr!	Danger!
Einbahnstrasse	One Way Street
Einbahnverkehr	One Way Traffic
Keine Durchfahrt	No Thoroughfare
Rechts fahren	Keep to The Right
Strasse im Bau	Road Under Construction
Kurve	Dangerous Curve
Kreuzung	Dangerous Crossing
Bahnübergang	Grade Crossing
Parken verboten	No Parking
Kein Zutritt	No Admittance
Frauen *or* Damen	Women
Männer *or* Herren	Men
Rauchen verboten	No Smoking
Eingang	Entrance
Ausgang	Exit

U. S. GOVERNMENT PRINTING OFFICE: 1944

Pages from the booklet that included translations of German signs, the importance of non-fraternization, no looting, property or food theft, a brief history of Germany, and reasons the U.S. soldier is fighting Germany.

CONTENTS

	Page
I. Your Job in Germany	1
II. On Guard!	4
Keep Your Distance	4
Keep Your Eyes Open	5
Keep Your Guard Up	6
What the Germans Think of the U. S.	10
"Alibis"	12
Health	16
Marriage Facts	17
III. Background	18
Nazi Vacuum	18
Glimpse of History	20
The German Empire	26
And Before the German Empire	27
Why You Are Fighting Germany	27
Landscape	30
Climate	31
IV. In Conclusion	32
V. Annex	33
Currency, Weights, and Measures	33
Language Guide	36

I. YOUR JOB IN GERMANY

Whether you fight your way in, or march in to occupy Germany under armistice terms, you will be doing a soldier's job on the soil of the enemy.

The occupation of Germany will give you your chance to build up a personal guarantee that as soon as you turn your back to go home, the German will not pick up his shooting irons and start throwing lead and lies at an unsuspecting world once more. One of the greatest challenges of the Peace to come is to make certain that the German people will take their place as law-abiding, useful citizens in the family of nations.

On German soil, you are expected to observe local laws and regulations except as modified or amended by your own military authority.

Local customs, especially those touching upon religion, are to be given consideration and respect.

Respect property rights. Vandalism is inexcusable. Rifling of orchards and fields and unauthorized appropriation of food stores are contemptible and punishable by court martial.

Remember that conquered and occupied nations will be critically short of food. Depriving the people

VALKENBURG RECREATION CENTER

✶ ✶ ✶

"Enjoy the Freedom for which you fought so gallantly."

WELCOME "HOME"

This is your Recreation Center — a town set aside solely for your enjoyment. It was created by men with combat experience, — men who best understand the problems you face when you go on pass. Their job has not been an easy one, but everything they did and are still doing is in keeping with a policy to please the soldier on pass.

Long before the defeat of Germany, Army officials realized the need of a recreation center — a center equipped with the same entertainment and other facilities a soldier would find in his own town back home. Valkenburg was chosen as a site for one of the recreation centers, chiefly because it already had some of these facilities. It offers you, for the most part, an opportunity to "brush up" on your civilian actions and manners.

You came on pass to get away from Army routine, to have fun and to enjoy yourself. Fully aware of these facts, the staff itself is devoting all its efforts to make Valkenburg a town you can call home for three days. It's work is still in progress — because it wants to make it possible for you to find increasing pleasure and enjoyment at the recreation center.

The welcome mat is always out to you — fellow soldiers of the U.S. Army. The staff is glad to have you here for three days and it hopes you have enjoyed the results of its efforts thus far. Pass the good word about the recreation center along to your buddies in your outfit. We want them to get in on the fun, too. And don't forget to come back yourself—soon.

MOVIES

Motion pictures are shown twice daily at the State Theater, the first show starting at 1330 and the second at 1830. It is a civilian theater, and is equipped with a modern motion picture machine and plush bottom seats.

POST EXCHANGE

Your pass entitles you to make one purchase at the PX. It is located at the Hotel Bellevue, in the heart of town. You'll need your ETO ration card to purchase rationed articles.

MONEY EXCHANGED

You'll need Guldens in this town. Get them at the Hotel Bellevue, where the finance clerk is on duty from 0900 to 1200 and 1300 to 1700 on the first and third days of your pass. Then, sometime during your last afternoon in town, change your money back into Marks at the same place.

MEALS DE LUXE

Our chefs are the best in Holland. They serve breakfast at 0800, dinner at 1230 and supper at 1730. Please be on time.

CENTER'S GROWTH.

The growth of the Valkenburg Recreation Center has been rapid. It opened on March 10, this year, with an enrollment of only 353 and, by June 1, this year, was capable of accommodating 1,150 soldiers at one time.

Major Maurice I. Fass, of the 95th Infantry Division, is director of the center. His working staff includes five officers, 53 enlisted men and 321 civilian employees.

The center's setup is designed to give you all the entertainment and rest you can jam into three whole days and three whole nights. Dances, movies, swimming and boating all comprise a part of the recreational program.

The center, now operated by the 19th Corps, formerly was under command of the Seventh Armored Group and the Ninth U.S. Army. It has provided rest and entertainment for more than 12,000 soldiers during the period from March 10 to June 1.

Twenty-two hotels are now used by the recreation center, in addition to a motion picture theater and two dance halls.

SEND PAPER HOME

Send your copy of the Recreation Center paper to the folks at home. They want to know all about the town in which you spent your three-day pass.

CONSULT DIRECTORIES IN HOTELS FOR LATEST DETAILED INFORMATION

Booklet from Valkenburg Recreation Center in Holland, where Dad enjoyed a three-day R&R pass. Note quote at top, "Enjoy the Freedom for which you fought so gallantly." Dad found it a pleasure to be able to speak freely with the Dutch people, some of whom knew English, and others who knew German.

CHAPTER 13

Guarding the MCC Near Helsa

ON JULY 7, DAD'S BATTALION relocated to a former German munitions factory complex, the *Fabrik Hessisch Lichtenau* in Fürstenhagen, just outside the small town of Helsa, about nine miles southeast of Kassel in central Germany. He had been through the area, in Hann. Münden, when the war was still on and had noticed then that it had been badly damaged. Now, Dad wrote to Mom about how "appalling the amount of damage that aerial bombs and shell fire can spew upon a city."

En route to Holland on pass the week before, his group had gone through Cologne in western Germany and he saw that Kassel, near Helsa, was almost as badly shattered as Cologne. But Kassel was still a big communications center, and the Army was using its facilities to ship equipment to France and from there to its final destination.

The munitions factory site now housed the Ministerial Collecting Center, called the "MCC." A complex of 800 buildings spread over a twenty-five-mile-square-mile, it had been chosen for its new purpose for several reasons. The site supplied space for storage and examination of documents, provided housing for German civilian workers in Camps Herzog and Teichhof, and offered easy access to highways leading both south to Frankfurt and north to cities in the plains. It was close to Kassel, which was in the northern part of the American zone of occupation, and near the British and Russian zones. And a prisoner-of-war camp could be established a short distance to the south, at Camp Führen, so that the inmates could be used as laborers.

The new responsibility of the 581st, now that antiaircraft artillery was no longer needed in Germany, was to guard the MCC. Dad wrote to tell Mom what his captain told them about their mission.

July 10, 1945

It seems that when the war was on, the Germans had dispersed their ministries from Berlin to small agricultural communities similar to Helsa, where we are now. The reason, of course, was due to the fact that their normal operations were harassed by the heavy bombardment that the cities got. Well, as you can see, the government of Germany was spread out all over the damn country. At first, they were able to communicate with one another, but the bombing became more intense so that eventually they lost contact with one another and didn't even know where to find one department or the next. By the time the war was over, there was no cohesive German government left. The personnel and records were hidden in out-of-the-way places. Now the Allies are attempting to gather all these together so that they can go over them and extract or file for future reference any information we may think important. The former ministerial employees are being housed in camps under government supervision.

In conjunction with a few other outfits, we are guarding everything that needs protection. Records, Army personnel, civilians, even prisoners of war who have been specially brought in to do the heavy and dirty work. As a matter of fact, we have about ten of them coming over to our area tomorrow, and we have a couple of men assigned to guard them and see that they work. We have been cautioned not to hit them but to shoot only in case they make a break. You know the U.S. We have to observe the Geneva Convention rules [which prohibit violence against prisoners]. We even have a lot of German civilians who are getting paid by Uncle Sam for fixing up the joint in which we live.

The Army realized it was necessary to explain the importance of the MCC's mission and how the unit's functions fit into the picture of reestablishing a peaceful Germany. So it created and distributed a booklet, *The 581st Antiaircraft-Artillery-Battalion Looks At The Ministerial Collecting Center*, which described the mission:

> The important files and up-to-date records of Germany's various ministries and leading political organizations were ordered by Adolf Hitler to be removed from Berlin to a place where the Government could function with more or less freedom from the innumerable and devastating air raids on the capital. Reports have it that the new capital was to have been Munich, deep in the now famed Bavarian Redoubt, where, theoretically the German army could hold out indefinitely.

When time ran out for the Nazis, the advancing Allied divisions "came upon trucks and houses full of records, directly from Berlin." They guarded these valuable documents, and experts were called in to appraise them. Since the U.S. had determined that Germany was to be "reborn again," it was urgent and necessary for the records to be assembled and evaluated. The operation was called "Goldcup," and its purpose was "to locate and control German Ministries and the Ministerial personnel which were known to have left Berlin in whole or in part." A huge quantity of documents and personnel had been located all across the country. According to the MCC booklet, "sixty-eight locations" had been found for "fragments of the Ministry of Food and Agriculture alone!"

The Goldcup operation was carried out jointly by the Americans and the British. For the United States, the MCC came under the jurisdiction of the Seventh Army, which was responsible for its security and administration, with duties delegated to the 49th AAA Brigade, commanded by Brig. Gen. E. W. Timberlake. Various tasks had been assigned to different units, and Dad's was responsible for the security of the MCC itself, to guard "all places where trouble may conceivably take place." They had to check the passes and movement of German civilian workers, POWs, and vehicular traffic.

Building a "Cathedral"

Only a few months before, the 581st had been a combat unit, and they were now being assigned tasks that the booklet author admitted "may strike you as the ultimate in drudgery, the very height of boredom." But the Army emphasized the importance of the MCC mission to help rebuild Germany so that it would be "fit to take her place in the family of nations." The booklet encouraged the men to remember the value of undertaking small jobs that are part of large projects, describing how very small jobs were vital to build a giant cathedral. Do not "submit to the temptation to waste your time in idle dreams and profitless chatter," the booklet author urged.

> It is, therefore, important for you to realize that the smallest job, even as the biggest, is essential in the making of the complete picture of our present as-

signment. Realize that if the work engaged in here is successful, you or your children will quite certainly not have to do this job again. Realize that if it is a good piece of work, YOU have made it so.

Isn't it better to build Cathedrals than chip stones?

Although the booklet made a good case, many of the men in the 581st, including Dad, just wanted to go home. Now that the war was over, Dad thought men who had not yet served or who had been found unfit for combat should come to Germany to do the police and guard work so that those who had fought and "lived in the field" could go home.

Mom had sent a photo of her and me on the beach in Far Rockaway, where we were spending the summer with her parents, and Dad noticed some "eligible males" standing around. "They look good enough to me to come over here and pull some of this guard. The fighting is over. They won't get hurt, if they mind their own business."

He was sure the Germans were not going to start anything for a while. "They still scare when an American plane comes over or an American tank rolls by." However, he tried to resign himself to the situation and be grateful that at least he would be "in one piece with a whole skin."

CLEANING UP GERMANY

Dad was also angry that his unit had to clean up their new quarters, as they had already done in their previous locations. The grass had to be cut and trash cleared away. Dad felt like they were cleaning up Germany, and he resented it. He felt there were plenty of Germans who could have done this work and thought his captain was ordering this work because he wanted to keep the men in the unit busy.

Again acting as an interpreter, Dad found a plumber he hoped could fix his group's showers if they could obtain the required materials—a difficult task because building goods were needed to repair and rebuild all of the bombed-out buildings. Dad said the quality of most items available was inferior to prewar merchandise and the prices were "way out of line."

In his July 10 letter, Dad said the Germans working at MCC were also angry because they saw how much damage had been done to the complex, which had been beautiful and fully equipped.

> But when the Amer. came, they [found that the Germans had] used it to house Russian slave laborers. The Russ. made a shambles of the place. Knocked out windows, destroyed plumbing, and generally raised the roof. Of course, I guess I would do the same if I were in the Russ. place after five years of forced labor in Deutschland.

Dad told Mom that they had been hearing and feeling heavy explosions for about two days that shook the barracks and the ground around them. Eventually, they discovered the Army was blowing up a tremendous underground ammunition dump that had been found about ten miles away from their base. It had been built into a mountain as part of the Germans' vast amount of underground construction.

The military had also discovered a large underground factory about two miles away that was so well hidden from the air it had to be pointed out when someone walked by or over it. "Trees, grass, and shrubbery grow right over it." As a result, it had never been bombed during the war.

Back home, the newspapers were publishing maps showing where the various divisions were deployed in occupied Germany, allowing Mom to get a better idea of where Dad was located. His unit was now attached to the 70th Infantry Division, although his particular group was located closer to the 78th, stationed about nine miles southeast of Kassel. Dad sent Mom a postcard with a picture of a beer garden and beer hall, which the Army had taken over to use as a club room where the civilian owner dispensed beer and soft drinks for the military men. A large building at the rear of the garden had been transformed into a movie theater.

During his off-duty hours that summer, Dad explored the munitions factory site, including a plant that had been built in the middle of a deep wood. "The structures are made of heavy reinforced concrete and are partly hung underground. The roofs have grass and vegetation growing on them, making them invisible from the air," he wrote.

Some of the buildings were now being used to store the records of the various departments, and stacks of papers were mixed in with rows of empty shells. "In other portions of the area, which is 3 miles long and about ¾ mile wide, are dynamite and other explosives in various stages of manufacture." He was moved by the thought of "how many slave laborers must have worked and died in these buildings for the future of Nazidom."

Dad also noticed evidence of hasty departure when he walked through the living quarters of the former employees. "Windows smashed, half-open closets with dirty litter [*sic*, linen?] half out of them and on the floor." He found a couple of German helmets and a pair of wooden shoes and decided to send those home as souvenirs. During the war, Dad wrote, he could have collected "a truckload of souvenirs" but had not felt like it. Now that the fighting was over, he had changed his mind and wanted "a few mementos from Deutschland."

One day, on a beer run to a small town called Malsfeld, Dad saw a trainload of Russians sitting along a railroad siding near the brewery. They were being returned to Russia but had been stalled for three days while trying to work out some red tape between the U.S. and Russian authorities.

"They were a wild bunch," Dad wrote. "Many had very oriental features. Long, drooping black mustaches. Black eyes. Others were European in appearance." Conversing with them in German, he told them his parents had come from Russia, and they were baffled that he had never been taught to speak Russian. The men, who were very anxious to return home, told Dad they thought that collectivism was better than capitalism, that they were proud to feel international, and that all people were the same. However, they admired Dad's clothing and wallet, remarking about their quality.

Dad wasn't surprised to learn that the Russians hated the Germans, but he was surprised to learn their authorities did not enforce a nonfraternization policy. He remarked to Mom, "Oh, well! I've stopped trying to figure everything out."

Summer of Rumors

Mom had heard a rumor that Dad's current APO address was that of a replacement pool, which reignited her fear that he would be sent to the Pacific. Dad assured her he was in the Seventh Army, Category 1, which was an occupation unit, and told her to stop listening to unsubstantiated rumors. He had just found out unofficially he had been granted another battle star for moving up with his unit when the Army was driving for the Elbe River line, which brought his point total to fifty and even closer to discharge. Encouraging, too, was that the redeployment program, operational only since V-E Day, was ahead of schedule. Outfits scheduled to sail in August were already at a POE (Port of Embarkation) in mid-July.

In the meantime, Dad had heard his own rumor — that his unit would move to Berlin after all of the documents that had been collected were cataloged. That would be good news, Dad wrote, because "then you can be sure that we are definitely occupation troops" and would not be sent to the Pacific.

The news in mid-July from the Pacific was that U.S. B-29 Superfortresses were continuing to raid Japan and the country was also being shelled by our surface fleet. Although Japan was being "pounded relentlessly," Dad did not expect the war to end until Allied troops invaded the Japanese mainland, but signs were accumulating that such a move might happen soon. In the States, more than 800 Pullman train cars were being converted to carry troops across the country to West Coast ports for shipment to the Pacific.

By late July, Dad expected a D-Day scenario in Japan would occur very soon. The Army was concentrating on sending troops directly to the Pacific and cutting shipments to the States. The sudden call for troops was unexpected, but since the Navy was now able to move with impunity in Japanese home waters, he felt those in charge must think the time was almost ripe for the invasion.

In early August, Dad expected the Allies would soon make a land invasion of Japan, which would be coupled with a Russian attack on Japanese forces in China. The double invasion would bring about the surrender, Dad thought, since Japan's factories, lines of communication, and morale were already "getting a terrific shellacking."

But he cautioned Mom not to get too excited about rumors of peace with Japan, even though there were hopeful signs. Japan was now allowing the Swiss to check on prisoners of war and speaking of making deals with "a more lenient U.S." When Japan was "riding high, they ran roughshod over everyone and didn't give a damn about international law," Dad wrote. So it was important now, when the enemy "was groggy, to keep punching while he is off balance" and not give him a chance to recover.

Both Mom and Dad continued to hear rumors that families would soon be allowed to join U.S. military men in Europe, and Dad asked several times if she would consider coming. Mom wrote that she was concerned about the possibility of epidemics, but Dad tried to allay her fear by saying, "Wherever the Army goes, disease and sickness disappear, except, unfortunately, for venereal disease, which spreads as the Army moves in."

The Army's sanitation standards were very high, which Dad thought prevented the spread of "violent, raging epidemics." Thanks to DDT (its ill effects unknown at the time), typhus was "squelched almost immediately," as civilians and their clothes and quarters were dusted and sprayed. Thus, he was sure the Army would take every precaution if families were brought over. He thought the hardest job would be to find transportation to move the families since all such resources were now taxed to the utmost. A further burden on the system, of course, would be to assure the flow of necessary supplies.

The weather in July was very warm, both for Mom in New York and Dad in the central German mountains. The weather again reminded Dad to be glad the fighting was over. "Digging gun emplacements, standing guard, and living under sunbaked tents is over for us." He was grateful for the relative comfort of the former German barracks where his unit was staying, because they were fairly sunproof, and the showers were "going great guns."

"Orientation Man"

When not on guard duty, Dad kept busy learning how to use a hammer and saw and taking courses on electricity and auto mechanics, skills that would be useful when he returned home and had a house and car to look after. Athletics, which the Army considered compulsory, and guard duties occupied the rest of his time.

Dad and another member of the battery had an additional responsibility in Helsa. They were called "orientation men," and their job was to closely follow the news in order to give several hours of classes a week to the others, an assignment Dad enjoyed so much he did not consider it to be work. He also read whatever books he could find or borrow, including *People on Our Side* by Edgar Snow and *Forever Amber* by Kathleen Winsor.

Dad's role as an orientation man probably played a part in his frequent comments to Mom about political and social events around Europe. He wrote Mom that British elections in the summer of 1945 seemed to show a "sharp swing to the left" and said he hoped it was "the end of Churchill and his Tory government." They had served their purpose, he said, but now it was "time they moved out." Dad was reading *People on Our Side* and thought Edgar Snow gave a clear—and unflattering—picture of the situation of India under British rule. He hoped the "socialistic plan" the British people had chosen in their last election worked out, and they did not "botch up the job."

August 7, 1945

> Britain is ripe for the experiment. She still has to put out for the war in Asia. Raw materials that could be put to better use building homes and necessities will have to go into that consuming furnace known as the war machine. If it—the experiment—works, we might see it tried in the States. The TVA (Tennessee Valley Authority) is one government project that has worked. The co-ops have worked out well. They work if they get a chance.

Dad also commented on the state of relations between the sexes in the postwar era, noting that it seemed the opposite of the nonfraternization policy was taking place all over Western Europe. As an example, he wrote how one of the fellows had lost his virginity to a girl he had met while on a pass in Brussels. She had invited him home after a dance, and her family insisted that he stay overnight. Then the parents went to bed, and her sister left to sleep in another room, indicating that he was supposed to sleep with her sister that night!

July 23, 1945

> You can believe it or not, but that is the sort of thing we ran into almost from the time we hit England, then Scotland and Belgium. Bearing an illegitimate child from a Yank seems to be an honor.

Many I have seen who would pat their swelled bellies and quite proudly say he was a Yank. In Scotland especially.

Personal Crusade Against Prejudice

Dad wrote several times regarding the unusual situations that black American soldiers faced in Europe. During World War II they served in segregated units, and some of those units had arrived there early in the war. As a result, Dad wrote, "a large percentage of the [Yank] fathers were some of the original negro troops who arrived early in the war."

July 23, 1945

If nothing else is derived from this war, the negro has discovered that racial discrimination among the masses stops outside the U.S. The Yank uniform is a magic wand. At first, the people were afraid of them, but their conduct was so exemplary that the people lost all fear of them. If you had read the papers, you'd find that there are very few instances of breach of conduct by the negro troops.

A lot of the southerners in our Army were angered by seeing a beautiful blonde-haired Scottish girl walking arm in arm or dancing with a negro as black as the ace of spades. But they couldn't do a damn thing. The civilians would look quite blandly and innocently at a protesting white soldier and, of course, prejudice being based on nothing logical, he was beaten for an answer and just turn[ed] and walk[ed] away.

Dad also wrote about the German people's reaction to the black soldiers. "Today, in Germany the people had a great fear of the black man. But, on being quartered in a village—perhaps in the same houses—he behaved like a gentleman, so that they went from one extreme to the other."

The Dutch people he had met in Valkenburg told Dad a similar story, and he wondered whether black Americans would be better off in Europe. The Russians Dad had met also seemed not to have a racist attitude, but were "proud of their internationalism." "We may be ahead of these people industrially, but we are behind in humanity to humans." He found it strange that "in our Army of democracy," some people could be so blind.

July 23, 1945

> It's not really a question of whether I want my sister or my daughter to marry a negro. That's the first thing they throw at you. It's just a question of allowing the black man the privilege of living on this world. I tell them [i.e., the men in his unit, especially the southerners] that but for the grace of God, their skin might have been black. That a power greater than mine put these people on the earth, and by God, they might as well accept it.

At times, it seemed like Dad was on a one-man crusade against prejudice in his unit. Some of the fellows were expressing negative opinions about the British, repeating what they had heard or read about them taking too much credit for winning the war. Dad defended the British "Tommy" as a soldier "same as you or I." He urged them not to hold against them what the English papers printed or "how Churchill feels about India."

To counter their opinions, Dad told them about a fellow he had met who was a driver for a British official working at the MCC.

The man came from Yorkshire, but his wife's family was from Bournemouth, where Dad's unit had been stationed for a few days before they were shipped to France. Dad said he had a nice time in Bournemouth and especially enjoyed the inexpensive fish and chips available from the little shops. The fellow immediately offered to give Dad his mother-in-law's address and said she would give him a place to stay if he ever went back.

In general, Dad had found all of the people he had met in the U.K. to be very friendly and kind. Although everything was strictly rationed during the war, he recalled that people would invite you to dinner and offer you everything they could from their meager store of goods.

Dad avidly read the GI newspaper, *Stars and Stripes*, which was then publishing articles attempting to cement relationships between the Americans and Russians. The journalists wrote about how friendly the Red soldier was and how well he got along with everyone, without mentioning politics or economics. Dad agreed that it was most important to understand the average person because he forms the basis of our society.

July 27, 1945

> Tear away the boundary lines and the language and racial barriers and see what you've got. A person just like yourself. If only a lot of these guys would wise up. Many are prone to follow the leader when it comes to ridiculing people other than themselves.

Dad believed that prejudice was not limited to people from the South but was displayed by anyone who had been raised in a prejudiced atmosphere. He also noted a difference in attitude between men who had served on the front lines, where "respect for the other fellow was developed the hard way," and the men like those in his outfit who had not contended with as much. The latter, he felt, "still haven't learned who the common enemy is."

He found the best way to argue with prejudiced people was to "give them plenty of rope, and by God, they really do hang themselves." But, on many occasions, he found it necessary to argue the "same old story against bias and prejudice."

Growing Frustrations

By late July, Dad and the other men in his unit were growing increasingly frustrated with the Army and the officers who seemed intent only on imposing "spit and polish and a raft of unnecessary guard duty." The Army had implemented an education program after V-E Day to help sustain the men's morale and keep them busy, hoping it would smooth "the transition to civilian life and compensate soldiers who had had their educations interrupted by the war," according to Ziemke in *The U.S. Army in the Occupation of Germany*. But only a few men in each unit were actually allowed to attend school. In Dad's outfit, only six out of 164 were allowed to attend classes. Although Dad was taking courses on the base in electricity and auto mechanics, he had not been selected at this time to attend a course off base.

The Army was also granting furloughs and allowing men to travel to other places in Europe, including England. However, in Dad's unit, a maximum of five or six men were ever on pass or furlough at a time. Everyone else was always on guard or some other duty. Even their time for sports or exercise was limited because they only had time to eat, sleep, shower, and serve guard duty.

When off duty at night, Dad would go to the movies. Every two days another film was shown, which was the only regular relief from boredom. Occasionally, the USO appeared in the area with its live shows. In Kassel, Dad got to see performances featuring Jack Benny, the pianist David Le Winter, Ingrid Bergman, harmonica player Larry Adler, and singer Martha Tilton. He wrote that Benny was a very good violinist, in addition to being a comedian. Adler performed classical music pieces on a harmonica, and Bergman did a monologue adapted from her forthcoming play, *Joan of Arc*. Needless to say, the show delighted the men and was a much-appreciated break from boredom and homesickness.

Some of the special services units also produced shows for the men. In Kassel, Dad got to see a hilarious satire of *Carmen (A Boilesk Voishin)* (in Brooklynese), performed by the 253rd Infantry Division Special Service of the Seventh Army, with all of the roles played by the male soldiers. The "Slopopolitan Opera Association" presented a "SNAFU version of Bizet's opera," and the 63rd Infantry Division contributed to the performance, with the men playing all of the instruments in the musical accompaniment. The mostly male audience loved it and enjoyed the inside jokes only the GIs would understand.

At home, there was talk about eliminating the draft and relying on volunteers to take on the duties of the occupying Army, which included police work, dealing with thousands of displaced persons, reestablishing all public utilities, rebuilding infrastructure, and reconstructing the educational system. Those duties were enormous and all-encompassing until about 1946, when civilian authorities assumed overall control of easing Germany back into the family of nations.

Dad found it difficult to believe that anyone would volunteer as an enlisted man in the military and willingly subject himself to the "autocratic regimentation of Army life." On the other hand, he thought the officers were "crazy about it" because they had better lives and enjoyed more privileges than they had ever had in civilian life. For him, life in the Army was contrary to what most civilians enjoyed in America, and he considered it "the direct antithesis of what we are fighting for." He looked forward to being out of it as soon as possible.

Dad was having no luck fulfilling Mom's request for nice linen or china, telling her that the Nazis had stolen a lot of the beautiful products and the black market had pushed prices of what remained sky-high. Of course, some American military men were acquiring what they wanted. Although it was forbidden by law to loot, Dad reported that fellows he knew were helping themselves to cameras, firearms, watches, jewelry, and anything else they found, believing that "anything goes" if the goods came from Germans. Dad was adamantly opposed to such behavior.

> It's stealing plain and simple, and even though the Nazis used to do it, that doesn't mean I can. Two wrongs don't make a right. After all, I do consider myself better than them.

In early August, President Truman decided not to allow Army wives to join their husbands overseas, saying conditions were still too unsettled and temporary. Although he was disappointed at the news, Dad reluctantly agreed that Truman was right. Units were still reassigned on short notice, decent living quarters would be hard to arrange, food supplies had to be shipped from the States, and little fresh food was available. Dad did not want his child living on a diet of stored or dehydrated meals.

Preparing for the Future

While marking time at the MCC, Dad was contemplating how to earn a living in the future. In addition to the courses he took whenever he could, he started studying up on the co-op movement in agriculture that the American government had established to help small farmers compete with large corporate farms. He discussed taking a two-month course in agriculture at the Army university in England and hoped he could get a postal position that would allow him to work a farm part-time until it was paying for itself, or he had learned enough to devote all of his time to it. He and Mom wanted a large family, and he thought it would be cheaper and healthier to raise children in the country rather than in the city. Although he had written earlier that he had changed his mind about farming because the work seemed too hard, based on his observations of German farmers, apparently he was still thinking about trying it, especially if he could get some help from the co-op movement.

Dad learned that the co-ops even helped their members professionally preserve their produce and sell and market their goods. His captain was familiar with some agriculture co-ops and told Dad it was best to specialize, recommending that he focus on poultry and eggs, for example, because those are year-round products. Dad also figured he could count on help from his kids for labor and believed a farm would give us a base to come back to whenever we wanted. This romantic view of rural life very much appealed to him, and he planned to research co-ops in and around New York State and Connecticut because he did not want to move west or south.

The more Dad spoke with the men in his unit about farming, co-ops, the Agricultural Adjustment Administration, and various county agents, the more excited he became. It gave him something to look forward to because he saw it as a way to make an independent living and support a family. He planned to ask some of his cousins if they were interested in joining him. Dad knew he might face anti-Semitism but did not expect too much in the New York or Connecticut areas he was considering, and he vowed not to let it stop him if he did encounter it. He was determined to make the enterprise work.

German Relations

For the most part, Dad found the German people very obedient and cooperative, and felt that was due in part to the way the Americans were treating them, which was not the way their soldiers had treated conquered nations. Otherwise, he speculated, the U.S. would have had trouble with underground resistance movements. He wondered if the German civilians' willingness to cooperate was because "they realize what a monstrous crime their nation is guilty of and hope we will be easier on them."

He wrote about one German woman he met who was working in one of the buildings where he had guard duty. To his surprise, she spoke good English, and he learned she had spent several years in New York as a governess. Her home was in Berlin, but she had lost everything in the air raids. After fifty air raids, all she had left were "two suitcases of threadbare clothing." The woman told him she thought the Germans had finally learned a lesson, but Dad was skeptical.

July 22, 1945

In every major war of modern history, Germany has had a hand in it. And as the years progressed, she acquired a more important role in each conflict until World Wars I and II, [where] she played a major part. Now, I said, we will have an American Army here for 100 years, if necessary. I'd rather have my kid come here for six months in 20 years around [*sic*] as part of an occupying force to make sure that it wasn't Germany who starts it again, than leave it to chance his fighting another long terrible war. I don't know. Maybe I am right, maybe I am wrong. Time alone will tell.

Some of Dad's interactions with German civilians fed his skepticism. On July 21, Dad wrote about "a little excitement" for their unit. The day before, on short notice, they were told to be ready to "fall out" at 3 a.m. By 5 a.m., Dad's unit was out in the streets of the town while all residents were restricted to their homes. Then the battalion began a house-to-house search for contraband, working with members of the Counter Intelligence Corps (CIC). They located an SS man, who was an escaped prisoner, and also found Nazi flags, books, and knives.

Dad was the interpreter for his search party. Although they did not find anything important, one family had a copy of *Mein Kampf*. Dad told them to burn it.

July 21, 1945

> At first, they protested that they never even read a word of it, and that it was just a gift from someone. I told them I didn't believe it, and the more they protested, the madder I got. Finally, I blew my top, tore the damn thing up, heaved it into a corner, and told them to burn it up at once. Without another word, they did as I said.

Dad's role as interpreter gave him an opportunity to interact with civilians at all levels, including an encounter with the burgomaster (mayor) of Helsa.

July [n.d.], 1945

> I got called downtown with an officer on an interpreting job. It seems that we are going to take over a building in town and in order to do that, now that the war is over, we must go to the burgomeister [*sic*, the German spelling is bürgermeister] and have him tell the people to get out by a stated hour. He must find new quarters for the evacuated people. Well, the old guy asked permission to have the people live in the cellar of the house and pleaded that they could close the door leading to it, and that they wouldn't bother the military. But we told him no soap. *Raus*. He begged that they had no place to go. All the houses in his village, Helsa, were full with evacuated families, and that the street was the

only place he had. I couldn't help but think of how much time a German commander would have given a Russian or Polish or Jewish family.

We're soft with these people all right. Me nichts Nazi. That's all they say in defense. For a nation with so few nazis, this nation raised an awful lot of hell.

Even though Dad sometimes felt America was too "soft," he also wrote that he felt conflicted about the German POWs forced to do some of the heavy labor at the compound.

July 18, 1945

They are a dirty looking lot. One of them had managed to beg a bite to eat from one of the cooks. He had nothing but his hat in which to carry it. He stuck his grimy fingers into the mess and licked his chops. One of the boys remarked, 'Look at them bastards.' I can remember when I used to see pictures of them in the movies, marching, throwing hand grenades, etc.

I know what he means because I feel the same way when I see them in their nondescript, raggedy, dirty uniforms. They are very docile and are probably happy that they are alive. We all get a peculiar feeling when we see them. Hard to describe. Hatred, yet you can't hate such miserable wretches; joy over their plight, yet you don't want to be guilty of kicking a guy when he is [down]. I don't know. I can't describe it. Can you let them go back to their bombed-out homes? If we do, perhaps they will start something in another 25 years.

At one point in the summer, Dad wrote that the Army was allowing German kids into its theater to view movies, possibly as part of a reeducation program or as a way to help them learn English, which many civilians, especially the younger ones, were attempting to speak. Dad was trying to understand how the civilians had been swept up by Hitler.

July 30, 1945

> They all claim they are not nazis or were not nazis. That they were forced to join the Hitler Youth and other Nazi organizations. It seems that it was similar to our compulsory school system. If a child didn't show up at meetings, the parents received a visit from the local big shot. If persuasion didn't help, then fines and other tactics were employed.

These civilians may have been telling Dad the truth about being forced to join the Hitler Youth and similar groups, because in 1936 all boys and girls ages ten to seventeen were required to belong to one of these organizations.

Early in August, Dad focused on news about the war crimes trials that were about to begin in Germany.

> The nazis are now living a thousand deaths. They are dying over and over again. When the trials start, they'll sweat even more. That's the only way we can torture them, and I believe that is one of the reasons they are not rushing the trials.

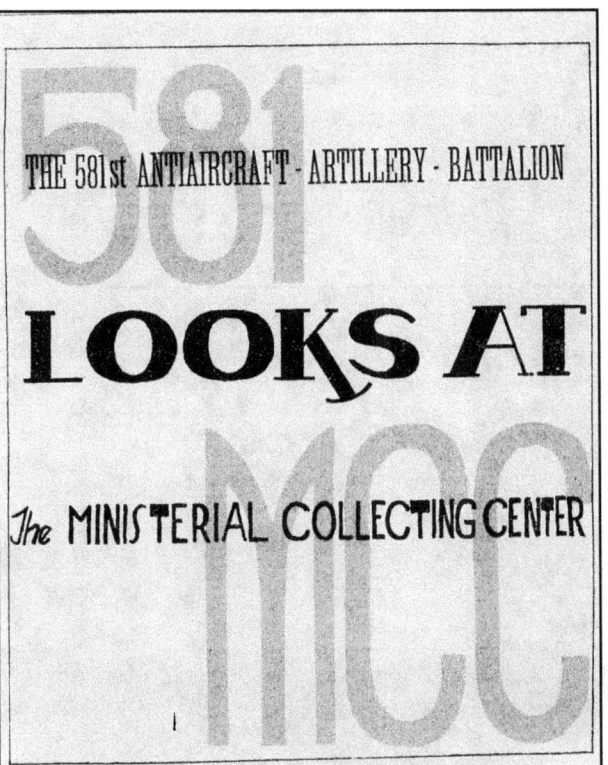

Cover of booklet explaining the purpose of the MCC to the 581st, Dad's unit that was assigned to guard it. (Written by Eugene F. Grewe, cover and design by Sergeant Henry Darbee, artwork by Pfc. William Grayell, published by U.S. Army Information and Education)

First page of booklet about the MCC with dedication by Brigadier General Timberlake calling the 581st Battalion by its nickname, "Rock of Remagen."

Page of MCC booklet showing its location near Kassel, the largest city; Helsa, the nearest town; and Fürstenhagen, where Germany's largest underground munitions factory had been located.

City of Kassel in ruins, as photographed by Dad just after the end of the war in Europe.

Dad's unit's barracks at the MCC.

Cover of program for *Carmen (A Boilesk Voishin)*, title in "Brooklynese," performed and produced by the Special Services 253rd Infantry, which Dad saw in Kassel. (Information Control Command Printing Plant Wiesbaden)

Dad and buddy at the guardhouse of the MCC, where they were stationed.

Dad and his bunkmates resting at their quarters at the MCC.

Dad waiting on line for "chow" with his mess kit.

CHAPTER 14

Hiroshima, Nagasaki, Victory over Japan

DAD FIRST WROTE ABOUT the atomic bomb on August 8, two days after the U.S. dropped one on Hiroshima. He had read about it in *Stars and Stripes*, the GI newspaper, but he did not immediately grasp its impact.

August 8, 1945

> The Stars & Stripes paper is full of that new atomic bomb. It must be a lulu. If it will end the war sooner than I hope, it is all they claim it is.

By the time he next wrote, Dad was far more excited to learn that the Soviet Union had declared war on Japan on August 8.

August 9, 1945

> My dearest darling,
> The entry of Russia into the war against Japan is the only thing I seem to be able to carry in my mind. I didn't hear about it until last night about 11 p.m. And then it was told to me by one of the boys who

heard it from another guy who caught it on the radio. I am dying to get hold of our newspaper and read about it. It is even greater news to me now than the day Germany surrendered. Of course, VE Day was a milestone in our march to V-Day. Now, with Russia on our side against the [Japanese], there is a strong likelihood that the war will be over this year. Just imagine, darling, the whole war over by New Years. I didn't believe it at first when they told me.

The Chinese Army that was being trained by General Wedemeyer is about ready for action too. What a tremendous squeeze play they can put on Japan.

The atomic bomb is creating a lot of furor and attention, but until I get more info on it, I will reserve comment.

Dad knew that scientists had been experimenting with "atom smashing devices" for many years. He feared their destructive potential but hoped the power could be harnessed for peaceful uses, like running motors, ships, planes, cars, or plants.

August 9, 1945

At first, when I saw the headlines about the power of the experimental bomb that was detonated in New Mexico, the thought that flashed through my mind was that they better stop fooling around or they'll be blowing the whole world apart. We are approaching the Buck Rogers era faster than we know. If only our sociology would keep abreast of our scientific advances, what a world this would be. There's that little word again, 'If.'

He felt personally vindicated by Russia's entry into the war against Japan because he had been predicting they would do so when the war with Germany ended ever since he had become the battery's orientation man while at Camp Stewart in Georgia. He only wished he could be as successful predicting his own future as he was in foretelling political events.

On August 9, the U.S. dropped its second atomic bomb on Nagasaki. Dad's letter of August 10 does not specifically refer to the Nagasaki bombing, but he must have heard about it because he refers to the eyewitness account of the bomber crew that dropped "the first one." Based on those eyewitness accounts, Dad was beginning to believe the stories about the destructive force of the atomic bomb. He also wrote that the Japanese "are beginning to squeal about it being outrageous and what not. So evidently, it must really be something. Not just some propaganda to scare the Jap[anese]."

On August 10, Japan sued for peace, and Dad's next letter bounced from ecstasy to disbelief.

> August 11, 1945
>
> I guess you know what's on my mind more than anything else. As a matter of fact, I can hardly believe it. That for which we have been waiting is here. It's not official, but it's over. The Japs would never have asked for any form of surrender if they didn't believe that further resistance was useless.
>
> Darling, I am confused. I am speechless. I can't even let out a healthy cheer. When I first heard the news, I was taking a shower. I thought the guy who told it to me was kidding. But then more guys came in and told me about the Japs offer. When I realized that it was true, I didn't know what to do or think.

Although he was "very happy and grateful that it was near its final end," he wondered, "Where does it leave me?" When would he be eligible for discharge and the long-awaited return home? The terms of his enlistment must have included a clause that his active duty would end six months after the end of the war, because he wrote, "Can the Army possibly keep me in for more than six months after V-Day?"

August 11, 1945

All these unanswered questions. I am really in a whirl. The thought that it is over is too much for me. The thing I have been ending my letters with, "Keep up your courage, it will be over soon," is actually here. Now all I have to sweat out is getting home. Baby, your daddy will be coming home soon.

Dad knew his discharge would depend in part on transportation and the needs for the occupation forces. The political situation at home would also be crucial. "That's where public opinion and your votes and influence come in. Make the Army show Congress why they need 400,000 men in the occupation army." He felt it was important that the voters and their representatives in Congress push back against an Army that had become accustomed to getting its way.

Dad reported that most of the fellows in his group "got plastered" when they heard the news, but he preferred to do his celebrating when he got home.

August 11, 1945

"When I see that familiar skyline. When I hit the doorstep of a certain address in Jamaica. At least that's what I say now. I'll probably be as speechless as I am now.

When "big things" happened, Dad said he did not cheer loudly but reacted internally "like I am living on a cloud. My heart feels warm, and I am joyful to no end." Most of all, he longed to hold Mom in his arms and see me again. He also wanted to wear civilian clothes, imagining that he would "look at myself in the mirror for hours on end." To prove he was not dreaming, Dad said Mom would have to kiss him "every minute or so." His letter of August 11 ended with, "Yes, darling. That day isn't as far off as I imagined only a letter ago."

The next day, one of his officers advised Dad about his discharge eligibility.

August 12, 1945

> I was batting the breeze with one of our officers today, and he says that it ought to take about eight or nine months for us to get out of Germany. He doesn't have anything specific to base his opinion on but guesswork. I asked him if he knew whether or not we were signed up for duration of the emergency, or duration of the war. He says it is the former. It was declared by Congress and President and is not over until they say so. Hell they can, at that rate, take their own sweet time about letting us out. That's where pressure from the public will have to come in. I hope Truman stays on the beam as soon as he can possibly engineer it. Well baby, in any event, I don't believe it is a two-year wait, the way we have been resigning ourselves. With a stroke of luck, maybe even sooner. Keep up your chin, darling.

Dad struggled to keep current with breaking news as his unit had only a few radios and contended with poor reception, so he assumed Mom heard more news than he did. He wrote on August 14 that the war was officially over, according to the latest reports. However, Japan did not officially accept the surrender terms until August 15, when the emperor's radio broadcast ensured his people and military would comply. The Japanese had been trying to ensure the continuation of the emperor's sovereign rule, but the Americans had insisted that the emperor and the government would be "subject to that of the Supreme Commander of the Allied powers," according to Willmott, Messenger, and Cross in *World War II*. This caused a second crisis, and Emperor Hirohito had to reaffirm his previous decision. Some junior officers rebelled and attempted a coup, "but army discipline, backed by royal princes who were sent to various commands, ensured compliance with the Imperial decision."

On August 15, the day the Japanese accepted the surrender terms, Dad could finally write, "Well! Now it's official." At this point, rumors began that the military would be releasing five and a half million men from service, and Dad hoped he would soon be one of them. He was encouraged to learn that the captured German liner *Europa* would be ready to ferry troops across the ocean in about a month. It would be outfitted to carry 10,000 troops, allowing it to haul 20,000 troops a month. The embarkation points in Europe were geared to ship almost 400,000 troops a month, but Dad did not think there would be enough ships to match that capacity.

The men in his unit finally had a radio down at the guardhouse, where they spent their off-duty hours.

August 15, 1945

> It's going 24 hours a day. As soon as a news flash comes on, everyone gets as quiet as a mouse or makes a dash for the thing. We have been having direct broadcasts from all over the world. Particularly, N.Y.C. We heard the crowds there going nuts.

Waiting to Celebrate

Although they were glad the war was over, the men in Dad's unit were not cheering much yet. They just wanted to know when they would be going home. But Dad said it was a little easier to withstand the waiting because "I realize what it must be to slave for the nazis."

At the document center, Dad had met a man who was doing research to determine who had benefited from the "crooked deals" that occurred when the Nazis had confiscated property from Jews and others. The researcher was a banker and politician on his fourth trip to Europe since 1927 and believed his work was important even though he told Dad that most of the Jews who had lost property were dead and could not be helped.

He asked Dad if he was Jewish and wanted to know if his family had come from Germany because "Klapper" sounded German. Dad explained that his father had come from a region in Russia where many Germans had settled, the Volga-Stalingrad area. The fellow then told Dad that a lot of people had moved from that area to Colorado about sixty years earlier to raise sugar beets. As a result, that area had a lot of people with German names who had immigrated from Russia.

As Dad was learning more about Nazi operations, he recalled what he had thought in 1935 when he read newspaper reports about Nazi atrocities to the Jews.

August 15, 1945

> I used to say to myself that no matter what happens, they must not come to America. If they ever did, then I was determined to retreat to the Canadian North woods. Become a guerilla. You may laugh at it now, but by God that was my intention. If I could take the folks with me I was going to. But I know that if they ever wanted me, they had to come and get me.

Dad again wrote about the German POWs working as laborers on the base, contrasting the way the Allies were treating the former Nazi soldiers with how the Nazis had treated their slave workers.

> We have them working for us around here. We can't work them outside when it rains. They must get a ten-minute break every hour. I don't know what they get to eat, but whatever it may be, compared to what they fed our boys and others, it's like a rare delicacy.

Still, when the men in his unit would gripe about their lot and envy those who were back in the States, Dad said, "I like to remind them of how much worse off we could have been. Darling, imagine the joy, the relief those poor people must feel that are about to be released from the Jap[anese] camps."

August 15, 1945

> I was almost going to write "God when will this war be over." You see, my darling, I still can't believe it. Maybe that's because I still have to perform the same damn duties as before.
>
> Now watch the rumors fly hot and heavy around here.
>
> It would be nice if MacArthur would sign the peace tomorrow. Then we could celebrate two events every year.

BIRTHDAY WISHES

I turned two years old on August 16, 1945, so in addition to his usual daily letter to Mom, Dad wrote one addressed to me. He compared the world that year to what it had been in 1943.

Helsa, Germany
August 16, 1945

To Daddy's dearest treasure,

Congratulations darling. Many, many happy returns this day. For it marks your second anniversary on this world. Looking back for an instant at the day you were born, we can see the devil's own triumvirate riding high. Dearest little one, today with God's will we are victorious over them. I shudder to think of what the consequences would have been had we not come out on top. It's left for your generation and whatever remains of mine to employ this victory to the fullest toward a lasting peace. That, my darling, is the least we can do to show our humble thanks for the sacrifices of those who gave their lives and limbs. Yes dear! They had to die so that I can sit here, deep in Germany, and tell you it is only a question of time before I come home for good.

It's been so long since I have seen you, I believe I'll be timid in your presence at first. It's going to be a new experience for me, dearest. When I saw you last, you were a tiny tot, barely able to walk. Now, you are a young lady. You must wonder how it feels to have a daddy. I will try my best to be a good one. We have so much time to make up. But time heals all wounds. We'll play, live, and grow together. As the years go by, we'll forget about these terrible years of war and try to make them only a memory. One that will remain dimly in the back of our minds as a warning to be ever vigilant against those who would usurp our liberty for their own selfish greed and power. We must make a long peace a reality. Then the sacrifice will not have been in vain.

Until I see you again dearest, which won't be long now, keep a stout heart and a clear conscience. They are like a beacon, guiding one straight and true to the hearth of our friends. With those two you can win the respect of your fellow man and, achieving that, you will always be happy.

My life and love are yours.

—Dad

In his letter to Mom written on the same day, Dad said he felt encouraged by rumors that Washington wanted to step up demobilization to 500,000 men a month. At that rate, about seven million troops would be home by the next fall. If true, he hoped to be back in the States by winter. He also referred to his letter to me, acknowledging that I would not be able to read it, of course, "but some day when she can, she will know that I didn't forget her birthday way back in '45." Although he expressed hope, Dad cut short his letter to Mom that day because he felt too low when he thought about how long it might be before he actually saw us again.

The next day, Dad wrote more about the Remagen bridge battle, describing it to Mom in more detail than he had been able to under wartime censorship.

August 17, 1945

By the way, I just happened to think about the time I wrote you when we were on the Rhine. It was back in March, and we had just moved up to the heavy artillery. I wrote and told you something about Paul Lukas. Inasmuch as the 1ˢᵗ Army was the only one that really was making the news those days with the Remagen bridgehead, I thought perhaps you would catch on as to where I was and with what army. Both facts were a secret at the time. The reason I mentioned Paul Lukas was because his most famous role on B'way [*sic*] was in "Watch on the Rhine." Did you understand honey? I knew you were trying to read between the lines those days of censorship, I thought perhaps you'd catch it.

Japan Still Coming to Terms

Although Japan had accepted surrender terms on August 15, it was not until August 28 that Allied warships entered Japanese territorial waters at Sagami Bay and, on the next day, Tokyo Bay. In that interim period, many people, including Dad, felt the Japanese were merely stalling. He proposed we continue the war and even drop another A-bomb on them until they unconditionally surrendered. He feared if given another chance that Japan would fight again in twenty-five or fifty years or gain time to discover the atomic bomb secret themselves and use it on us. Even so, he realized the latter scenario was probably remote because the U.S. would have a large occupation army "to keep a sharp eye on all goings on in Japan." Also, Dad believed the Russians and Chinese had a lot of manpower to deploy if necessary.

Dad was disturbed that he was hearing "rumblings" of civil war in China, but he was not surprised as he had read Edgar Snow's book *People on Our Side* about the situation. At this time, too, the Russians had been having success in defeating the Japanese in Manchuria. On August 19, the Japanese surrendered to the Russians at Khabarovsk in Manchuria, and Soviet forces had overcome heavy Japanese resistance in the Kuril Islands by August 23.

On August 19, Lieutenant General Jonathan Wainwright, the U.S. Commander after General Douglas MacArthur had departed from the Philippines, was rescued by the Russians from a prisoner-of-war camp in Manchuria. He had been captured by the Japanese during the U.S. surrender in May 1942. Although Dad assumed Wainwright was glad to see the "Red star," he figured he had probably been treated much better than the "little guys who always get it in the neck." Nevertheless, when General MacArthur saw Wainwright at the end of August, he was shocked by his "haggard and emaciated" appearance, "with snow white hair and parchment-like skin." MacArthur was reported to not be able to eat or sleep that night.

By that time, Japanese peace envoys had landed in Manila, so Dad hoped our troops would start moving into Japan very shortly. "MacArthur is mad as a hornet anyway at them. He knows enough not to trust them, and he is a very clever, if not brilliant, man. Once the Japs [*sic*] surrender their arms, they will be done for good." He also wrote that more and more Japanese troops were reported to be surrendering, even in New Guinea and Northern Luzon in the Philippines.

On August 27, Dad heard radio reports that our fleet had finally started to move into Tokyo Bay. The weather in Helsa was beautiful that day, and Dad felt compelled to describe the landscape he saw.

August 27, 1945

> The blue sky has only a few white fleecy clouds. From the top of the hill where we sit, you can see for miles around. The heavily wooded hilltops are dark green. Below them on the sloping hillside lay the geometric pattern of plowed fields. The colors

> are varied and look unreal. On one field is wheat about ready for harvest. Golden and rippling as the wind gently brushes it. In the next is a red color. That's the ground that has been turned over and made ready for the next planting. The people know they must feed themselves and are not wasting any time in raising their crops.
>
> Also, as you look at the panorama, you will see a lone figure looking tiny in the distance, like a toy doll, with a horse and plow. It's beautiful, darling, and a sight I'll always remember.

He again contrasted the beautiful landscape with the horror the people had brought on themselves.

> I feel sorry for these people, like I'd feel sorry for a fool. They had so much, and now what have they to look forward to? They and their children will see foreign soldiers on their soil for a long time to come. Yes! Germany was seeking total victory, but instead she found total defeat.

He longed to have Mom by his side to enjoy the beauty he saw, feeling that was the only way he could fully appreciate it. Dad fantasized that when he was home, on days like this, he and Mom could pack up a picnic lunch and take their children to the country or the beach. That would be their way of "getting the most out of nature's gifts."

On August 28, Dad heard on the radio that our first occupation forces had landed in Japan. "The next few weeks should see a tremendous influx of troops into Japanese territory. Both on the continent and the homeland," he wrote.

Preparing for Peacetime

Although everyone was celebrating the end of the war, Dad and the rest of the world were starting to adjust to the changes that would come with peace. Many large Army and Navy contracts were going to be canceled, potentially leaving millions of people unemployed until a reconversion to peacetime production could absorb them. Dad hoped many of those affected had saved enough money or would get enough unemployment benefits to get through that period. Dad felt very lucky to know that his job in the post office would be waiting for him when he returned to civilian life because he had held a regular—as opposed to a temporary—position before he joined the military.

To further his plan to farm, Dad was considering trying to transfer into the Railway Mail Service (RMS), a branch of the postal service that sorted and processed mail on moving trains. Positions in the RMS paid more than those in regular post office stations, and employees worked forty-hour shifts and then had three or four days off in a row. To Dad that would seem like "frequent short holidays," and he thought the schedule would give him more time to work on a farm.

RMS jobs were considered the "elite" in the post office, and many former GIs sought these positions when they returned home after the war. Dad had written to his senator in May to ask for help in procuring one of the assignments. Senator Robert F. Wagner responded later that month, promising "every possible assistance." He told Dad to get in touch when he returned to New York. Dad hoped he could accomplish such a transfer without too much red tape but said he would probably refuse a substitute position if that were offered to him.

Wartime rationing and restrictions were being lifted at home, and Dad wanted to know if tires were still hard to get and whether the prices on food were level or going up and down. He expected a certain amount of governmental price control would still be necessary "to keep things at an even keel." Otherwise, he feared goods would be caught up in the black market and prices would skyrocket.

Dad was familiar with the dangers of a black market since it had become so rampant in Germany that the Army had to restrict the amount of money the men were sending home. Dad was very much opposed to the black market and saw it as "akin to killing a man when he is down. We came here for a purpose, to liberate these people. Not to take advantage of them."

By August 20, Dad was happy to report that guard duty in his unit had been reduced from eight hours a day to four, giving the men more time to rest, shower, and eat. They could also see a movie more often.

But he was not happy about the increasingly erratic mail system, which deeply affected the men's morale. Dad was miserable on days when he received no letters, especially from Mom. He suspected the delays were being caused by the imminent return home of large numbers of troops because the post office units would have to redeliver mail to home addresses if it arrived overseas after demobilization. For the first time, Dad was glad he had not been assigned to the Army post office because the deluge of mail might have caused him to be declared essential personnel, which could keep him "stuck in some remote APO for a helluva long time."

The redeployment process based on the point system established after V-E Day was finally beginning to function on a somewhat systematic basis. Men in Dad's battalion who had accrued at least seventy-five points were not being given passes so they could be ready to move out on short notice. After being alerted for shipment, the man would be transferred out of his original unit and sent to one where others had the same number of points. The entire unit would then be shipped home. Dad had fifty points, so he assumed he would have to wait a while longer. But the redeployment news continued to improve. Just a few days later, men with seventy points, down from seventy-five, were being put on alert and restricted from passes.

With an election coming up in November, Dad expected many politicians to vie with each other over who could bring the troops home the quickest. He predicted they would first try to bring home men over twenty-one because they were eligible to vote. If Dad was right, that meant the eighteen-to-twenty-year-olds, who could not vote then, would be the bulk of those who would be shipped overseas as occupation troops.

Future in Farming?

As he had asked, Mom was continuing to investigate cooperative farming possibilities. She had contacted his cousin Marty, who had responded positively, which encouraged Dad. He also asked her to make some preliminary inquiries into farms in upstate New York and Connecticut and have his cousin gather as much information as possible.

Dad's time in the German countryside had made him eager to try farming at home. He loved the way the fields looked when the wind blew over them. "At a distance, it looks like the waves of the ocean in a sea beige color." He had enjoyed his time in the open and grown to prefer the woods and fields. "The rustle of the wind in the tall trees that sway so gracefully. The sounds that the different birds make."

Although he liked going into the city to see a show or other such entertainment, he had grown to dislike city streets and noise and said he did not want to live there again. He believed he would be able to spend more time with Mom and thought their parents would like to see them settled on a farm, "happy and contented," before they passed away. Most of all, Dad wanted to be his own boss. He was already dreading the night shifts he would have to work in the post office. Although Dad recognized that "a civil service job is more independent than a private one," he wrote that "a man still has to put up with people he doesn't want to. It's a lot like the Army. The soft jobs go to the guy with the longest tongue and the blackest heart and conscience."

However, he was bothered by an article he had read.

August 29, 1945

> I read a rather discouraging article in *Yank* magazine about a GI farm loan. I will try to enclose it in this letter. It seems they really put the screws on a guy when he applies. According to the article, a guy gets a better break from the FSA (Farm Security Administration, which had been established during the Depression) than the VA (Veterans Administration).

The article Dad enclosed detailed how difficult it was to obtain a farm loan from the VA, which would guarantee 50 percent, up to $20,000, of a loan made by a private party to purchase a home, buy a farm, or start a business. It seemed the FSA was far more generous in granting loans to both veteran and nonveteran farmers.

The *Yank* article made Dad realize how difficult it would be to convince the VA he deserved a farm loan when he had no farming experience. He felt deflated because his dream of owning a farm had helped raise his spirit during the war and especially in the postwar period, when his days were filled with boring tasks. Even so, Dad continued to hope for a way to achieve his dream.

> There's a new show on at the movies tonight, but I don't feel like going. I kind of got the wind knocked out of my sails by that article, I guess. It looks like I may have to purchase a farm outright and then take my chances. Well, I won't worry about it much. First I have to get home.

Dad suffered another blow the next day when he learned that the Army had denied his application to take an agricultural course at its University Center in England.

August 30, 1945

When I returned to the battery, I was told that I and another fellow were to see the battalion I & E officer (Information & Education). We knew it must have something to do with the applications we had put in for agriculture courses in the army's University Center in England. I was rather tickled and I might even say overjoyed at the prospect of going. I thought at last, here is my chance to start learning about farming. When we got to see him, it developed that he could only let one of us go out of the five who had applied for the agric. [*sic*] courses. Furthermore, the basic requirements of the course required a fellow to have at least two years experience on a farm and about two years of schooling in that field. Of course, I was left out even if I was the only man applying. I guess as the saying goes in the army it was TS. When I get home, if I remember, I'll tell you what that means.

I suppose now that my farming career will have to start another way. After all I can't, as most other farmers have done to get started, do sharecropping. I can't throw up my job and take a hit or miss on something like that. My responsibilities are too much.

Dad's final hope was to find a solution in the Jewish co-op movement or that he could somehow save enough to buy a farm outright or in conjunction with others. He continued to explain his dilemma to Mom in the same letter.

You see, baby, I just don't want to burn my bridges behind me by giving up my job entirely and devoting all my time to the new field.

Even the VA isn't much of a help in what I wanted to do. According to that article I sent you yesterday, the farmer-to-be had to have his own farm equipment and some livestock before they considered him a safe risk.

Personal Touches

Mom had moved back to her apartment in Jamaica at the beginning of August, and she let Dad know that she was glad to be free of the feuding and tension at her parents' place. Now, Mom could be on her own turf when her mother visited, a much better situation.

She had also mailed Dad absentee voting ballots, but he had been away for such a long time that he was not familiar with the candidates. He asked Mom her advice and told her he was inclined to just vote for the American Labor Party (ALP).

Sometimes Dad enclosed Bill Mauldin cartoons, which regularly appeared in *Stars and Stripes*. Now that Mauldin was a civilian again, his cartoons of Willie and Joe focused on the GIs' reactions to civilian life, with their usual combination of acerbic wit and hilarity.

Dad also told Mom that men coming back from leaves were now comparing the women they met in different cities in Europe. Paris seemed to have "cheaper" women than those in London, and Parisian women had fancier hairdos, "dyed all sorts of colors," and beautiful clothes. "You'd never believe there was a war on or that they had been occupied for five years." Dad was hoping to have a chance to take a tour of Paris—although not for the women, as his dreams were all about Mom.

He kept envisioning his homecoming and told Mom to wait for him in the apartment in Jamaica. He urged her not to run down to the subway or the bus, and that he wanted first to meet her and me alone, without any "confusion and decorations."

August 28, 1945

I am no conquering hero. I just want to slip quietly and unostentatiously into my place in society. Believe me, honey, that's the way I want it. I'll be so grateful for being home. It will be like such a sacred moment that a lot of cheering and noise and hilarity would be blasphemous. It's more a moment of prayer than anything else. I believe you understand how I feel.

> Helsa, Germany
> 8-16-45
>
> To daddy's dearest treasure
>
> Congratulations darling. Many, many, happy returns this day. For it marks your second anniversary on this world. Looking back for an instant, at the day you were born, we can see the devils own triumvirate riding high. Dearest little one, to-day with Gods will we are victorious over them. I shudder to think of what the consequences would have been, had we not come out on top. It's left for your generation and whatever remains of mine to employ this victory to the fullest towards a lasting peace. That, my darling is the least we can do, to show our humble thanks for the sacrifices of those who gave their lives and limbs. Yes dear! They had to die so that I can sit here, sleep in Germany and tell you it is only a question of time before I come home for good.

First page of letter from Dad to me on my second birthday. Helsa, Germany, August 16, 1945. In it, he contrasted the situation in the world on this date to the one in which I had been born, when "the devil's own triumvirate [was] riding high." Unfortunately, I didn't see this letter until after Dad had passed, and I was moved to tears upon reading it for the first time.

CHAPTER 15

Waiting It Out at Fifty-Eight Points

AT THE BEGINNING OF SEPTEMBER, the "high-point guys," those who had earned seventy or more points, were transferred out of Dad's unit to prepare for discharge and shipment home by September 20. Although he envied them and was becoming more impatient by the day to go home, Dad acknowledged they had put in more years than he had and many had endured much more combat.

On September 2, Dad reported on the latest rumors about what would happen to his unit.

September 2, 1945

Nothing happens except rumors. They fly thick and fast. The best one this morning has it that our outfit will now be built up into a high-point unit by adding high pt [*sic*] men and transferring the low pt men out. By low pts they mean men with less than 35 pts. They are just a few in our battery. Also, they expect to add the new pts to our score to raise our point average. Then the payoff of the rumor says we will be in the States within two to four months. I know it's only a lot of hot air but can you blame us for believing stuff like that, that is supposed to come from unimpeachable sources. It's so good to hear and we want so much to hear good news that we are suckers enough to believe it. We can only pray that it's true.

In early September, the military announced that everyone thirty-five or older would be sent home, but Dad was only thirty, so that didn't help him. But it was a sign that the military was working to get men home as quickly as possible. The number of points needed to go home had been lowered from eighty-five to eighty and would be progressively lowered as shipping became available. Men with at least seventy points had already been placed in the redeployment pipeline, and Dad had received eight more points for service between May 12 and September 2 of that year, bringing his total to fifty-eight. He now believed he would be out in six months or less.

Although everyone wanted to go home as soon as possible, it was also difficult to think about separating from the men who had become so close during their years of service. Dad said he felt funny seeing the men over thirty-five, who were now eligible for immediate discharge, handing in their field equipment and arms as they prepared to leave. He told Mom to expect telephone calls from some of them, who would be calling just to say they had recently seen him, because he thought she would find that comforting.

Robert Klinefelter, who the men called "Tubby," left a note on Dad's bed expressing his feelings. Tubby came from a small Baltimore suburb and never had much "schooling," but Dad described him as a "good kid and a rugged little son of a gun" who everyone liked, especially because "in combat and maneuvers, he had proven to be a worthy soldier." Dad sent Mom the letter, which I include here as it was written—poor spacing, misspellings, and all.

September 1945

Headquarters Six Section in the behalf of the fighters

E.A. Bullard Commander Six Section i ask this of you only

Mr. A. Klapper,
We have all made friends in our Two years Together. But if it is as i hear you are about to go home leaving us all hear sad and broken-hearted so we ask one Thing of you. Please get your rags packed and take off before all knows of This great misfortune that is about to take place. If you should wait at New York for us to come an then say So long To us all we well fell much better about it all. So please spare the Tears an broken hearts and go while all is sleeping.

Thank you very much AEB

Appealing to Congress

Unfortunately for Dad, his departure was not as imminent as Tubby had seemed to think. Although his unit was now in Category IV, the latest redeployment news indicated they might not get home as soon as he had expected, and it made Dad furious. Servicemen were not supposed to write directly to their congressional representatives or senators about expediting discharges, so Dad organized a letter-writing campaign, urging the men in his section to ask their families to write their representatives on their behalf. He told the men what main points to make but told the men and their families to use their own words in their letters.

Dad's main points were that the draft should continue, and that the men in Category IV units should be shipped home as quickly as possible. Family members were told to explain that their group had been overseas for almost a year, had served in combat, and had earned two battle stars. The letters should include a reminder that appreciation for any action on the servicemen's behalf would be demonstrated at the polls in the coming election. Dad told Mom to write such a letter and to ask her father to also write to New York Senators James Mead and Robert F. Wagner. He did not know their congressional representative since he had not really lived in Jamaica before he had left for the service, so told Mom she would have to inquire about who he was and how to contact him.

Dad wanted Congress to be bombarded with letters saying it was essential not to cut the draft so the Army would have sufficient men to deploy for the occupation in Europe and the Pacific. He thought the occupation would require more than a million military members and was convinced "a million and a half men" would not "gladly volunteer to submit to their regimentation [and] petty tyranny. Especially with the war at an end."

Dad overestimated how many would be required for the job, though. Even the Army's own planners, in an analysis called the "Occupational Troop Basis," initially expected to have only 404,500 troops for the occupation of Germany and Austria within a year after the surrender. Public pressure to bring the troops home had forced it to keep reducing that number, first to 370,000 and later 337,000. In Japan, fewer than 200,000 troops were deployed after 1945. Despite the reduced figures required, Dad remained justifiably concerned that a reduction in the draft would delay his discharge date.

September 12, 1945

It's a democracy we are supposed to have, and that means everyone shares the burden. Well! How

> about some of them not so essential workers taking a crack at this for a while. The shooting is all over. It's quite safe. They won't get hurt. They might lose a little sleep, but otherwise nothing will harm them.
>
> The way the news reads and sounds, it makes a fellow choke with disgust. The way some of it sounds, we won't be back for a year yet.

He also thought it was important to continue the draft in order to have young people experience a year or so of training so they would appreciate what they had left behind.

September 13, 1945

> As a matter of fact, the worse the Army treats him, the more he'll hate it. In that way, the future generation will be careful to keep an eye on world affairs and be on the alert so that events somewhere in a remote corner of the world that threaten the peace don't get so much out of hand that he will be forced into the Army he has learned to hate.

He thought Mom might disagree with his views, thinking they could lead to militarism, but he felt "the little people must always be vigilant against those who usurp our freedom." He said in our system, people's votes determine who gets into Congress and the presidency, and they control the military.

Shortly after writing this letter, Dad found out he would probably only get six points instead of eight for his post-May 12 time in the Army, and he was hearing reports that the legislators were deferring to the Army regarding the demobilization program. Dad asked Mom to send him the name of their congressman, because he wanted to find out where he stood on the issue. If Dad were allowed to write him directly, he was planning to tell him he would never vote for him if he did not help bring the troops home quickly.

Dad was also angry and disappointed because he thought the inflation that was taking hold in the U.S. would foil his dream of buying a farm and a house soon after his return. He now estimated that he and Mom would have to wait for about five years before they could afford to purchase either.

At home, Mom was starting to envy some of Dad's better-off relatives. One of his uncles owned a big, fancy house in an expensive New York City suburb. Dad's brother-in-law, an accountant who had not been drafted due to a 4F exemption, was able to provide his sister with the economic security and comforts Dad did not expect to afford on his post office salary. But Dad assured Mom that when he got home they would be happier than any other couple because of their love for each other and because he did not think they were asking for that much. He just wanted a house, a car, children, and to be together "until the end of our days." He also tried to comfort Mom by telling her she was the reason he had fought.

September 18, 1945

Better that we came over here and fought it out, than for them to have bombed our cities. You've never seen a bombed city, or seen a wreath laid on a pile of rubble that was once a home. The people that lived there couldn't get out in time and lie buried under the ruin. Their grave is marked with a wreath. All the fellows feel that way, and we realize how dreadful a catastrophe we prevented from happening to our own homes. For a brief instant, I could easily see Far Rock, or Jamaica, or 99th St. like that. Do you see what I mean, baby?

I came here to fight, rather than let them bring the fight to us. You and Bonnie don't have to get up in the middle of the night and race for a crowded shelter. If you're lucky, you can make it. You don't have to look up at the sky with fear when you hear planes. These people still can't believe that a plane overhead doesn't carry their destruction in its belly. Yes, darling, I came to fight for you here so that you'd be safe over there.

Toward the end of September, Dad was encouraged to hear that a legislator had introduced a bill in Congress to expedite the discharge of men who were fathers and those who had served for two years. Until he saw some "action," though, and not just talk, Dad was bracing for serving for another nine months.

Unexpected Opportunity

Dad had decided he wanted to go to Switzerland when he had a chance for a furlough, so he turned down his first chance at a furlough in the Riviera. He was interested in Switzerland because he had heard it was possible to buy good watches there for much less than they cost in the States, and he wanted to buy gifts for Mom and his sisters. He had heard rumors that some Swiss merchants allowed the GIs to arrange for payment to be made at their offices in the States, which would have been helpful because the currency the GIs were using in Germany was "Allied Marks," not dollars.

Dad sent Mom some Dutch gulden notes to keep as a souvenir. He also sent her a collection of other prewar European bills, including some prewar German marks. Some of those were in very large denominations, reflecting the tremendous inflation Germany had experienced between the two wars.

On September 17, 1945, the battery threw its first party since it had left the States. During the party, the executive officer asked Dad if he was interested in attending the Information and Education (I & E) school in Bavaria to learn to lead discussion groups. He told

Dad it was located in a beautiful area—Oberammergau, the town where the famous *Passion Play*, the oldest continually performed passion play, was produced. Dad immediately agreed to put his name on the list and less than a week later was on his way for a week of I & E school. The night before he was to leave for Bavaria, he could not resist writing about the beauty of the countryside.

> September 21, 1944
>
> It is about 6 p.m. now, and I am sitting in the woods. The sun is starting to set, and the few stray clouds are coloured by it. In the distance, I can hear the chug of a locomotive, and overhead the birds are chirping. Otherwise, it is still. Quiet, yet it has sound. Rather like the silence of an audience just as the curtain is about to go up. It is a living thing, that sort of silence. Occasionally, a leaf, yellow or red, tumbles from a tall tree and falls crazily through the branches until it comes to rest ever so lightly on the matted earth about me. We haven't had rain for several days, but the ground is moist. The sun finds it hard to get through the ceiling of limbs and branches overhead. It's always cool here. Nature's own air conditioning.

CHAPTER 16

Oberammergau, I & E School

ON THE WAY TO the Information and Education School in Oberammergau, Dad's group stayed overnight in the small town of Seckenheim, which was about two or three miles from Mannheim and about seven from Heidelberg. The Army had evacuated the town's civilians and turned it into a transit camp for the GIs, assigning men to the various houses in town, and Dad found it very comfortable. Polish civilian workers served the chow, and one was an artist, who sketched a charcoal portrait of him. When their transport truck developed mechanical difficulties, Dad decided to take the opportunity to visit nearby Heidelberg.

Although he usually hated organized tours, Dad joined one as it was his only option for seeing Old Heidelberg. He enjoyed visiting the old castle but wished Mom could have been with him. As he walked from room to room or examined various paintings, he kept saying to himself, "Lil would like this." He also regretted not having time to wander through the halls of the famous old university in town.

Heidelberg had remained "quaint" because it had not been bombed during the war, and Dad imagined how the picturesque atmosphere could inspire someone to write his memoirs. He also saw the old Red Ox Tavern, which was "jammed with soldiers and WACs drinking beer from big horns." He could feel the "good living that must have dwelt inside its walls" and "almost hear the sound of singing and gaiety that many students used to enjoy."

Dad described the differences he noticed between German and American cities, towns, and villages, observing that the German ones seemed to be nestled between mountains and "belong to the landscape," while "our cities seem to rise up out of the ground in stark relief against the horizon. But these towns seem to have been there as long as the mountains or the river that flows by."

He was also impressed by German hydroelectric and agriculture resources. "Nothing seems to be wasted. It's going to be a tough job to keep a nation like this down." He predicted Germany would expand without Americans even being aware of it. "After all, we won't use the Nazi tactics of mass murders and forced mass migrations."

But Dad found the scenery on the route to Oberammergau so breathtaking that he said he did not have the words to describe it. Oberammergau is famous for the *Passion Play* performed by the local populace every ten years (except in 1940 because of the war), and Dad met the man who was going to play the role of Jesus that year. He was a very skilled woodcarver and autographed a small booklet Dad bought from him.

Although he claimed to lack the words, he was able to describe some of the mountain scenery.

> Oberammergau, Germany
> September 25, 1945

> This morning, I saw for the first time in my life a snow-capped mountain. The weather wasn't very clear, and the swirling mist and clouds sweeping around the peaks were so awe-inspiring, I could hardly talk. Oh, darling, if only you were with me. Tonight, some woman singer from Vienna will give a recital here.... I hate to admit it, darling, but I am really enjoying this. Never in all my born days did I ever expect to see all this. These things I have read about.

Dad was also able to visit Garmisch-Partenkirchen, the site of the 1936 Winter Olympics and the tallest mountain peak in Germany. Again, the scenery was so beautiful as to be almost indescribable, although the weather was very bad the day he visited.

> Garmisch-Partenkirchen
> September 26, 1945
>
> [The clouds] float along the valley floor until they bump up against the steep side of a mountain. As a result, one minute it appears to be foggy, then when the cloud starts breaking up against the mountain into mist, the view clears and stays like that until the next cloud comes along. Rain is intermittent, and sometimes the sun manages to break through. Nature seems to be engaged in an eternal struggle with the elements. Now I know where Wagner must have come for his moods. I can very easily picture how a superstitious people might have evolved those mythical gods. It all seems more powerful than any ordinary mortal could dare defy.

The church in town was not as "bright and shiny" as the one in Oberammergau, but he was tiring of seeing so much ornate, elaborate artistry. He missed the simple straight lines of modern art.

In these towns, the Red Cross had set up and operated centers for the men, and Dad was sure they were run "a whole lot more efficiently" than the Army would have been able to do. The Red Cross staff included women, and Dad especially enjoyed hearing a pretty American girl speaking "real American slang," rather than listening to the language being "mutilated" by a German.

Training to Lead

On September 27, Dad began classes at the I & E School, which was run by the 681st Ninth Army for the purpose of adult education and "teaching personnel the skills necessary to provide a training and education service to U.S. Army personnel." It was one of the methods the Army employed to combat morale problems and keep men occupied while they were awaiting their discharge. It was also intended to help transition them back to civilian life. Dad was enrolled in a three-day intensive program to train discussion leaders, covering current events in Europe and the U.S., and he was very impressed by the quality of the instructors, both enlisted men and officers.

The participants were taught how to start a discussion, choose subjects, conduct the session, and "keep everyone in line if the thing starts to get emotional and out of hand." He learned that it was important to make a discussion "profitable so that the men leave your room with something more than when they entered." It was a "really touchy job" because many of the subjects were "so hot and highly controversial that a guy could get his fingers burnt more times than once."

Although Dad thought the project was terrific, he recognized that military duty would always come first when he returned to his unit. From personal experience, he knew it would be difficult to get permission to pull men from guard duty and other responsibilities for informational discussions. But he loved the mental stimulation the course provided and said he could have stayed there for weeks without getting bored.

He was also pleasantly surprised by the attitude of the officers involved in the program because "they accept most of the enlisted men as something more than a mental midget." He concluded that his view of relationships between officers and enlisted men had been limited to those in his outfit, and that he had "foolishly jumped to conclusions about all the brass." He admitted he had made "the same old mistake of jumping to conclusions and generalizing" and reiterated his belief that "each person must be judged on his own merits."

When the three-day course ended, Dad returned to his unit in Helsa, about 350 miles from the school. He described what he had learned to his battery commander, explaining the course's aims and methods and asking for his cooperation. To properly carry out the programs, Dad would need time to prepare lectures, discussions, and other related projects. The commander recognized the value of the program Dad had described and promised to help. Dad realized he had probably talked himself into "a load of work," but he enjoyed it, so he hoped the program would be successful.

Dad spent the week preparing the first lecture. He put in a lot of effort because he knew it was important to catch the men's interest right away if the program were to succeed.

He was also looking forward to an upcoming furlough and wanting to go to Switzerland. He was hoping to buy a watch for Mom as an anniversary gift but knew that getting enough of the right kind of money would be difficult. The Swiss merchants wanted payment only in Swiss francs, and GIs were allowed to change only about $40 into Swiss francs just before they crossed the border. And because there were no shortages of basic goods, there was no black market in Switzerland, meaning the GIs could not sell the Swiss any of the usual items they sold in other countries, such as cigarettes, coffee, or chocolates.

Dad was still dreaming of becoming a farmer. Mom's father had spent his summer vacation at a farm in Walden, in upstate New York. The property was in exactly the area where Dad was thinking about purchasing a farm, so Dad had lots of questions for him. He wanted to know what the acreage was, how long the family had been there, and what they raised. He asked how far it was from the city, if there was a cooperative in the neighborhood, and if the family lived there year-round.

Patton

About this time, Dad wrote to Mom about his reactions to a widely publicized event. On September 28, General Patton was ousted from his position as military governor of Bavaria after he defended to the press his decision to allow former Nazi Party members to keep their political and civil servant positions. He had compared the former Nazis to members of the Democratic and Republican parties in the U.S., arguing that anyone with infrastructure management experience had been forced to join the party. He also claimed that many civilians would starve in the coming winter if he dismissed the officials.

Eisenhower was angry and, after a "heated exchange" with Patton, relieved him from his position. On October 7, Patton was also relieved of command of the Third Army and accepted a position as commander of the Fifteenth Army, which had only a small headquarters staff and a responsibility to write a history of the war in Europe.

Dad had never forgiven Patton for slapping a young soldier with battle fatigue a couple of years earlier. Patton had actually slapped two soldiers suffering from combat stress (what we now call PTSD) during his visits to the wounded in military hospitals in August 1943, but only one incident had been made public. Drew Pearson, a journalist with the *Washington Post,* reported the incident on his nationally broadcast radio show in November 1943, and Dad knew of that case. He read about Patton's ouster from the governorship of Bavaria on October 3 and wrote to Mom about it the next day.

October 4, 1945

> Yesterday's paper told about Patton's ouster. That's good. He may know how to maneuver tanks, but I think he'd do the same for any country if he were a member of that country. He is not an idealist or a democrat. He is strictly a soldier and disciplinarian. One of the worst in the Army, as far as I am concerned. Good riddance, is all I can say.

Charcoal portrait sketch of Dad drawn by a Polish civilian worker in Seckenheim, Germany, while Dad was en route to Oberammergau for I & E School, September 1945.

Cover of *7th Army Guide Book Tour of Heidelberg* that Dad received when he visited there in September 1945 en route to I & E School. (Under the auspices of Seventh Army Special Service Recreation Section)

German postcard depicting a military building in Oberammergau flying a Nazi flag, obviously taken before they were defeated. Dad was still able to purchase this on September 25, 1945, per his handwritten date, months after V-E Day. (Photo: Verlag H. Kronberger, Oberammergau)

Title page of a booklet about the famous *Passion Play* performed by the citizens of Oberammergau in 1930, the last one performed before the war. (Wm. May & Co., Ltd., Aldershot, England)

Postcard with photo of the man who had played Jesus in the *Passion Play* in 1930, who was also a skilled woodcarver. Dad met him on his visit to Oberammergau, and the man signed a small booklet Dad bought from him. He told Dad he was to play the same role the next summer. (Photo: Aufnahme W. Pfingst, Ansichtskartenwerlag, Oberammergau) However, subsequently, that performance was canceled by the U.S. Army, as the denazification process was still ongoing at the time, and some members of the proposed cast were found to have been members of the Nazi Party. John Q. Barrett, "Oberammergau and the Bubonic Plague (1946)," April 12, 2020. www.yonkerstribune.com.

CHAPTER 17

"Till the End of Time," October 1945

DAD GAVE HIS FIRST LECTURE on October 8, and although he didn't mention the topic in his letters, he wrote that he thought most of the men enjoyed it. Some of them grumbled because Dad's new responsibilities got him out of guard duty, but he said it was much more work to prepare material for lectures and discussions than guard duty had ever been. He had to read and digest a lot of reference material while trying to focus on something other than the constant conversations about redeployment.

Dad reported that his second lecture did not go as well as the first, as most of the men seemed to resent being forced to attend and were not interested in the subject, which again Dad did not mention. They just wanted to focus on redeployment and when they could go home. The negative reaction almost made Dad give up on the whole project, but he resolved to try it a few more times. He felt most of the men in his unit represented the "masses of the country" who were just not interested in important issues, even though those issues directly affected their lives. Dad estimated only about a dozen men were interested enough to get the most out of the lectures, describing the rest as not stupid but only "phlegmatic," probably meaning apathetic.

But Dad was encouraged by the success of his third lecture on the Potsdam Conference that had been held in occupied Germany in July through early August. The Army wanted the troops to be informed about this important postwar event, and Dad had spent a lot of time studying the material available to him so he could pass on the information. The Allies had met from July 17 to August 2, 1945, to determine how to administer and punish Germany and discuss other postwar issues, such as maintaining order. The men were interested in this topic and told Dad he was giving them a chance to learn about important issues the easy way. Ordinarily, when they looked at a newspaper, they would first turn to the comics or sports section.

Dad continued to give lectures and lead discussions throughout the month of October. One was on the need for an occupation army, and Dad was pleased that he had prompted the men to admit that such a force was needed, even if they were the ones in it. In late October, there was going to be a vigorous debate in Congress over the issue of a peacetime draft, and Dad was convinced the draft had to continue because he could not see any other way to keep up an occupation army both in Germany and Japan.

He also led a discussion on the Army's effort to recruit men eligible for discharge to civilian jobs overseas in civil service positions. Dad thought the jobs would be enticing for single men as they offered inexpensive room and board and a chance to save a lot of money due to the lower cost of living in Europe. For example, chauffeurs and messengers were being offered around $2,500 per year and would also receive room and board at a nominal cost of about $600 a year.

Men in these jobs could travel more easily and cheaply to many countries, and they would not have to worry about winding up unemployed during the reconversion stage in the States. They could return home in two or three years after having seen a good part of the world and then be ready to settle down. But the jobs offered no provision for bringing families to Europe, so they had little appeal for married men like Dad.

After a few lectures, Dad was gratified to be getting more positive feedback. Although many of the men were reluctant to speak up during the discussions, Dad wanted as many as possible to participate, not just "a few courageous souls." The men told him they liked the discussions and felt they were getting a lot out of them. Even his captain told Dad he wanted to sit in on one of the lectures, and he also asked Dad to come to one of his officers' "bull sessions" (informal group discussions), especially when they spoke about Russia. While the officers did not care for Russia, the captain felt the future peace of the world depended on how well the U.S. and USSR. got along.

One of Dad's lecture and discussion sessions concerned the somewhat controversial subject of labor strikes. Although striking had not been allowed during the war, workers in many industries were now trying to improve their wages and working conditions, and a longshoreman's strike had threatened to slow redeployment of the troops. Although the discussion had "lagged a little about halfway through," Dad said it had "picked up steam" when a lieutenant voiced some antilabor sentiment.

> October 22, 1945
>
> I believe he was trying to sway the group's thinking. I tried to keep neutral, but I could sense that the group realized that the strikers perhaps had a legitimate reason for their actions. Many of the guys really felt that the strikers should be drafted into the army, but as the lecture and discussion progressed they began to waver. Then the lieutenant sounded off. There wasn't one of the fellows who agreed with him. Maybe men with his point of view are disturbed by the attitude of the worker groups. Actually, I believe a lot of our officers in this army are of the same opinion.
>
> I told the fellows, when the lieutenant asked to speak, not to let the bars overawe them. Because this discussion was a civilian problem, and as civilians, his vote didn't count any more than theirs. PFC, PVT, or Corporal.

After the discussion, many of the fellows came up to me and asked 'I wonder what the lieutenant used to do for a living?' If I made them think a little bit about their part in the labor picture, then all my time has been paid for. The problem the way I saw it was to snap them out of their lethargy and the 'To hell with it all' attitude. . . .

I still have another lecture to give tomorrow on the same subject. I guess the captain will be there to stick his two cents in. But we all have a right to criticize, so let him have his say. I only hope it goes as well tomorrow as today's did.

REDEPLOYMENT AND RUMORS OF REDEPLOYMENT

A topic of great interest every day was the redeployment process and news and rumors about the latest scores needed to go home and how many men were being shipped per week. Dad continued to watch the shipping statistics that helped him track how many troops had been sent home, and by early October, he estimated he would be in Germany until at least the end of the year. He was hoping to avoid ending up in what the GIs called a "repple depple," slang for replacement depot. He heard through the grapevine that some men who had left their unit more than a month ago were still waiting in France to be shipped home.

Back in the U.S., the longshoremen's strike was threatening to slow the troop movement home. Although Dad was a strong supporter of labor, he had a hard time understanding this action, and he began to worry that he would not be home before spring. "I sure wish I knew what the hell they are striking about. Anything that interferes with my redeployment so acutely better have a damn good reason." However, the authorities vowed they would not permit the strike to interfere with shipping troops home, even if it meant sending the transport vessels back to Europe empty.

In mid-October, the men were discouraged to learn of another possible delay when Great Britain reclaimed a number of its ships to carry British soldiers home. Dad was fuming at the delay but opposed to the anti-British rhetoric being spewed by some of the men and, even worse, some American politicians. He felt it was important not to create hard feelings between the Allies because "the future welfare and the peace of the world" was at stake. He hated how some politicians would use the situation just to get votes and attention in the newspapers. And he was encouraged to hear reports that Congress would pressure the Navy to use some of its warships and airplanes to offset the loss of the British ships. Dad hoped it was true because it might allow even more men to return home sooner.

Rumors continued about when Dad and other "high-pointers" would move into the redeployment lineup. He had heard that troops in his unit who had fewer than forty-four points would be transferred out, so the remainder would become "a real close-out unit" with scores of forty-five to fifty-nine. They were already a "Category IV close-out" group, meaning it was a unit with sufficient points for deactivation and discharge. Dad did not understand why any remaining work in Europe could not be handled by "Category I units" composed of soldiers who were to stay in Europe as occupation troops.

The constantly changing conditions and ever-present rumors discouraged Dad, and to make matters worse, his mail stopped coming for a couple of weeks. He thought it might have been held up due to the longshoremen's strike, and the delay made him so blue he could hardly force himself to write.

By the end of October, the low-point men had been shipped out of Dad's unit and replaced by men who had about fifty-five points, keeping the average of the unit between forty-five and fifty-nine. By this time, the Navy was allowing some of its ships to be used to carry troops home, helping to alleviate the "bottleneck" responsible for the delay in the Army's planned redeployment schedule.

Rumors continued to circulate. Although Dad said he did not believe most of them, he wrote about them to Mom. One was that the unit would be relieved of its present mission by February 1. Another was that Dad and others would be shipping out of the unit the following week to join the sixty-pointers who had left the week before and who were now rumored to be leaving by the German port of Bremerhaven. Dad just hoped he would not be shipped out of his unit until he was ready to move out of Europe because he did not want to be "knocking around in some other outfit for a few months until our shipping orders come through."

Issues on the Home Front

In one letter early in October, Dad responded to a letter from Mom, who had been upset when Dad's father had asked her for $100. Money was so extremely tight for Mom, who was struggling to save whatever she could from Dad's meager Army allotment and her own occasional nursing jobs to go toward a down payment on a house. She had asked Dad's advice about what to do.

October 9, 1945

> You know how fond I am of my folks, but you must know how much I love you and Bonnie. I don't believe, however, that anyone will ever know what a struggle went on within me when I first had to make that decision. But I finally did, thanks to you, and now although my loyalty to mom and pop is strong, my loyalty and responsibility to you that can only come from loving you so much is primary and first in all considerations when they conflict. I hope you understand what I mean, darling. I wouldn't want you to misunderstand that for anything. I love you and Bonnie so much. I don't know if that clears up anything about the $100.

I guess the best thing I can tell you is to use your own judgment.... I also believe you are right about the reason he didn't ask Sylvia. Pop thinks a lot of me. Maybe it's because I am the only son. So much for that.

Dad also wondered why his father needed the money because he had not written anything about it to him. In the end, Dad left this uncomfortable decision to Mom. We don't have a letter from Mom telling Dad about her decision.

Later that month, Mom wrote that she was planning to find someone to care for me so she could accept more nursing cases. Dad discouraged her, though, because he was concerned about leaving me with strangers and also worried that working so much would impact her health. He reminded her of her fears about coming home alone late at night and said he did not think it was necessary for her to start working more now as he expected to be home in four or five months.

Mom reported that she had been in Walden, New York, when Dad's cousin Marty Ellman and his wife visited and unexpectedly decided to buy a farm there. Dad was surprised that they were able to put up $20,000 to $30,000 for the farm and disappointed that the purchase would prevent a cooperative venture between them and Dad.

But he was still full of questions for Mom about the area. He wanted to know the size of the town's population and whether many Jewish families lived in the area. Since he planned to keep his post office position, he asked her to inquire if the office there was first or second class because that would affect his pay scale, which would go further in the country than in the city.

Friends and Comrades

Since Dad was now thirty, some of the younger men looked up to him almost as a father figure. Dad wrote to Mom about one of them. "Wick," short for Wickersham, was about twenty and would often ask

Dad to explain things to him. Dad called Wick his "morale booster" and described him as "the perfect mentality for the Army. Nothing ever bothers him. He is so dumb, sometimes he is funny." Wick came from a small town in Ohio. One of the men snapped a photo of Dad explaining something to him. He said, "I usually am. He has a very high regard for me and thinks I must be a walking encyclopedia." Unfortunately, although Dad wrote that he had enclosed that photo, I did not find it in the collection.

One of Dad's good buddies in the unit was Frankie Greco, a young Italian from Brooklyn who had lived in a mostly Jewish neighborhood and worked in the Navy Yard as a coppersmith. Dad told Mom he hoped to continue seeing Frankie when they both returned home. Frankie's sister sang with Louis Prima, a famous big band leader in the 1940s, under the name of Lily Ann Carol.

One day in October, Dad had an experience that illustrated how small the Jewish world was then, even in the U.S. While in the latrine, he met a young man who asked if he could translate "Jewish script," meaning Hebrew. Dad replied he could not and then asked where the young man was from. He told Dad he came from Bay Ridge, Brooklyn. Dad had cousins in Bay Ridge, and it turned out the fellow had come overseas with one of his younger cousins, Marty Klapper. Then Dad realized that he had often heard his parents speak of the young man's family, because they had owned a store near Marty's father's place for many years.

During the war, the U.S. government and many American journalists, including those who worked for *Yank* magazine, encouraged feelings of comradeship with the Soviet Union and the Russians. For example, on the cover of its August 31, 1945, issue, *Yank* published a photo of a GI and a Russian female soldier dancing together. The caption read, "Russian Partner."

Dad saw a demonstration of such warm feelings in early October at a semiclassical concert by an all-female American orchestra. The concert had been held up because a general and his party were late. As the men began to complain and grow angry, the general arrived with a surprise.

October 8, 1945

When the General did show up, he had some men with him in strange uniforms. He escorted them to a reserved section. Then he turned around and faced us all and said in his typical gruff manner, 'Gentlemen, tonight we have with us our God damn, good fighting allies, the Russians.' Boy! You should hear the applause and approval that went up from the audience.

By coincidence, most of the pieces the orchestra played that night were by the Russian composer Tchaikovsky.

Dad, along with many others at the time, believed the Soviet Union had much to offer its people, such as less racial discrimination. But he was also beginning to question why the Soviets would not allow the rest of the world's journalists to see and report on what was going on within its borders and those areas under its control.

October 26, 1945

I had a little discussion today with the captain when I went in to get my box o.k.'d. He used a couple of articles in the Readers Digest [*sic*] as a basis for discussion on Soviet Russia. Frankly darling, I am confused as hell. The main question that is unanswered in my mind is: 'Why don't they allow the world to send newspaper men to the USSR and those places under its control like we do in our country?' I know there is a lot of suspicion and mistrust still existing between us and the USSR. But wouldn't it make for a healthier state of affairs if they'd open up. Have they got something to hide. Let's have the bad with the good. I don't believe we can really discuss the USSR until more is known about what goes on inside. Is she building up a privileged class as the article in the RD suggests. If she isn't then let's have the real story. I don't know what to think. Basically there must be something better there than what the Nazis had to offer. There is a great deal less racial discrimination or none at all, if we are to believe certain other articles I have read. I wish I could know more about that nation. The future peace of the world depends on our relationship with her. Any other country is small time compared to the US and the USSR.

Current Affairs

Russian relations was just one of many topics Dad discussed in his letters. He wrote several times about the trials and fate of war criminals. Pierre Laval had been France's head of government under the Vichy regime and had signed orders permitting the deportation of foreign Jews from France to the death camps. Although Dad thought Laval was guilty, he believed he should be given a fair trial "for the sake of history and posterity." But Dad guessed the temperament of the French and Italian people would prevent a real trial. His hunch was correct as most observers and writers concluded Laval's trial was a mockery. Laval was found guilty of plotting against the security of the state and collaboration with the enemy and then executed by a firing squad.

Robert Ley, a Nazi politician and head of the German Labor Front from 1933 to 1945, had committed suicide in prison in October while awaiting trial. Dad wrote, "I don't believe you can say he cheated justice however. He sweated out a thousand deaths since his capture. I don't care how he died, just so long as he is dead."

Another accused Nazi war criminal, Otto Abetz, had just been caught. He had been the German ambassador to Vichy France and had been captured in the Schwarzwald (Black Forest) in October 1945. He was later sentenced to twenty years in prison for his crimes, "particularly his role in arranging the deportation of French Jews to the death camps." Dad believed that some war criminals would get away, but that others would be caught eventually and made to pay for their crimes.

Dad also wrote about what was happening in Spain, which was then ruled by Francisco Franco. "Even the Spaniards will show the world how hot and excited they can be when the bubble bursts around Franco's head. I just wonder if there are active revolutionary forces in Spain now, trying to foment a revolt. The prisons are filled to overflowing with political prisoners." Unlike Dad's prediction about Laval's fate, he turned out to be wrong about an impending fall of Franco, who managed to suppress all opposition and ruled Spain as a dictator from 1939 to 1975.

Dad wrote at length about a short film he saw in October about the Tennessee Valley Authority (TVA), which he had mentioned in earlier letters to Mom. Dad was excited by the changes it had brought to the previously impoverished areas it now supplied with power, especially because it was a government project, owned and operated by and for the people of the valley it served. The project encouraged them to try new methods of farming, enabling them to produce more, hold back soil erosion, increase flood control, and reforest their land. The film celebrated the TVA's advantage in providing cheap electric power, which had raised the standard of living of "those who used to use oil lamps." Dad noted that efforts to create a similar project in the Missouri Valley, to be called the MVA, were being blocked, probably by the big utility companies. The same forces were also blocking the St. Lawrence Seaway project, but Dad felt those projects, too, would succeed eventually.

Holding on Till the End

During this time, Dad was promoted to corporal. Although he had been up for a sergeant position, his captain refused to let it go through because Dad had so frequently refused to "take stripes" (accept a promotion). He was not too impressed by this current promotion either, as all positions were in an "acting" capacity now and did not receive the pay grade that usually accompanied the rank. In Dad's case, his new rank of corporal received the same pay as his previous rank of T5, but the corporal had more responsibilities.

Dad's hatred of the regimentation of Army life made him empathetic to how German civilians had been treated in Germany during the war. He described how civilians would stand at attention when an American officer spoke. The behavior had been most pronounced during and shortly after the war, especially when American Army units would move into a new town. Although the behavior seemed to be declining somewhat, Dad predicted that it was "going to be a snap" for civilian bosses or foremen to enforce discipline among German workers.

Fall brought magnificent colors to the German countryside, and Dad tried to describe the scene to Mom. Dad knew a fellow with a color photo camera and planned to ask him to take a shot of the mountainside opposite their barracks—another image to contrast the beauty of nature with the devastation caused by war.

The men were beginning to go to dances with German women, who were eager to dance and then have sex afterward. Dad went to one dance with a buddy, but they left early. He said he had no desire to embrace women who a short while ago had been "heiling all over the place." As a loyal, faithful husband, Dad was sometimes left alone in his barracks while many of the other men were out drinking or "shacking up with the frauleins." On those nights, Dad would sit glumly on his bed, overcome by homesickness.

Despite the pain of separation, Dad felt lucky because Mom's constant stream of letters confirmed her love and loyalty. Unfortunately, not all the men were so lucky. One of the fellows in his unit had not heard from his wife in about a month. They had been married just before he had been shipped overseas and had no children, and his wife was not working. He was so upset by the lack of mail that he asked Dad to write to his wife to tell her how badly it was affecting him. Dad agreed to do so, even if he risked being told to mind his own business. He told Mom it was his hunch she was probably "two-timing" him and contrasted her with Mom, who found time to write every day despite having a child and working. He felt very sorry for that fellow. "No matter how crummy I feel, at least I know I have you and you know I am yours."

Number one on *Your Hit Parade* (a music program broadcast on the radio at the time) that month was "Till the End of Time," sung by Perry Como. The men in Dad's unit had not yet heard the song, but one of the wives had sent her husband the sheet music. It was an appropriate song for the men still stationed overseas who were waiting to go home and longing to see their wives and loved ones again. The lucky ones felt sure their loved ones would still be there when they got home. Dad believed he was one of the lucky ones.

Even so, Mom was becoming increasingly impatient about when Dad would be able to return and began to ask about getting him an emergency furlough. Dad warned her it was very difficult to obtain such a furlough, describing how a fellow he knew had been unable to get one even when his father had died. The complicated procedure required the Red Cross to certify the emergency at home was legitimate. Then the request had to go through the usual Army channels and red tape until it got to the commanding officer, a long and aggravating process. It seemed the Army was reluctant to let a man go, and Dad speculated that might be because of jealousy.

But by the end of October, Dad was sure that the redeployment news was improving. The Army now expected to have every seventy-pointer out of the ETO (European Theater of Operations) by November 30, and Dad expected that would mean all of the 335,000 men with sixty to sixty-nine points would start to be moved the same month. Then those with fifty-six to fifty-nine points, including Dad with his fifty-eight points, could start to move by the latter part of December. By the end of January, at the latest, Dad expected his group would be out.

He felt optimistic about his predictions as he had heard on the radio that more than 350,000 troops would be shipped in October, which was more than the Army had anticipated. Based on these reports, he expected to be on a boat the latter part of December or sometime in January. His letter of October 31 concluded happily, "Soon, in a few months, we'll be living like normal human beings."

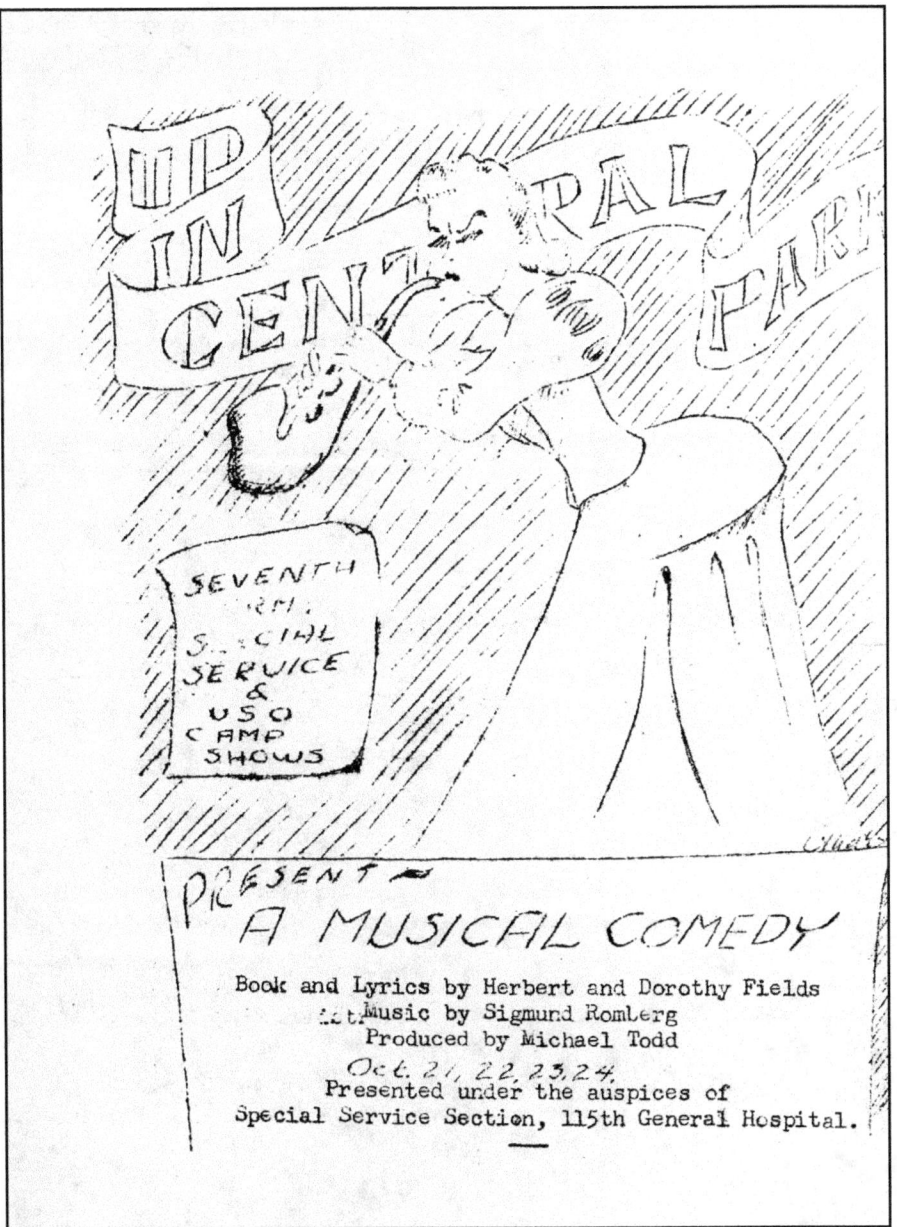

Cover of program of *Up in Central Park*, a musical Dad saw in Kassel, Germany, on October 23, 1945. He had enjoyed the show and especially liked hearing American girls speaking English. Note the producer is Michael Todd, another example of the many talented famous people who contributed their efforts to supporting the morale of the U.S. troops abroad. (Under the auspices of Special Services Section, 115th General Hospital & USO Camp Shows)

CHAPTER 18

Pass to Paris, Farewell 581st, November 1945

IN NOVEMBER, ALTHOUGH THE waiting seemed almost unendurable, Dad sensed he would not be in Europe for longer than three more months. He would have liked a chance to explore a little more of Europe in that time, but the pass he was hoping for seemed more and more elusive as new men were transferring into his unit who were due for a furlough or pass sooner than Dad was.

Finally, Dad had moved up far enough on the list for passes that he was certain he would get to make the long-awaited visit to Paris. But the trip was coming very close to his wedding anniversary, which dampened Dad's excitement. November 5 marked Mom and Dad's third wedding anniversary—and the third anniversary they had spent apart. He felt too depressed to even write much about it that day, other than tell Mom they would celebrate when he got home and were together again. Although he wished Mom could travel with him to Paris, he hoped to at least buy her some perfume there, if he could afford it, because the black market there was very bad.

Dad reached Paris on November 8 after a grueling, all-night ride in a third-class coach. He and his buddies rode the whole night sitting up, and he wrote that his spine "felt as though someone had been beating the hell out of it at the ass end." Even as he arrived in Paris, Dad was already dreading the ride back, and he wrote that he came only to buy gifts for Mom and his sisters.

The first night in Paris, the other men in his group left him in charge of their money while they all went out looking for "mamselles." Dad wrote that the women in Paris were so bold in their pursuit of GIs that some would grab them "by the privates from behind, and then they giggle and ask if you want a good time." He wrote that if he got through this place "without touching a woman, it will be the supreme test."

But Dad stuck to his plan. He spent his whole first day in Paris shopping and found himself warming to the city. He described the people as extremely friendly and helpful, and he quickly learned to use the Paris underground Metro lines to get around. He sent Mom a list of his perfume purchases and told her to compare the prices to what they would cost in the States.

November 9, 1945

> Here is the name of the brands. You can use your own judgment.
> "Tabu"—two sizes, $6.00 and $8.00
> "Chanel"—one bottle, $5.80
> "Molyneux"—two bottles, $4.00 ea[ch]
> There you have it.

He also bought her a half dozen lace handkerchiefs from Switzerland for $3.30.

The next day, Dad wrote in his daily letter that he was planning to take a sightseeing tour and shoot lots of photos with the small camera he had borrowed from a buddy. He probably went alone, since he reported that he was the only one in his group of eight men who had stayed sober and slept in his own bed the previous night. In the evening, he was planning to go to a GI nightclub run by the authorities with a few of his buddies who were "tapering off" from the night before. Even though the club served Army food, the items were prepared by French chefs, who managed to make it "tasty."

After his GI nightclub visit, Dad reported, "Never again will I be shocked by what I see in America. Now I know why they call it 'gay Paree!' The girls are not only not hard to get, but you have to fight them off." The club had three different floor shows, and Dad told Mom that he drank only orangeade while his buddies got "high."

He woke early on his third morning in Paris and enjoyed a two-hour tour of the city. Dad found Paris to be beautiful and was especially impressed by Notre Dame's age and architecture. Dad wished he could spend a few more days in Paris so he could see the Latin Quarter and the Louvre, although only a third of the famous museum was open to the public since the French were still recovering items stolen by the Nazis.

In his daily letter, Dad wrote that he planned to go to bed early, while the others went to Pigalle, "the red light of red-light districts." He did not feel like testing himself again. But he was pleasantly surprised at how comfortable he felt in Paris, saying he was running around "just like I would in New York." He realized then he was just "a big city fella, and I might as well admit it."

Living Conditions

Although Dad's trip to Paris reminded him of his love for the big city, he felt fortunate he was not stationed in one because living conditions for the civilian populations in large cities were far worse than they were in the countryside. Returning from Paris, Dad had noticed cold and hungry people in Kassel while he was waiting for a truck to take him to the base in Helsa.

November 14, 1945

> Even though they are Germans, you can't help but feel some compassion for their misery. It's one thing when someone asks for 'shokolade' [choco-

late], but when they ask you for bread, that's different. The city has taken a terrific shellacking, and many of the people live in the still habitable cellars. The rubble is piled high. The whole city stinks. There are still people buried under the ruins. In a town like Helsa, which is a farming community, you don't see much of starvation or cold. It's plenty tough and cold, but nothing like the big cities.

In light of those living situations, Dad understood why the women looked for soldiers.

They know the GI has plenty to eat, and they'd gladly sacrifice a few morals for the K-ration or piece of candy or cigarette that he will throw them. It's so commonplace that most of the people don't notice it. At least they don't seem to condemn. The boys who shack up sleep right in the same house with the family of his fraulein. So much for what goes on in Germany today. The worst is yet to come.

Mom had mentioned bicycles in an earlier letter, and Dad told Mom how Europeans relied on bicycles for basic transportation. He said the abundance of bicycles in England, Scotland, Holland, and Germany highlighted the difference in the standard of living between Europe and the U.S.

November 1, 1945

Because of the high cost and unavailability of cars and gas, bicycles are a favorite form of transportation. It's better than walking, I guess. To us, cycling is just a lark, a means of exercise. To these people, it's a serious thing. They don't think anything of walking several miles to the next village to shop or visit. We Americans are spoiled. Who'd think of walking several miles when all you gotta do is hop a trolley or subway. That's where our standard of living is higher than theirs.

Dad continued to be called upon to interpret for his officers, which allowed him glimpses into the lives and problems of the German civilians around him. One incident involved a woman with a sick child in an underground hospital in Kassel who had pleaded with the battery commander to get an ambulance to take the child to another hospital in Witzenhausen. Her child was suffering from a lung or heart disease and needed fresh air and sunlight. After the commander had approved her request, the civilian ambulance driver told her he had no gasoline. When the commander checked, he found the driver did have gas and was just stalling, so Dad had to go to the driver with the woman and "lay down the law to him."

Another situation concerned the high number of children in small towns who had been killed by GI vehicles. His officers asked Dad to tell the local burgomaster to remind civilians to observe traffic rules and regulations. The streets in these small towns were very narrow and were "usually filled with cow manure, which is very slippery. Stinks too."

The Nuremberg Trials began during Dad's final days in Europe. He said he hoped they would run smoothly and each of the defendants would be found guilty and sentenced to death. Dad was able to follow the progress of the trials by listening to a fifteen-minute summary on the radio at 9 p.m. each night. "These are, indeed, historic days. I hope and think each will hang. They mustn't let that Krupp guy get away with it either." Alfried Krupp was a German industrialist whose father, Gustav, began the illegal rearmament of Germany in the 1920s and 1930s. In 1941, Alfried became more active in running the company after his father had a stroke, and in 1943, he officially replaced him as head of the firm under a special law proclaimed by Hitler to preserve it as a family business. The company had been a major arms supplier of weapons and materiel to the Nazis and German army during World War II.

The weather was growing colder again, and Dad was grateful the war was over so that he did not have to be outside on the alert for the enemy. The nights were "pitch black, so you can't see your hand in front of your eyes. The mist is very thick around our barracks. Indeed, it is a night unfit for man or beast." He promised to tell Mom once he was home about the strain of being on watch night after night.

For Thanksgiving that year, the Army attempted to give the men a real "American feast." They even rearranged the tables and chairs in the mess hall, but Dad could not help comparing the feast to the typical conditions of the local people.

November 22, 1945

> The tables were laden with nuts, hard candy, and cream cake that the baker in town must have made for us, with our ingredients, of course. I think the office hired five or six frauleins to wait on us, and we really had 'beaucoup' turkey and trimmings. Probably the biggest inducement that was offered the girls to work was the promise of a square meal. These days, that seems to me to be their major preoccupation. Eating. The rationed food supply consists of about half of our normal wants. In a way, I guess that's why they don't take much interest in politics these times.

The shortages of food made it easy to get almost any kind of work done for a small can of meat "that I can't even look at, it tastes so lousy," Dad wrote. Cigarettes were worth more than money. For a few packs of cigarettes, a German craftsman built almost a dozen boxes for the men to ship home some of their souvenirs. The craftsman was "overjoyed" when Dad also slipped him a small can of dehydrated beef in exchange for his wooden box, which he was going to use for his souvenirs from Paris and other items he had collected.

Dad also noted some positive interactions with the local Germans, including at the movies. The officers allowed local kids, the German women who worked for the unit, and Germans who were accompanied by soldiers to watch the movies too. Dad enjoyed observing the "Krauts" laughing hard and screaming at the antics of Abbott and Costello. Since the actors' humor was mostly slapstick, it did not require a knowledge of English to understand it.

"Redeploymentitis"

Within a couple of weeks after returning to Helsa from Paris, Dad's departure from his unit seemed imminent. By that time, he and other men in his group who had accrued fifty-six to fifty-nine points were next in line to be moved into the redeployment pipeline.

Dad was beginning to feel optimistic again about being home sometime in January or early February, especially when he read in the *Stars and Stripes* that the Army expected to ship 400,000 men by the end of November. The seamen's union was also lending its support to transporting the troops home as soon as possible, announcing that its members would not man a ship capable of carrying troops that was being diverted to private commercial channels.

Rumors continued to abound about various dates and destinations. Dad heard that he had enough points to be moving through a port by December 15. But he also heard that his unit was going to break up, with people assigned to different places based on point totals.

Dad even coined a new term for the confusion and stress: "redeploymentitis," writing that the worst part of the waiting was "they build you up and then let you down. . . . A fellow feels like he wants to bust."

The uncertainty was causing many men to grow bitter against the home front and especially toward the Army. Newspapers reported that some men had rioted and "raised hell in general." One man in D Battery could not stand the uncertainty any longer and shot himself in the head.

Dad believed that every person eligible for discharge could be home before Christmas if the Army used all possible ships for moving troops home, but he and others were becoming suspicious that the redeployment was being held up because of "big officers in the armed forces who want to hang on to their jobs."

Dad also thought that the government did not want to "dump" too many men on the U.S. labor market at the same time, writing that the "big shots" did not want too many returning GIs on the labor market just yet, in part because they did not want a "full employment bill" passed. "[A]nd a lot of unemployed might create too much pressure for its passage. It's the same old rotten race. Hoorah for me, the hell with you."

He wrote again about the news of the talk in Congress about ending the draft, which made him furious. He felt that the occupation would not succeed if it were to rely solely on "volunteers," fearing it would allow the Germans to start another war machine enabling them to "make more fat profits in another war in about 20-25 years." He also predicted that not too many guys would volunteer because the Army was not "such a picnic."

Mom was feeling the stress back home too. As more and more men came home, she began to feel even lonelier and more envious. The husband of one of Mom's neighbors in Jamaica had returned, isolating Mom even further because she did not want to intrude on her friend's private time with her husband. She complained bitterly to Dad about watching couples together enjoying a night out, while she stayed home alone. Dad begged her to be patient just a bit longer and reminded her again of how lucky they were.

November 14, 1945

It's true a lot of guys are back and I am still here, but remember darling that while those fellows were sweating it out in foxholes in France, wallowing in mud, rain, snow, freezing weather, and the enemy, I was still in the States, getting a pass or furlough now and then, or when I was away, it was only simulating the real thing. That's why I am still here, and they are home. A great many of the boys will never come home. . . . Many have come back without an arm or a leg. Things could be a whole lot worse.

Dad told Mom to watch his letters for a change of address. If the return address was no longer the 581st, then she would know he was on his way, as the initial step would be to move out of his unit into one close to being shipped.

He again discouraged her from applying for an emergency discharge to try to get him home earlier, illustrating the futility of the process with two stories. The mother of one of the men in his group had suffered a stroke, which left her partially paralyzed, and she was now on the verge of death. But the Red Cross told the family that they could not call the son home unless there was a death in the family. However, he knew of another fellow who tried to get an emergency furlough when his father died. That man was told that because his father had died, the emergency was over and he could not be released.

Concrete News

On November 16, Dad finally had some concrete news to report to Mom about his redeployment. According to Dad, the guy who brought up the mail "burst into the room and said, 'Hey! You're going home.'" Dad told him to relax and just hand over his mail, but the fellow said, "Honest. They sent in a list of all the men with fifty-six to fifty-nine points. They expect them to leave the battalion by the end of the month."

He told Dad he would go to one of three homebound units — the 49th AAA Brigade, the 100th, or the 84th Division. One of the "kids" who worked at battalion headquarters told Dad he had already made out the paperwork that goes with transfers. Dad wanted to alert Mom right away to give her time to absorb it. Her neighbor and friend Sylvia in Jamaica literally had a breakdown when her husband returned without notice. Dad definitely wanted to avoid that scenario. He wanted his return scene to unfold as he had envisioned it.

November 16, 1945

> I want to come into the house, ring the bell downstairs, run up the stairs and see you open the door for me. No hysterics, just our hearts full of gladness and gratitude that at last we are together. The perfect homecoming. That's the way we want it.

The next news he heard about redeployment came from his lieutenant, who said the shipping orders for his group were expected at battalion headquarters on November 30. Dad wrote that he would be on "pins and needles" until then. He had also heard that 75,000 replacement troops were due in that area of Germany in December to replace men in Dad's category.

News about when Dad would be leaving and where he would be going continued to change, almost daily it seemed. But Dad could mark tangible progress toward home when he turned in his rifle on November 20. This was the first time he had been without a rifle since joining the Army, and Dad said he was glad to be rid of it.

As an I & E noncommissioned officer, Dad had to attend a meeting late in November focused on informing the men about reenlistment in the regular Army. Not surprisingly, he reported his group was "tremendously uninterested."

Looking Forward—and Backward

In contemplating his return to civilian life, Dad was very glad he had a job waiting for him so that he did not have to worry about finding one. He also planned to write to Senator Wagner again, asking for help in transferring to the Railway Mail Service, which would be a harder job but would pay more and provide a more appealing schedule.

He said he was glad he didn't have to worry about finding housing, which was becoming harder to get as more men returned home, and was happy Mom had decided to hold on to their apartment in Jamaica, even though she was becoming increasingly uncomfortable there. Mom complained the units were not being taken care of, and she was nervous about "stories" she was hearing about events occurring in the area. But Dad was just happy the apartment would give them some privacy for a while after his return.

In his letters, Dad began to wonder what it would be like to again face the rush, competition, and need to strike out for oneself. He called it "the every man for himself attitude." As much as he despised the regimentation of Army life, at least "you are more or less always working as a team."

At night, during their "bull" sessions, the men would often talk about their experiences during the war days, and Dad observed that those experiences seemed different now, looking back on them. "The things that stand out in a man's mind sometimes are the little things." He wondered what those memories would seem like "ten years from now."

Sometimes, he listened to GI radio programs that told about the war experience of different units. Listening to one about the 359th

Infantry landing in Normandy, he again felt grateful he had not served in an infantry unit. "Man, what a beating the infantry took. We were fairly safe compared to them. We fought the enemy at a distance. The infantry man slugged it out man to man."

Packed and Ready

On November 25, Dad moved with his battery from Helsa to Hessisch Lichtenau. The living accommodations were not as comfortable because the men were housed in civilian homes instead of being billeted in barracks, while the German inhabitants of the homes lived in the cellars.

Dad didn't enjoy being "smack dab in the middle" of civilians. Because he could understand German, they often came "acryin" to him about their troubles, and he had to serve as the interpreter for his unit. But Dad said the situation was ideal for the men who liked to "shack up" with the frauleins because now they did not have to go into the women's homes but could bring them into the house where they were billeted. "What a life," Dad observed. "Soldiers come and soldiers go. But sex goes on forever."

Dad was also unhappy about the mail situation, as no one in his unit had received any mail for quite a while. He speculated bad weather was causing delays, and that a lot of the mail was being returned to the sender because so many men had already left. Letters often followed the men for several months after they had left one place, creating a great mix-up in the post office.

But Dad had to endure the new living arrangements for less than a week. On November 27, he received official word that he was to leave at 7 a.m. on November 29 to join the 84th Division, 333rd Infantry Regiment, located near Mannheim. That unit was rumored to have a shipping date of December 15, but Dad told Mom not to count on seeing him until sometime in January. He advised her not to write until he had a chance to determine how long he would be stationed with the new outfit because he figured the mail would only follow him back to the States.

On November 28, Dad was so excited he could hardly sit still long enough to write. His stuff was "all packed and ready to go." He wrote that he had to be up at 5:30 the next morning to "roll up our bed rolls and eat early breakfast. Then we go to the railroad station and board the train." He recalled the times when he used to come home on pass or furlough and how he had a "sinking feeling inside my chest," when the time drew closer for him to leave. Now he also had a funny feeling.

> November 28, 1945
>
> If you can realize how the opposite sensation must feel, then you will realize how I feel now. Soon it will all end. We will start our lives anew. I think it will be a richer and a better one. Because we have suffered, so much sweeter will we make our lives. To me, the most extravagant luxury I can think of now is just being able to see and hold you and Bonnie in my arms.

Dad's group of GIs on pass visiting Paris, November 1945. Dad is in front row, second from left.

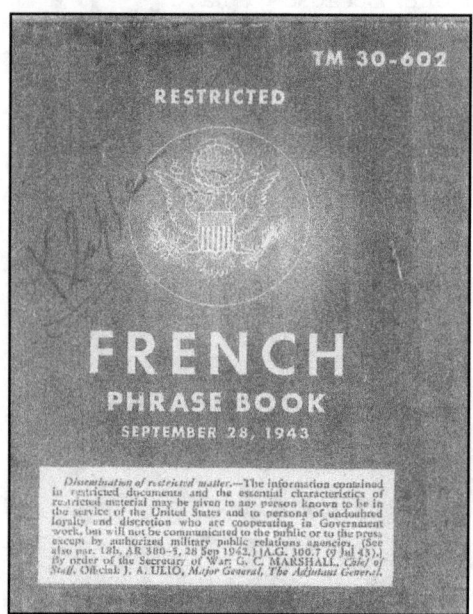
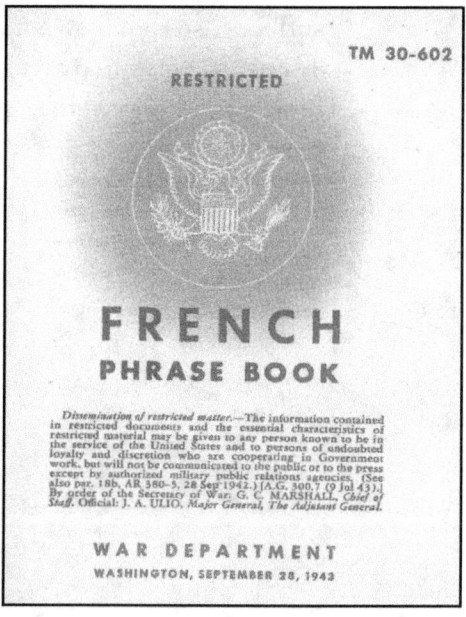

Cover and first page of *French Phrase Book* the Army gave GIs on entering France. Note restrictions printed on cover and first page limiting its use to only those in the U.S. service or to "persons of undoubted loyalty and discretion who are cooperating in Government work . . ." (War Department, Washington, 1943)

 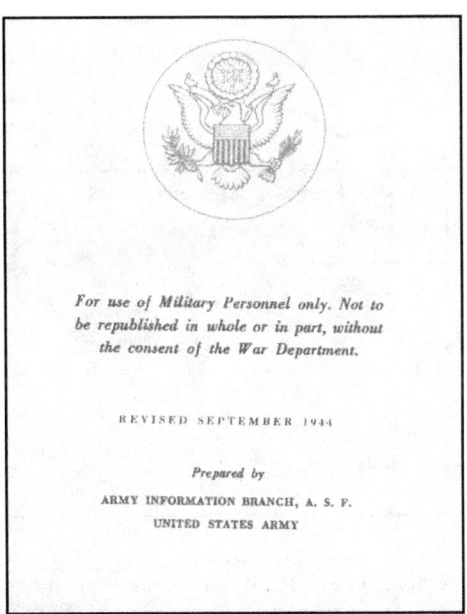

Cover and first page of *Pocket Guide to France* given to GIs on pass in France. (Army Information Branch, A. S. F., United States Army)

Linen handkerchiefs Dad bought in Paris for Mom, November 1945. She kept these for the rest of her life.

Phantom German Capital Works on Reich Secrets

FÜRSTENHAGEN

By ROBERT MARSHALL
Staff Correspondent

FÜRSTENHAVEN—Top governmental agencies of Hitler's Reich are in operation today on a wooded hilltop near this village in one of the most fantastic settings every contrived for any nation's bureaucracy.

In a hundred carefully camouflaged buildings which once turned out explosives for the Wehrmacht, millions of records, dossiers, files, maps and charts are being handled by the same persons who once worked over them in Berlin before Allied bombs drove them to seek refuge in obscure corners of Germany.

This study is being conducted by the Allies to salvage a priceless fund of information about every phase of German life for use of the four powers now occupying the country.

The history of this capital-in-captivity began in September, 1944, when government functions centered in Berlin were scattering across Germany to elude Allied troops. The American army set up an operation known as "Goldcup" to locate the personnel of the ministries and their documents.

The choice of a one-great munitions factory to house the skeleton government was due more to necessity of war than to the sense of the macabre. It was decided such important documents should be easily accessible to all Allies. The vicinity of Kassel—nine miles from Furstenhaven—was selected because it was the most central location in the American Zone for the other Allies.

Today, Reich ministries carry on in buildings with jagged eaves to break outlines in air observation and with a flourishing natural growth on flat roofs. Four of the buildings even have artificial lakes above them for camouflage.

The operation is now known as the ministerial collecting center and is under the supervision of Col. Henry C. Newton, of Hollywood. More than 1,200 tons of documents are already assembled here from virtually every German ministry. At present, 1,252 Germans from ministry staffs are also at the center.

A study of the documents provides a steady flow of new light on the "low days" when Germany was cut off from the rest of the world. One set of papers turned out to be a complete set of staff planning and operations documents of the Battle of the Bulge, down to a field order with last-minute penciled corrections.

Article from *Stars and Stripes*, November 1945, describing the Ministerial Collecting Center (MCC) in Fürstenhagen, Germany, that Dad's unit was assigned to guard. Note misspelling of name of town and Dad's correction. (*Stars and Stripes*, n.d.)

Wooden box Dad had a German civilian make for him to pack souvenirs to ship home.

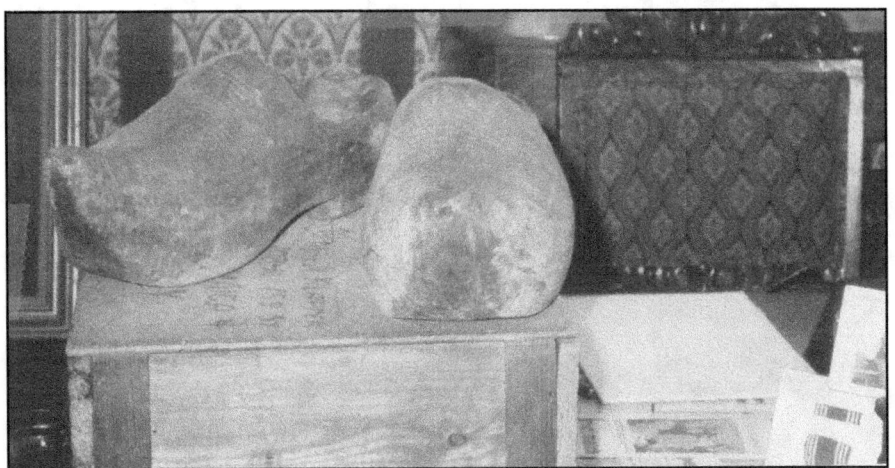

Wooden shoes Dad found in the underground munitions factory in Fürstenhagen, Germany, the site of the MCC, probably worn by a slave or foreign laborer during the war.

Ammunition box Dad used to ship home souvenirs.

CHAPTER 19

"Processing," in Limbo, Death of Patton, December 1945

ON THE LAST DAY OF November, after a rough twenty-four-hour ride in a boxcar, Dad and the departing group from the 581st ended up in Heidelberg. They called for trucks from the 84th Division, their new outfit, to transport them to their new—and what Dad hoped would be very temporary—quarters.

In his first letter from his new place, Dad told Mom that he could neither pronounce nor spell the name of the town, but he could tell her that the small city of Weinheim was nearby, and that he was about ten miles from Heidelberg. The 84th had a "readiness date" to be shipped of December 15, and they were supposed to sail about ten days later.

To prepare for their "readiness date," the division first had to go through a processing period. Everyone had to have his papers checked and turn in all but necessary clothing as well as equipment, such as weapons and vehicles. The processing was done at a staging area. Shortly after the war, this process had taken as long as thirty to forty-five days, but the Army had changed its procedure to do it all at the unit's point of origin, which in Dad's case was his new location. This was easier on the men and eliminated "long layovers in drafty tents." Instead, they were now in houses with much better protection from the winter weather. Again, he advised Mom not to write because their Army post office was to close on December 4.

In his December 1 letter, Dad could now report that he was staying in the "one-horse town" of Lützelsachsen. The food was not nearly as good as what he had been eating while guarding the MCC, but Dad was willing to endure almost any hardship as long as he was going to be on his way home soon. "Like one fellow put it, he is 'ready to crawl through a mile of manure if it's necessary.' It's an exaggeration, of course, but it's an idea of how we feel." They hoped the processing for their group would start the following week.

He expected to turn in his unnecessary clothing and equipment the next day as the first step in the procedure. And he was hoping to be on a boat home by the end of the month. Men with fifty-six to fifty-nine points were arriving at his location in small groups from all over the American zone of occupation. On December 2, Dad recalled that his foreign service had officially begun almost a year earlier.

December 2, 1945

> Darling, do you realize that our waiting has been cut down to weeks instead of counting months. Pretty soon it will be days we are sweating out. Right up to the minute I set my eyes on you. I can hardly push these weeks by quickly enough. . . .
> You know my foreign service started on Dec. 26, 1944. This Dec. 26, I expect to be on the water. Just a year later. I would not have believed that a year ago it would be possible. But so far I am hale and hearty and just rarin [*sic*] to come home. A year older and a lot wiser, I hope.

On December 3, he wrote, "Now that the waiting is almost over, I can't even write about it. I am just like a horse straining to get to the finish line. That's a hell of an analogy, but what can I do? I feel that way." He was also a bit worried about how I would react when he returned.

December 3, 1945

Bonnie will probably be a little puzzled and jealous to find her mummy now has someone else to love too. I think she'll snap out of it quickly. . . .

I'll close now, darling. Soon I'll be kissing Bonnie good night myself, and soon I'll whisper in your ear how much I love you.

—A

To break up the tension and monotony of waiting, Dad requested and received a pass to Heidelberg. One of the only large cities in Germany that had not been bombed because it had surrendered before it was attacked, Heidelberg still offered its charm and beauty, but it was crowded with civilians in search of housing and food. The food shortage was so severe that German women frequently propositioned American GIs, willing to exchange sex for food. It was not just the young women who were involved either, as Dad wrote that many of the women were "well beyond the age of 30."

After returning from Heidelberg, Dad learned "unofficially" from one of the officers that their readiness date for moving to a port had been advanced from December 15 to December 10. Since the division was going through processing twenty-four hours a day, things seemed to be moving "at a good clip."

Dad could hardly believe that he might actually be home before January, but he learned that his unit's departure date had been advanced because another division of men with slightly higher points had been quarantined when some of the men contracted scabies, a contagious skin disease. Dad could only imagine how disappointed that group must feel, but he was overjoyed that his unit might be leaving earlier. The 84th Division was now told to be ready to move on a moment's notice beginning December 10, although their official date remained December 15.

Marseille was rumored to be the destination port, which would bring a long, uncomfortable ride in a boxcar. But Dad hoped they would land in New York because he thought they would then be taken immediately to Shanks, the Army camp in Orangeburg, New York, that had been the embarkation point for troops being sent overseas. From Shanks, the troops would travel to Fort Dix in New Jersey for separation. Dad hoped he would be able to call Mom from Shanks and wrote again that he could not believe all of this waiting would soon be over.

In these last bull sessions, the men loved to talk about their favorite foods and how their parents and loved ones prepared them just the way they liked them. Dad asked Mom to bake him an apple pie with a flaky crust, topped with a bit of real ice cream, and wrote about how much he longed to taste real butter and fresh milk again. The Army's dehydrated powdered food had sustained the troops, but it had long ago lost its appeal. The chow they were now receiving was very poor, Dad wrote, although he credited the mess sergeant with doing a "helluva job." Although the company was by that time way over strength, the mess sergeant had managed to stretch the rations enough to feed everyone.

On December 8, Dad expected to be on his way to port in five days or less, and he reminisced about how he had felt when his ship was pulling out of New York Harbor on the previous December 26.

December 8, 1945

> I silently prayed that I would see Brooklyn and Staten Island again. I dreaded the thought of possibly coming back a cripple. But someone has been watching over me, and I've come through without a scratch. I am not home yet, but things look a lot better than they used to.

He could not wait to see Mom and me and to hear me speak for the first time. "Her voice will be a new sound to my ear."

Dad was called to help with the processing by checking personnel records, which kept him busy all day on December 9. His unit was slated to clear out on Wednesday night, December 12, but he did not know their port of embarkation or their destination in the States. All he knew for sure is that he would be separated from the Army at Fort Dix in New Jersey. Based on other GIs' experiences, he could then expect to be headed home a few days later.

Delayed, Then Delayed Again

Although the men in the 84th were processed and ready to move on twenty minutes' notice, they found out on December 10 that they would not be leaving until around the 15th, their originally scheduled date. Their disappointment was bitter, as was the weather, which was so cold that the open sewers in the small towns had frozen over. The men spent their days huddled together in the kitchen of the house in which they were billeted because the stove provided the only heat.

While trying to stay warm, Dad kept trying to figure out how he could obtain a loan to buy a house. Congress appeared to be ready to liberalize the GI Bill of Rights to make it easier to buy a house. Despite this, he expected he and Mom would have to wait a year or two to save up enough money, and also give prices a chance to come down. He wrote to Mom that it might be best to take out a combination of Veterans Administration and FHA loans, which would allow a veteran to purchase an $8,000 house for a payment of about $50 per month for twenty years. Living outside the city limits would be more affordable, he wrote, and if he could obtain an RMS appointment, his commuting time would be cut way down.

He also wrestled with whether to buy life insurance underwritten by the government. The premiums were fairly small, only $11.15 per month for a twenty-payment life policy or $8.30 per month for a thirty-payment one, if he wanted to backdate it to the day he entered the Army. Still, he wondered whether they would be able to afford it along with their expected home mortgage payment.

On December 12, the men discovered that their later moving date was now in jeopardy, as it was rumored that the 82nd Airborne had been bumped ahead of them so it could be in New York for some sort of parade. Dad was furious and depressed by the news.

December 12, 1945

> I hope the people who are demanding those damn parades and flag-waving demonstrations will be happy. Oh, what's the use in blowing off. I'll have to get home in spite of those things.

Unfortunately for Dad and the other men in the 84th, the rumor turned out to be true. The 82nd Airborne and the 2nd Armored, which were not even Category IV outfits slated to go home, were shipped ahead of Dad's division to participate in a parade.

December 13, 1945

> They rushed us through our processing and got us ready to ship in a hurry. Now we hear we won't ship until early Jan. The dirty____[*sic*] have slipped in two units ahead of us. Why? So that the flag-waving sons ____can have a parade. . . . Burnt up? I can hardly think straight. The bastards are using every trick they know to keep as many men here as possible. The USS Geo [*sic*] Washington that we came over on last Dec. has just left for the States with about 4,000 men. But when we came over, it carried damn near 7,000 (I can't even write). Why the sudden drop . . . ?

I can't tell you when the hell I am leaving now. Expect me when you see me. I think it still will be about Jan. 15.

What Dad did not know was that Mom had contacted the Red Cross to request an emergency furlough for him. I had become very ill with a serious kidney problem about this time, and she must have asked my pediatrician to write a letter for her to send to the Red Cross. The procedure required the Red Cross to send a wire to the serviceman's commanding officer. On December 13, the same date that Dad wrote the angry letter above, the Queens chapter of the Red Cross notified Mom that they had sent the information to the military authorities for a decision on her request.

Frustrated, Desperate, and Foolish

Probably as a result of the redeployment delay, the Army lifted its restriction on men in Dad's unit moving, so Dad was able to visit Heidelberg again. He purchased a camera and took it along to take photos, including some of the old castle. In addition to touring and taking lots of photos, Dad could swim in the Red Cross pool, which he found refreshing, although the pool was not nearly as nice as the one he had enjoyed so much at the St. George Hotel in Brooklyn. In Heidelberg, he could also see movies, including *The Story of G.I. Joe*, which he found a bit over the top for his liking.

He also tried to change his attitude to cope with the new delay. "We have waited so long now to get to this point in the redeployment pipeline, I guess I can stand it." He said it was better to think this way rather than feel "frustrated and desperate." He felt certain they would have a definite shipping date by the end of the month because they were about the last big division left in Category IV already processed for redeployment.

While Dad spent his extra time in Germany touring Heidelberg and writing to Mom, many of the men dealt with their disappointment by beginning to "run around with the frauleins again." They had stopped when the departure seemed imminent because a man would not be shipped with his unit if he had venereal disease. Dad thought their behavior was foolish. "It's like saying, 'I'll contract VD, I'll show them.'"

Dad wrote Mom that the house he was sharing was becoming a caricature of Army men deployed in Germany waiting to be shipped home.

December 16, 1945

> So here I am, sitting in the kitchen of our house, keeping warm near the stove. In other rooms, some of the boys have brought in their frauleins or frauen, as the case may be. Through closed and open doors, the sounds of silly giggling and laughter can be heard. The things that happen around here or any place since I am [*sic*] in the Army ... would make some of those risque books look like a Bible.

He found it "interesting and somewhat alarming to see the change in the young fellows." He lamented that many who came overseas with him "couldn't talk to a girl without blushing. Now they cuss and complain when they can't sleep with a babe after talking to her for half an hour." He asked if they had noticed the change in themselves. Some had noticed but did not give a damn.

Unfortunately, Dad wrote, many of those young guys and even the older ones were now "running to the medics with dripping penises." Even after shots of penicillin, some were not cured. One doctor told them they had weak prostate glands, a middle-age complaint. Dad concluded they had overworked their sex glands so much that "at 25 or 20, they are 45 years old. They've sowed their wild oats, now they are reaping."

"Sex is the cheapest commodity in all Europe," Dad wrote, "and most of the men made gluttons of themselves. Men like myself who have steered clear of them are few and far between." He said he was not looking for a "pat on the back" from Mom but wanted her to know he had stayed away from other women because he loved her too much to be untrue. Dad said others seemed to take as their motto, "The cat's away, the mice will play." He could not help but think about those men, especially the married ones, who had contracted syphilis or another venereal disease, which is "more insidious and harder to cure than gonorrhea."

He was glad the Army had adopted policies that encouraged men to seek early treatment rather than "wait until it has a death grip on them." Similar to what the government had found with Prohibition, it was impossible to outlaw sex, he said. Dad wrote that for a while, the men in his outfit going out on pass were required to take along condoms, which were issued free and in large quantities. The authorities—including the unit's chaplain and doctor—told the men to use prophylactics if they were going to have sex. There was a "pro station" in every big city or every Army unit, down to a company, that was open "24 hours a day so that a man can never say he came in too late or too early."

December 16, 1945

> Imagine them bringing that stuff home with them. The Army is doing a good thing now that they didn't do after the last war. If a man has VD when it's time for him to get on a boat, he is scratched from the shipping list and is committed to a hospital for about 90 days or until he is cured. If a man got it here, by God he should leave it here and not take it back with him. This whole VD problem is serious and very large in scope. I don't know what these guys would do if it wasn't for the miracle of penicillin.

Death of Patton

While Dad was waiting to leave Germany, General Patton was badly injured in an automobile accident near Mannheim, not far from where Dad was stationed. Patton had been on a pheasant hunting trip in the countryside on December 9 when an Army truck struck the car he was riding in at a railroad crossing. The impact caused him to hit his forehead, breaking his neck and injuring his spinal cord. Patton was paralyzed from the neck down and rushed to the military hospital in Heidelberg.

No fan of Patton, Dad was far from sympathetic when he heard about the accident.

December 16, 1945

> As far as I am concerned, he can remain in his present condition. There are few enlisted men who were under his command who have any use for him. 'Blood and guts Patton.' His guts and your blood, they used to say.

Patton died twelve days after the accident, on December 21, of a pulmonary embolism. Dad heard the news on the radio, and his reaction was in keeping with his earlier comments.

December 21, 1945

> I won't say I am glad he died, but I am unconcerned. A quarter of a million American boys died here too. He is just another death. I feel sorrier for them than I do for him. They died a dirty, violent death. He's just another general who died in bed. I'll never forgive him for slapping that soldier at the beginning of the war.

> Now the flag wavers and professional weepers will probably have a big thing. They'll probably make us mourn him by passing in review or some other crap. Very few of the men who were under his command that I have spoken to have ever expressed any use for the bastard. He was as chicken as they make them. Enough of this talk about the dead. When the heck do I go home. That's what I want to know.

Even on December 21, Dad still had no date for moving out. All the men did now was eat, sleep, and wait. Even reveille and retreat had stopped. The latest rumor was they would leave Germany on December 26, but Dad no longer believed "those flimsy things that are rumors." His unit was facing another inspection of clothing "by a regimental team." They had been told it would be the last one, but he had heard that message before. Cynically, he wrote, "I'll be home when I get there."

Dad was right about the public ceremony for Patton. On December 22, members of the 84th Infantry Division were on the streets in Heidelberg, where Patton's body lay in state, and they were back the next day for his funeral.

But Dad probably did not have to attend after all.

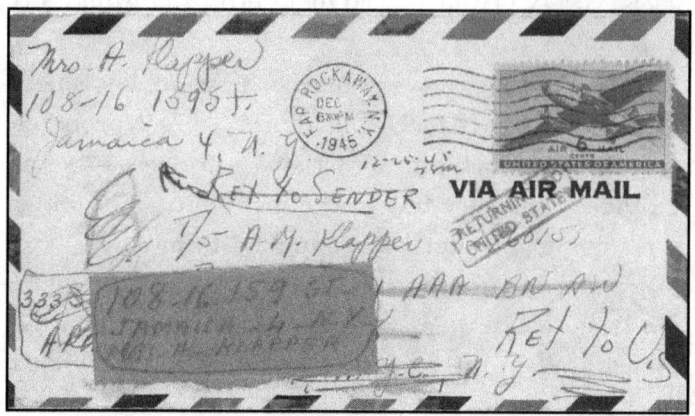

Envelope of letter Mom mailed to Dad on December 1, 1945, that was returned to her on December 25, 1945, after Dad was already in transit to return home. This is an example of the Army Post Office's elaborate system of tracking a serviceman's location.

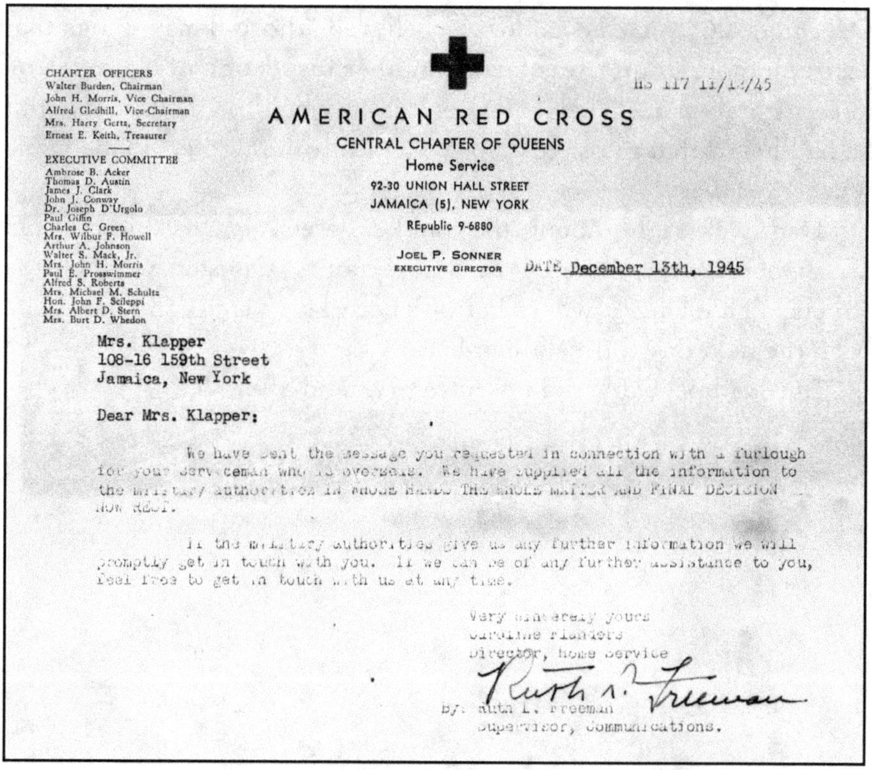

CHAPTER OFFICERS
Walter Burden, Chairman
John H. Morris, Vice Chairman
Alfred Gledhill, Vice-Chairman
Mrs. Harry Gertz, Secretary
Ernest E. Keith, Treasurer

EXECUTIVE COMMITTEE
Ambrose B. Acker
Thomas D. Austin
James J. Clark
John J. Conway
Dr. Joseph D'Urgolo
Paul Giffin
Charles C. Green
Mrs. Wilbur F. Howell
Arthur A. Johnson
Walter S. Mack, Jr.
Mrs. John H. Morris
Paul E. Prosswimmer
Alfred S. Roberts
Mrs. Michael M. Schultz
Hon. John F. Scileppi
Mrs. Albert D. Stern
Mrs. Burt D. Whedon

HS 117 11/13/45

AMERICAN RED CROSS
CENTRAL CHAPTER OF QUEENS
Home Service
92-30 UNION HALL STREET
JAMAICA (5), NEW YORK
REpublic 9-6880

JOEL P. SONNER
EXECUTIVE DIRECTOR

DATE December 13th, 1945

Mrs. Klapper
108-16 159th Street
Jamaica, New York

Dear Mrs. Klapper:

We have sent the message you requested in connection with a furlough for your serviceman who is overseas. We have supplied all the information to the military authorities in whose hands the whole matter and final decision now rest.

If the military authorities give us any further information we will promptly get in touch with you. If we can be of any further assistance to you, feel free to get in touch with us at any time.

Very sincerely yours
Caroline Flanders
Director, Home Service

Ruth L. Freeman
By: Ruth L. Freeman
Supervisor, Communications.

Letter Mom received from the Red Cross, dated December 13, 1945, informing her that they had forwarded her request for an emergency furlough for Dad to the military authorities for a decision. Mom had not told Dad of her decision to apply for this furlough, as he had previously discouraged her from doing so.

CHAPTER 20

Emergency Furlough, Home!

WHILE DAD WAS DEALING with delays and fretting about life insurance and future home loans, the Army had decided on December 19 to grant Dad an emergency home furlough due to my serious kidney illness. This decision had been made as a result of Mom's request through the Red Cross, but Dad knew nothing about it until December 22 when the 84th Division headquarters received a special order relieving him from his present assignment and attaching him "unassigned to Camp Herbert Tareyton, Le Havre, France."

Dad was to proceed there "without delay, reporting upon arrival to the CO thereof for transportation by top water priority to an appropriate port of debarkation in the U.S., reporting to the CG thereof for reassignment for emergency reasons." The order authorized him to travel by "rail, motor, and/or surface transportation" and to use air transportation to Le Havre, France. It was a "permanent change of station."

Although I don't know for sure, this special order probably allowed Dad to skip Patton's December 23 funeral. Because the order authorized him to leave his unit and travel to France "without delay," he probably left his unit on December 22.

I can only imagine Dad's complete surprise at his sudden change in status because I do not have any letters from this period. The only correspondence I found after this date was a telegram he sent to Mom from Le Havre, France, stamped December 29, 1945.

N703 INTL=CD HAVRE VIA COMMERCIAL
19 1945 DEC 29 PM 9 53
VLT MRS A KLAPPER
108 16 159 ST JAMAICANY=
DARLING ARRIVING JAN 10 DELAYED
WEATHER SAILING TOMORROW=
:AXE.
AXE 10.

However, a letter written to him at the end of February by one of his buddies, Frank Greco, fills in some of the blanks. Frank and some of the others from the 581st were still in Germany waiting for processing to be shipped home. He acknowledged that Dad must have been very worried when he received the emergency furlough and agreed Dad made the right decision in accepting the furlough rather than waiting a bit longer for his expected discharge. Frank also wondered why the Army would grant a furlough when they could have just discharged him by that time.

I was not surprised that Dad decided to take the furlough because he probably felt he had to get home as quickly as possible since my illness was the basis for his furlough. However, according to Frank's letter, by the time Dad arrived home, I had recovered.

According to his official record and report of separation, Dad departed from Europe on December 31, 1945, and arrived in the U.S. on January 5, 1946. Based on a booklet about Camp Kilmer I found in Mom's collection, I assume he was first sent there. The camp, located near New Brunswick, New Jersey, had been activated in June 1942 and was the Army's largest staging area in the U.S. Men returning from Europe landed here for their initial processing and preparation to be sent to the separation center nearest their homes or to a reception station for leaves and furloughs. From Kilmer they would take trains to their next destination. Dad was officially separated from service at Fort Dix, New Jersey, on March 5, 1946.

Sometime between arriving at Kilmer and his separation from service at Fort Dix, Dad was able to make a surprise visit to the apartment in Jamaica. He decided not to call ahead but to just show up. The family story is that Mom had been mopping the kitchen floor with her hair wrapped in a *shmate* (rag), when he knocked on the door. When Mom saw Dad, she jammed her fist into her mouth to keep from crying out.

I've been told that I was sitting in my highchair in the kitchen, and although I had not seen my father since I was a baby, I immediately recognized him. I said simply, "Hi, Daddy." Knowing how many times my father pictured his return and how much he wanted a "normal" homecoming and family life, I can only imagine that this simple greeting must have thrilled him.

As a strange parting coincidence, Dad's official discharge date from Fort Dix on March 5 was his birthday. He had been in active service for two years, eight months, and eleven days. At thirty-one, he was a civilian again and home for good.

The "Special Order" from the Army that Dad received granting him a furlough home for "emergency reasons," dated December 22, 1945. This order was a complete surprise to Dad, as Mom had not told him she was applying for one.

The telegram Dad sent Mom, stamped December 29, 1945, telling her he would be sailing from Europe the next day and his expected arrival date in the U.S. on January 10, 1946.

Cover of booklet about Camp Kilmer, where Dad was probably first sent on his arrival in the States to be processed for his emergency furlough. (Special Service Branch, Camp Kilmer, N.J., 1945)

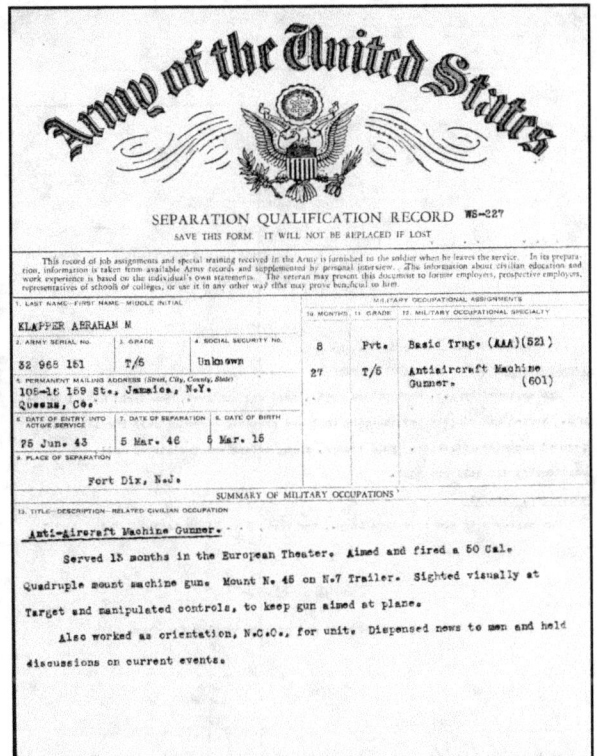

Dad's Separation Qualification Record, indicating his date of separation, March 5, 1946; place of separation, Fort Dix, New Jersey; and description of his antiaircraft duties while in the service. It also included his duties as an "orientation, N.C.C, for [his] unit," where he "dispensed news to men and held discussions on current events."

Dad's Enlisted Record and Report of Separation and Honorable Discharge. It includes his term of service, military specialty, battles and campaigns, medals received, and reason for separation.

Dad's Honorable Discharge certificate with his separation center, Fort Dix, New Jersey, and date, March 5, 1946, his thirty-first birthday.

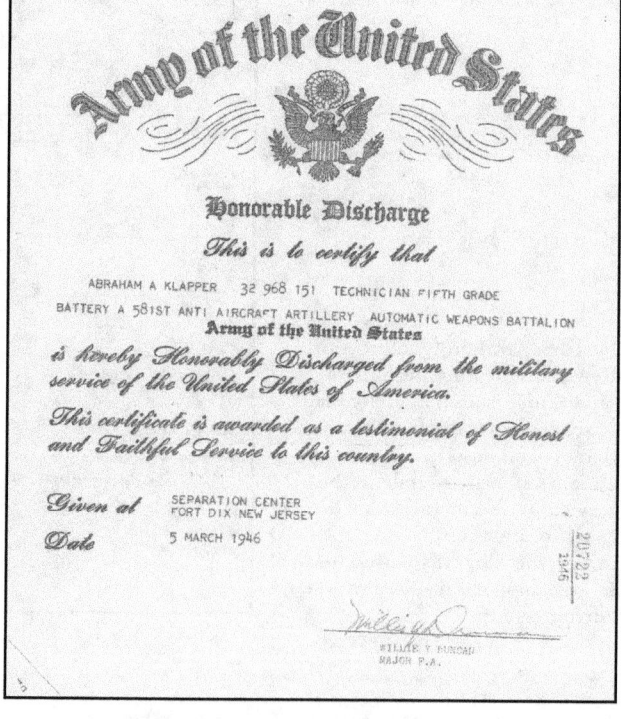

EPILOGUE

AFTER HIS DISCHARGE FROM the Army, Dad went back to his old job at the post office. I never remember him speaking about his dream of owning a farm in the country or trying to obtain a position in the RMS that he had written about during his years in the service, so I conclude by his actions that he opted for the security of the familiar. He returned to the job that was waiting for him and settled down in Mom's hometown, where they purchased their first house.

For several years, he worked at the large Church Street Station in Manhattan, commuting first from our apartment in Jamaica and later from our house in Far Rockaway, New York. Dad had worried so much about buying a house when he was in the Army, at times speculating that it might take them up to five years before they would be able to save enough money. But with the help of the GI Bill and a loan from a private lender, Dad and Mom were able to buy their first home sometime before the end of January 1947, less than a year after Dad's official discharge.

That property was in Far Rockaway and consisted of two wood shingle buildings, one behind the other. There were two apartments in each, one upstairs and one downstairs. My parents figured they could live in one unit and rent the other three, which would help them pay off the mortgage, and it did. They first moved into a small, two-bedroom upstairs apartment in the front building.

Mom took on private-duty nursing cases, with breaks between jobs so she could juggle work and family responsibilities. As her children grew older, she increased her hours and the types of jobs she took, even working as the nursing director of a nursing home for a while.

Although Dad was fortunate to have survived his service without a major injury, he did lose quite a bit of hearing, especially in one ear, from the loud percussion of the machine gun he had helped operate. He also suffered a permanent back injury, which he had never mentioned in his letters, probably because he was more concerned with surviving and then getting home as quickly as possible. He filed a disability claim with the Veterans Administration in April 1946, just a month after his discharge, but the claim was denied. However, many years later, when he needed hearing aids, the family successfully refiled his claim. Dad's back never really healed, despite visits to many doctors and chiropractors over the years, and he always walked with a twisted posture.

At the end of January 1947, my sister Havela was born. A heavy blizzard piled drifts so high that my parents could barely drive home from the hospital. But when they brought their newborn back into their own house, they must have felt they had really begun to live their postwar dream.

A year or two later we moved into the downstairs apartment in the rear building, which was more convenient and a bit larger. Though still small, the apartment seemed more spacious because it faced a yard, where Dad set up a swing set and built an arbor over the driveway that was eventually draped by fragrant, pale pink roses and grapevines my parents planted. Later, Dad built an enclosed front porch, which added more living space to the apartment, and turned the garage adjacent to the apartment into a woodworking shop.

"Golden Hands"

After a few years of teaching himself basic skills by repairing his own houses, as well as taking a course paid for by the GI Bill, Dad began to do jobs for other people, eventually developing a small carpentry and cabinetmaking business. With the help of a loan from his Uncle Phil, our family benefactor, he purchased some of the expensive tools of his craft.

Eventually, he was able to transfer to the post office station in Far Rockaway, cutting his commuting time from hours to minutes. He could conduct his carpentry business in the early part of the day and then work the swing shift at the post office, a schedule he kept until he retired from the post office. To assist him, Dad hired Leo McCray, an African-American man, and they worked together for many years,

On Saturdays, Dad visited potential customers and prepared estimates and bids, often creating hand-drawn artistic renderings to illustrate the final project. Although he never made a lot of money from his business, Dad greatly enjoyed the work and was proud that his assistant never had to collect unemployment insurance because there was always enough money to pay Leo's weekly wages. As Dad's reputation grew, he gained many customers throughout the Rockaways and in the nearby wealthier Five Towns in Nassau County. Some of his customers were so pleased with his work they sent him letters of appreciation along with their final checks. More than once, we heard some of them say he had "golden hands."

Jonni, my parents' third daughter, was born in 1951. We were still living in the downstairs apartment, but it was becoming cramped. When Jonni was about two, my parents bought a three-bedroom, one-story ranch house in a new development closer to the center of Far Rockaway. They kept their first property as a rental, though, and Dad continued to work out of his shop there.

In 1956, Mom had her first son, but our family happiness was short-lived. Matthew Charles, or "Chuckie," was born with a congenital heart defect that could be repaired by a pediatric surgeon in a fairly routine procedure today. But there was nothing doctors could do at the time to save him, and Chuckie died at about four months old.

Mom was so distraught that she did not want to live in the house any longer, so my parents signed a contract with a builder who was setting up a new development in a wealthier section of town called Bayswater. They were able to select many of the features they wanted, including some custom work. Although keeping busy with plans for the new house helped distract her, Mom always mourned her beloved Chuckie and talked wistfully for years about missing his "blue eyes."

In about a year, the house was ready, and we moved into the much larger, split-level home with a basement. Since most of the owners had moved into the new development at about the same time, the community grew close quickly. Because of Dad's carpentry business and Mom's nursing skills, neighbors and others were always dropping by to socialize, obtain advice, or get help in emergencies.

In 1957, about a year after Chuckie died and soon after we had moved into the new house, Mom gave birth to my brother, Robert. She and Dad finally had their long-awaited son. With a new baby, three young daughters, and sporadic nursing jobs, Mom was constantly busy. She and Dad lived in the Bayswater house for many years, until they retired and moved to Florida in the late 1970s after all their children had finished college.

Florida Years

In Florida, they first lived in a small house in an adult community in Pompano Beach, later moving a bit farther north to another adult community in Delray Beach, where they had a lovely home and yard. Mom kept working as a private-duty nurse throughout her seventies, even taking her last case in her early eighties. But Dad needed quadruple bypass heart surgery when he was in his early seventies, and he was only able to handle a few part-time jobs after that.

Dad's health began to fail when he was in his early eighties due to a series of TIAs and mini-strokes that affected his balance and cognitive ability. By the time Dad was in his mid-eighties, he grew too incapacitated for Mom to care for by herself, and he entered an assisted living facility and then a nursing home as his condition deteriorated. Mom sold their house and moved into a small condo at Kings Point in Delray Beach.

Final Visits

I last saw Dad in early July 2004, when my family and I traveled to Florida from our home in California to attend my oldest niece's wedding. We visited with him in the nursing home, and although he was worn out and frail, Dad, now eighty-nine, recognized all of us and was lucid enough to carry on a conversation. We left Florida shortly after the wedding to fly to Europe for a long-planned trip to visit World War I and II battle sites. My son was then in high school, and we wanted to help him prepare for an upcoming European history course.

Our itinerary included a stop at the remains of the Ludendorff Bridge at Remagen, where Dad had fought in 1945. The Germans have created a "peace museum" in the towers on the western side of the bridge where they display many photographs of the immediate aftermath of the battle, including photos of the huge number of German POWs who had been corralled in the area by the U.S. Army after they had surrendered. In the gift shop, we purchased souvenir metal chips from the bridge encased in plastic blocks with an inscribed ink drawing of the intact bridge and mailed one to Mom to give to Dad.

After seeing plaques mounted on the outside wall of the tower commemorating some of the Army units that had participated in the battle for the bridge and its crossing, we called Mom and my sisters, who were by Dad's bedside in Florida, to tell them where we were and what we were seeing. But Dad was too debilitated to speak on the phone or understand what we were saying.

We continued on to Kassel, the city nearest Helsa, the small town closest to where Dad had been stationed in 1945 after the war had ended. We entered the only government building we found there, but unfortunately, we were not able to speak with any city official who knew anything about the MCC (Ministerial Collecting Center) that Dad's unit had helped to guard. However, one of the clerks was kind enough to call someone who knew an old man from the area who said he remembered the installation. Since I had not yet read all of the letters and could not discuss the matter with Dad, I did not know then that the MCC had actually been located in Fürstenhagen, about nine miles southeast of Kassel, and that it had previously been the site of Germany's largest munitions factory. That information might have jogged some memories. Time was growing short, though, so we never made it to Helsa, as we had to move on to Berlin, our next scheduled stop.

When we reached Berlin, I called my family, who told me Dad was in the hospital and had grown much weaker. At that time there were no direct flights to the U.S. from Berlin, so I had to wait a couple of days until we arrived in London to book an emergency flight to Florida. By the time we arrived in London, the family reported that Dad was near the end. Mom, my sisters, and my niece Mierka were at his hospital bedside in Delray Beach. Later that day, July 23, Mierka called to tell me Dad had passed away. I was devastated that I had not been able to say goodbye and sad that he had never received the piece of the bridge that he helped defend or knew we had visited the site.

Saying Goodbye

Dad's funeral was held in Boynton Beach, Florida, a couple of days later, but I could not get a flight from London in time. I arrived at the airport in Miami, the earliest flight to Florida I could get from London, just as the family was leaving the cemetery. I took a cab north to meet them at Havela's house in Royal Palm Beach, where my sisters, my Aunt Shirley, and Anne Ellman, the widow of Dad's cousin Marty Ellman, recounted the highlights of the funeral service for me and played a cassette tape they had recorded.

Even though I was not at the service, they told me my presence had been felt when Aunt Shirley read a poem I had written for Dad on the sixtieth anniversary of D-Day. My brother Robert spoke about how much he admired Dad and wanted to be like him. To honor Dad's Army service, two uniformed enlisted men attended to deliver an American flag to Mom. They folded it into the traditional triangle before handing it to her, and my sisters told me she held it during the entire service.

At first, Mom appeared to be relieved from the burden of having to care for Dad and looked forward to having more time for herself. She wanted to travel and visit her children and grandchildren more often. But Dad had adored Mom and looked up to her until the end, and now she felt that lack.

In early 2006, Mom decided to spend more time in California with Robert and his family, who live in Encino in the San Fernando Valley. She was enjoying her stay at his weekend home near the beach in Ventura when she suddenly fell ill. Blood tests revealed that she was suffering from an aggressive form of leukemia. For a couple of months, my sister-in-law, a pathologist specializing in blood disorders, arranged for her medical treatments in Los Angeles. In August, as her condition worsened, my brother and I decided she would be more comfortable in her own home in Florida, where she would be near close friends and neighbors as well as my sisters.

In August 2006, I accompanied Mom to Florida, where she seemed glad to be in familiar surroundings again. We hired an aide to care for her and take her to doctors and hospitals for treatments and transfusions. Her brother Aaron, who as a youngster had spent time with Mom, me, and Grandma in Georgia when Dad was based at Camp Stewart, came from New York but could only stay a short while.

I returned to California to care for my own family but flew to Florida about every three weeks from August until the end of October, and my sisters visited her as often as they could.

Mom passed away on October 30, 2006, at eighty-six, a little more than two years after Dad's death, in Delray Medical Center. I am grateful I was with her on that day, along with my sisters, brother-in-law, and Mierka. We called my brother and sister-in-law in California, and we all mourned together. The nurses who had cared for Mom were very moved too. She had shared their profession and regaled them with stories about nursing "in the old days," making the nurses feel like they had lost one of their own, not just another patient. At the end of that week, we buried Mom next to Dad at Eternal Light Memorial Gardens in Boynton Beach.

After reading and rereading my parents' letters from the war years, I can now say that they achieved much of what they had dreamed of when they were apart. Their postwar lives were a mixture of sad and happy times, as are all lives, but my parents were able to purchase homes, raise a large family, and see all of their children graduate from college and professional or graduate schools. They lived long enough to see all of their children marry and have children of their own. They weathered many stresses, especially financial, but Abraham and Lillian remained together for sixty-two years.

Their four surviving children all became professionals in different fields. I was formerly a labor lawyer in New York and Washington, D.C., and have been a writer for many years. Since 2015, I have also assisted my husband, an accomplished Ph.D. polymer/organic chemist, in running a biopharma start-up in Newbury Park, California, near where we live. Before her retirement, my sister Havela was a prizewinning middle school math teacher and longtime chair of her department in Royal Palm Beach, Florida. Jonni initially became a nurse like Mom, but later went to medical school and now serves as a pediatrician with the school district in Tampa, Florida. Robert is a well-known orthopedic surgeon in Los Angeles, who also hosts a sports medicine radio program on ESPN.

It is a Jewish custom to gather in the cemetery a year or so after a parent or other close relative is buried. The ceremony is called an "unveiling" because that is when the headstone is "unveiled" and seen for the first time. We recite special prayers, called the Kaddish, and offer a few memories and anecdotes about the deceased. I gathered with many family members in 2007, a year after my mother died, and appreciated the chance it gave us to support each other and gain much-needed closure.

My parents share a headstone with their names and birth and death dates carved into the gray marble slab. Dad's side says, "adoring husband, loving father and grandfather" and includes a pair of hands symbolizing the "golden hands" of a master craftsman. Mom's side is inscribed with the words, "beloved wife, mother, nanny" and "dedicated nurse." The caduceus medical symbol appears above her name, reflecting her many years of service to her patients.

Whenever I visit my parents' graves, I am comforted to see them together. After spending so much time reading the letters they wrote during those "long terrible years," I am especially grateful that Mom and Dad were granted their primary wartime wish that they never again be separated.

Mom and Dad, February 1946, just after Dad's return home, probably still on his emergency furlough, before his official discharge from the Army on March 5, 1946.

Mom and Dad and other family members at his parents' apartment in Manhattan, spring 1946, attending the first Passover seder the family held after his return home. (Martin Klapper, *From Four to Forty and then some*)

PHAIR Family Circle Meeting, May 11, 1946, the first one held after the war, and after Dad and his cousin Marty had returned home. Mom and Dad are seated at the front table, turning to face the camera. Dad's younger cousin Marty is next to Mom, and next to him is Dad's mom, Mary. His mother's extended family was very important to Dad, and during the war he wrote about looking forward to seeing them again. (Martin Klapper, *From Four to Forty and then some*)

Mom with her daughters, baby Jonni, Havela, and me, ca. 1952, in front of my parents' first house in Far Rockaway, New York. By this time, we had moved to the lower downstairs apartment in the rear building of the property. Dad's woodworking shop was in the attached garage next to our apartment.

Dad's carpentry, cabinetmaking, and contractor business letterhead he used for customer bids and invoices. Note the additional phone number at the top right, which he had to add to handle his business calls, in addition to our residential line.

Dad "race-walking" in Central Park, Manhattan, a few years before his heart bypass surgery, mid-1980s.

Mom, Dad, and me in Central Park, Manhattan, mid-1980s. Mom had knitted and sewn the jacket I am wearing.

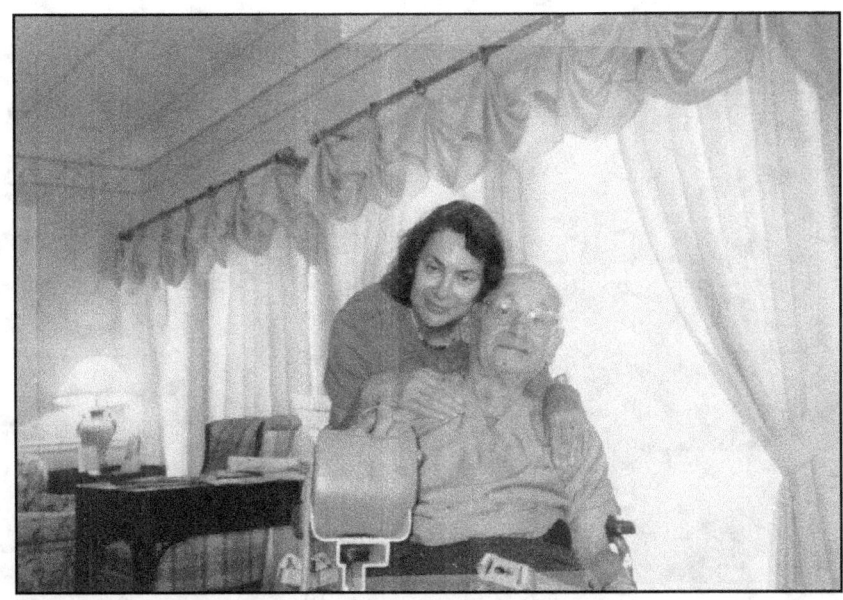

Last photo of Dad and me together at his nursing home in Boynton Beach, Florida, late June 2004, just before I left with my family for our trip to Europe, which would include our visit to Remagen, Germany.

Road signs in Germany on the way to Remagen, July 2004.

Remains of the Ludendorff Bridge sunk into the Rhine River across from Remagen, Germany, July 2004.

Sign in front of the Peace Museum Bridge at Remagen in Remagen, Germany.

Exterior of remains of the Ludendorff Bridge at Remagen.

Memorial plaques on one of the remaining towers of the bridge representing some of the American units that fought there during the battle. Dad's unit, the 581st, was not represented, presumably because the units' associations themselves had paid for the plaques, and apparently Dad's (if it had one) had not at the time of our visit in 2004.

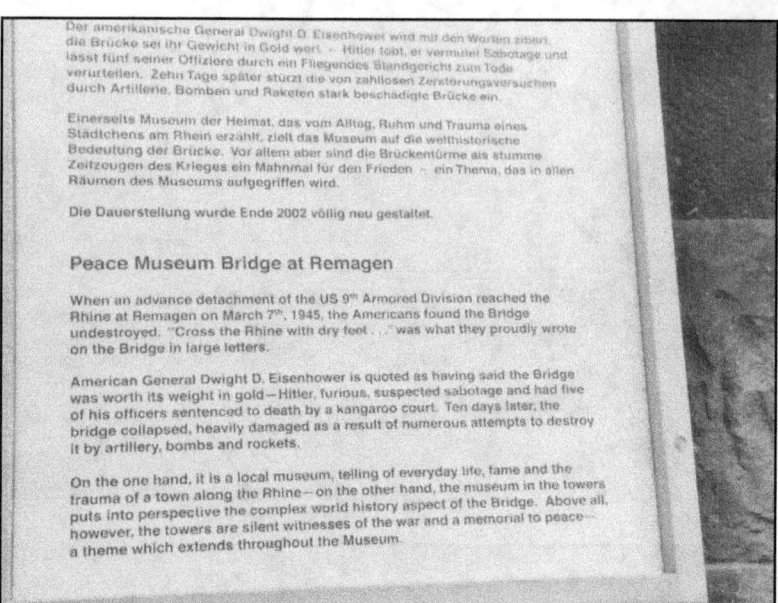

Displays from the interior of the Peace Museum Bridge at Remagen, including artifacts from the battle. The museum exhibits included artifacts from both German and American soldiers. The text accompanying the exhibits is in German and English. One excerpt explains the museum's overall purpose, "Above all, however, the towers are silent witnesses of the war and a memorial to peace—a theme which extends throughout the museum." (Author photos taken in museum)

A small remnant of the Ludendorff Bridge retrieved from the Rhine River and encased in a plastic cube, which we purchased at the museum. It includes a certificate of authenticity. We sent one to Dad, but it arrived after he had passed. (Author photo)

My son Samuel, then age 16, standing next to me at the entrance to the *Stadtarchiv* in Kassel.

The entrance to the *Stadtarchiv* in the *Stadt Kassel Magistrat* building in Kassel, Germany, where we were disappointed at being unable to find information about the MCC. We visited there before I had discovered the exact location of the MCC and that it had been an underground munitions factory, which might have yielded more information about it.

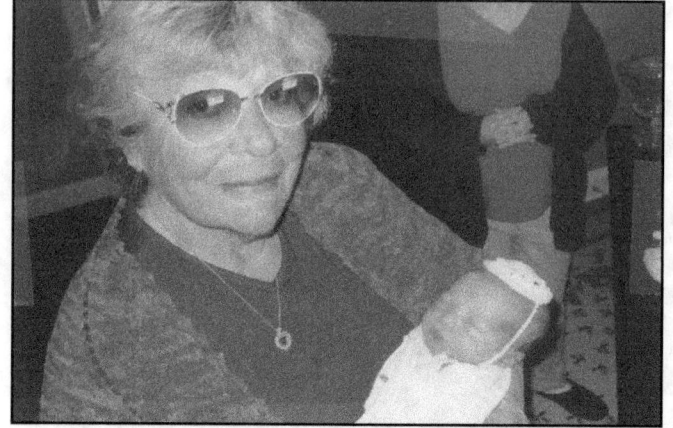

Mom, holding my cousin Rachel's baby Luke at his circumcision in New York, a few months before she contracted leukemia, March 2006. Rachel's mother had died years earlier, so Mom came up from Florida to help her.

Last photo of Mom and me taken in her condo in Delray Beach, Florida, shortly before she died, October 2006.

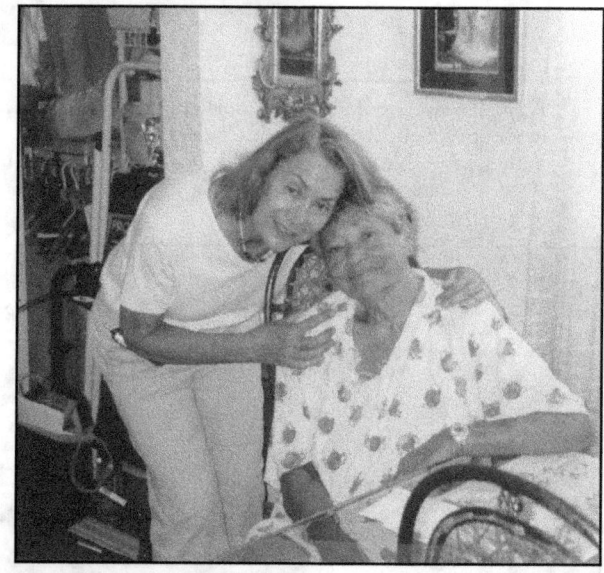

Mom and Dad's gravestone in Eternal Light Memorial Gardens cemetery, Boynton Beach, Florida.

NOTES

CHAPTER 1. A WARTIME COURTSHIP

6 *a Galitzianer:* The area called Galicia in eastern Europe changed hands several times from the Middle Ages on, but it had been part of the Austro-Hungarian Empire when Grandma was growing up there before World War I, so she always proudly claimed to be "Austrian." After World War I, when she immigrated to the U.S., the area became part of Poland. The Soviet Union occupied the area during World War II and made it part of the Ukrainian Soviet Socialist Republic after the war. When the Soviet Union disintegrated, Galicia was included in the newly independent Ukraine. *Encyclopedia Britannica,* 15th ed. (1998), vol. 5, 84.

   Many Jews from this area were actively engaged in commerce as traders and middlemen because they were not allowed to own land to farm. Therefore, they had a reputation for having shrewd marketing and sales skills. Jews from other areas in Europe, such as those from Russia or Lithuania (known as "Litvaks"), were often wary of them for this reason.

8 *doing her best to help:* Postcard from Ceil Klapper, dated November. 26, 1942, Brooklyn, New York. After reading her postcard expressing support for the marriage and her warm, humorous correspondence to him when he was in the Army, I now see why Ceil was one of Dad's favorite relatives. In her later years, she chose a nursing home near where my parents lived. Despite their very busy lives, they visited her often and took her bagels, lox, and other Jewish delicacies she loved.

8 *financial support for his mother and Shirley:* Dad's strong feeling of responsibility for supporting his family had precluded his signing up for the military earlier in the war, as had so many other eligible young men, and he never expressed a sense of "shame" for not enlisting earlier than May 1943.

9 *Order to Report for Induction:* Selective Service System. "Order to Report for Induction," May 27, 1943.

9 *June 25, 1943:* H. M. Kurtzner, Major, Infantry, Adjutant, Armed Forces Induction Station, Grand Central Palace, Special Orders No. 84. Asn. 32968151, New York, N.Y., June 11, 1943.

Chapter 2. Camp Upton, New York, to Fort Eustis, Virginia

13 *Camp Upton*: For a brief background of Camp Upton, see "Camp Upton: U.S. Army Reception Center," *Long Island During World War II* website, http://www.skylighters.org/; Donald Bayles and Paul Infranco, *The History of Camp Upton, World War I through World War II* (Scott the Printer, 2017). According to the website, the camp had first been a World War I camp; today, the Brookhaven National Laboratory occupies the site. During World War II, it received recruits from New York, Connecticut; other New England states after they reported to their local draft boards. At Upton, they were mentally and physically evaluated and then assigned to different military branches and training camps. They were also given their first uniforms and a series of inoculations, which were often quite painful. Upton was the beginning of the servicemen's "adaptation and acceptance of the Army lifestyle."
13 *document from the Red Cross*: American Red Cross postcard, New York, chapter serving Manhattan and Bronx.
14 *before being sent to active duty*: Gertrude Johnson, "Manpower Selection and the Preventative Medicine Program," in *Preventive Medicine in World War II*, ed. John Boyd Coates Jr., *U.S. Army Medical Department Office of Medical History* website, https://achh.army.mil.
14 *block-counting test*: "The Army General Classification Test of World War II," http://en.copian.ca/library/research/adlitus/page25.htm.
14 *a case of gonorrhea*: "Venereal Disease and Treatment during WW2," *WW2 US Medical Research Centre* website, https://www.med-dept.com/articles/venereal-disease-and-treatment-during-ww2/.
15 *On July 5*: The July 5 card had a slightly different address from the one on a card mailed the previous day.
15 *Dad wore glasses*: However, even with his poor eyesight, Dad would later receive a marksmanship award during training.
16 *enjoying the vegetables very much*: In my parents' World War II memorabilia, we found two pamphlets on how to grow "victory gardens" in urban areas. One was "Victory Gardens," Miscellaneous Publication No. 483, issued February 1942, revised January 1943, published by the U.S. Department of Agriculture. It included a supplement from Macy's, "Macy's Handy Vegetable Planting Chart for Victory Gardeners." The other, "Victory Gardens in Greater New York," was prepared by Specialists of the New York State College of Agriculture for the Greater New York Victory Garden Council. It was sponsored by the New York State War Council, Governor Thomas E. Dewey, Chairman, and distributed by the Greater New York Victory Garden Council through the Civilian Defense Volunteer Office.
17 *aid the war effort*: U.S. produce shortages during the war were aggravated by the internment of Japanese Americans who had grown about 40 percent of

the vegetables in California, which supplied produce for much of the nation. Although the land was confiscated from its rightful owners and given to others, primarily refugees from the Dust Bowl and immigrants from Europe, those farmers were not as familiar with the California climate and soil and thus not as productive as the Japanese had been. "Victory Garden," *Wikipedia,* http://en.wikipedia.org/wiki/Victory_garden; and G. Hansen's May 1998 article on the website, *The Virtual Museum of the City of San Francisco,* http://www.sfmuseum.org/hist9/harvest.html.

17 *40 percent of all the country's vegetables*: "Victory Gardens at a Glance," *The National WWII Museum* website, http://enroll.nationalww2museum.org/learn/education/for-students/ww2-history/at-a-glance/victory-gardens.html, 1–2. See also "Victory Gardens," *Wessels Living History Farm* website, http://www.livinghistoryfarm.org/; and "History," *Victory Gardens 2007+,* http://livinghistoryfarm.org/farmersinthe40s/crops-3/victory-gardens.

18 *"nice Southern names for boys and girls"*: That is probably how I ended up with the middle name of Sue.

27 *quota for their post*: Unfortunately, Dad never did receive the opportunity to attend OCS.

29 *hoping the end*: Of course, Mom did not know that the Germans would replace the Italians or that the war in northern Italy would continue almost until the end of the war in Europe. See H. P. Willmott, C. Messenger, R. Cross, *DK World War II* (London: DK Publishing, 2009), 275. Dad's letter of September 16, responding to her excitement about Italy's surrender, shows he understood the importance Hitler placed on defending the Italian front.

33 *family circle group*: The "PHAIR Family Circle" was an acronym made up of the first letters of the given names of several of the ancestors of its founding members, although not everyone in the family agreed on which family members were represented. Dianne Schwartz and Alte Schiller, *The Ancestry of the PHAIR Family Circle,* (Privately published: October 1965), 10. Retyped and footnotes added, September 1988. My cousins Harold Shultz and Nora Mandel updated and expanded this family history in 1991.

Chapter 3. Camp Stewart, Georgia

43 *"negro detachments"*: The Armed Forces did not officially desegregate its troop units until July 26, 1948, when President Truman issued Executive Order No. 9981, although full integration was not achieved until the Korean War "when heavy casualties forced segregated units to merge for survival." "This Day in Truman History: July 26, 1948. President Truman issues Executive Order No. 9981 Desegregating the Military," *Harry S. Truman Presidential Library & Museum* website, www.trumanlibrary.gov. There was much opposition to integration by the different branches of the Armed Forces, with

the Army and Marine Corps resisting the most. See "Harry Truman and the Desegregation of the Military: A Timeline," *theGrio.com* website, https://thegrio.com/2012/05/28/harry-truman-and-the-desegregation-of-the-military-a-timeline/;and "Desegregation of the Armed Forces," *Truman Library* website, www.trumanlibrary.gov. Fifteen years later, on July 26, 1963, Robert S. McNamara had to issue Directive 5120.36, "obligating military commanders to employ their financial resources against facilities used by soldiers or their families that discriminated based upon sex or race." "Executive Order 9981," *Wikipedia*, http://en.wikipedia.org/wiki/Executive_Order_9981.

46 *The Allies promised Stalin*: Although Stalin had been pressuring Churchill and Roosevelt for a western land invasion earlier in the war, it was only at the Tehran Conference in Iran, held from November 28 to December 1, 1943, that they promised to launch a land invasion (Operation Overlord) in May 1944. Stalin then agreed to mount a major offensive from the east at the same time to keep German troops engaged there so they could not be transferred to the west. Willmott, Messenger, and Cross, *World War II*, 217. See also "Tehran Conference," *Wikipedia*, http://en.wikipedia.org/wiki/Tehran_Conference.

48 *"The Battle for Russia"*: The film was *The Battle of Russia*, produced by the U.S. Office of War Information and released in 1943. Frank Capra, who was then a lieutenant colonel in the Army, and Anatole Litvak directed it, according to the entry on the *Turner Classic Movies* website, http://www.tcm.com/tcmdb/title/564013/The-Battle-of-Russia. It was an overtly pro-Soviet Union propaganda piece that portrayed the past failed attempts in history to conquer the country and her victorious battles against the brutal Nazi forces, concluding with the siege of Leningrad and Battle of Stalingrad, "The Battle of Russia," *Wikipedia*, https://en.wikipedia.org/wiki/The_Battle_of_Russia. It achieved its purpose at the time for Dad, who was very moved by the film and admired the courage of the Russian people.

CHAPTER 4. CHEROKEE HOMES, PORT WENTWORTH, GEORGIA

55 *MacEvoy Shipbuilding Corporation*: Jan Skutch, "Hitch Village faces demolition with stimulus funding," https://www.savannahnow.com. See also "World War II on the Savannah Waterfront—MacEvoy Shipbuilding Company," in *World War II on the Savannah Waterfront in the American Theater of Operations: Wartime Production and Service in Savannah*, prepared by L. Spracher (City of Savannah: Research Library and Municipal Archives, August 29, 2008).
55 *Housing Authority of Savannah*: Jan Skutch, "Hitch Village," 3–5.
55 *affordable housing*: "Other Housing for the Southeastern Shipbuilding Corporation Workers," *History of the Southeastern Shipbuilding Corporation* website, http://cvsolarbear.com/PGNR%20HOA%20hoods.htm.

56 *promotion to technical corporal . . . "T5"*: Jos. G. Howe, Lt. Col., 581st AAA AW Bn (SP), Commanding. Army of the United States. Typed communication appointing Private Abraham M. Klapper to Technician Fifth Grade (Temporary), effective December 21, 1943.

58 *"During the war emergency period . . ."*: Jennie R. Bouhan, Acting Chairman, First District Nursing Council for War Service. Board of Examiners of Nurses for Georgia. January 11, 1944.

60 *Hunter Field*: Hunter Army Airfield is located in Savannah and is now part of Fort Stewart. It began as a municipal airport in Savannah in 1929 and became an Army Air Corps base in 1941, Website for Hunter Army Airfield Museum, http://www.stewart.army.mil/haaf/haafHistory.asp, 1. During the time Mom and Dad were in Savannah, Hunter Field had become "a final staging base for B-17 crews on their way to the European Theater of Operations." The Army's Eighth Air Force was activated there as well. Hunter Field is still in existence today, with about 5,000 soldiers stationed there from different units. It is also home to the Coast Guard, including its largest helicopter unit. See also, Hunter Army Airfield, Georgia website, https://www.hunterarmyairfieldhousing.com/history.

CHAPTER 5. FURLOUGH, RETURN TO CAMP STEWART, D-DAY!

64 *South Jamaica Houses . . . New York City Housing Authority*: New York City Housing Authority Developments Portal. My NYCHA Developments, "Development Description," https://my.nycha.info/DevPortal/Portal, 1.

66 *unaware of the large number of casualties*: There are numerous accounts of the enormity of the casualties suffered by the Allies—and by the Germans as well. One interesting analysis of the invasion and subsequent battle in Normandy that details these losses is from British author Max Hastings, *Overlord: D-Day and the Battle for Normandy* (New York: Simon and Schuster, 1984). His views reflect the British perspective.

CHAPTER 6. AWAITING OVERSEAS DEPLOYMENT

76 *Although we were never able to determine*: After the war, my great uncle, Samuel Bergwerk, Grandma's oldest brother, tried unsuccessfully to find out what had happened to the family. His inquiries through HIAS, a Jewish organization that helped relatives find survivors, turned up no information. When I visited Israel many years later, we searched for records of my family at Yad Vashem, the Holocaust museum and memorial in Jerusalem. We found nothing for my immediate family but discovered some records for a few other relatives, who had been murdered in concentration camps.

Later, I filed an application with the Red Cross Tracing Service, but that also yielded nothing. Then I hired a Ukrainian researcher based in

Lviv (formerly Lwów) to search for any record of them. He even went to the apartment house where they had been living when the Germans invaded the city, which was still intact, but could find no one who had any information about them. He told me that after the war, the Russians, who were in control of Poland then, forced much of the population in that area to relocate.

78 *complete control of the Philippines*: Dad was wrong about this prediction, as the Philippines were not under Allied control until almost the end of June 1945. Alexander Swanston and Malcolm Swanston, *The Historical Atlas of World War II* (New York: Chartwell Books, 2010), 356. Dad simply did not realize the fierce, "fanatical" resistance the Japanese would mount, even at this point in the war, or the enormous toll it would take to liberate the Philippines. Iwo Jima was not finally subdued until late March 1945 and Okinawa until late June 1945. Wilmott, *World War II*, 260.

78 *port of Antwerp in Belgium*: Allied ships were indeed able to dock at Antwerp on November 26, 1944. "1944: November,"*World War II Chronology*, http://members.aol.com/vetcenter1/ww2dates.htm, excerpted from *Compton's Interactive Encyclopedia*.

78 *He also expected the winter*: Of course, when he wrote these lines, Dad could not have foreseen the onset of the Battle of the Bulge, which began on December 16, 1944. For a brief summary of this important battle, see "Battle of the Bulge," *Wikipedia*, https://en.wikipedia.org/wiki/Battle_of_the_Bulge. There are many longer works on this important battle, including H. P. Willmott, C. Messenger, and R. Cross, *World War II* (New York: DK, 2009), 234–235, and Rick Atkinson, *The Guns at Last Light* (New York: Henry Holt, 2013), 412–492.

80 *If Russia declared war*: Dad was correct about this prediction. As they had promised the other Allies at Yalta in February 1945, the Soviet Union attacked Manchuria on August 8, 1945. In addition to the dropping of atomic bombs on Hiroshima and Nagasaki by the United States on August 6 and August 9, the Soviet invasion of Manchuria also played a crucial role in the Japanese surrender. Swanston and Swanston, *Historical Atlas*, 372–73.

81 *prohibited subjects. . . . The censoring was done*: War Department pamphlet No. 21-1. July 29, 1943. "Censorship and Protecting Military Information in Letters Home," *Well, Happy and Safe* website, http://igreenbaum.com/2012/01/05/censorship-and-protecting-military-information-in-letters-home. See also "Censorship," *PBS American Experience* website, http://www.pbs.org/wgbh/americanexperience/features/general-article/warletters-censorship/, excerpted from *Compton's Interactive Encyclopedia;* "Letter Censorship During WWII . . . . Censor Stamp Examples," *WWII Letters: Actual Letters Written During WWII* website, https://wwiiletters.blogspot.com/search?q=Letter+Censorship+During+WWII.+Censor+Stamp+Examples.

83 *the Battle of the Bulge, and my parents later*: See information above regarding the Battle of the Bulge.
83 *the Battle of the Hürtgen Forest*: See Antony Beevor, *Ardennes 1944: Hitler's Last Gamble* (London: Viking, 2015), and Atkinson, *The Guns at Last Light*.
84 *probably the last letter*: The last three letters Dad wrote before he sailed were undated, so I had to construe their order from the content. On one he had only written "Thursday night," on another "Fri.," and the third had no day at all. Mom had scribbled in pencil "12–22–44" on all three of them, but that did not seem accurate. From what he wrote in the letter labeled "Fri.," I assumed that was his last. After checking the calendar for December 1944, I was able to determine the exact dates of the Thursday and Friday letters, which were the 21 and 22 of December, respectively. However, I am still unsure of the exact date for the unlabeled letter. The next letter we have is dated December 30, 1944. It was on a V-mail, and he was already sailing. See chapter 7 for information about the V-mail system used during the war.
84 *December (?), 1944*: As noted above, Dad's last few letters were undated for security reasons, but later he was able to write that his ship had pulled out of New York Harbor on December 26, 1944, the day after Christmas.

Chapter 7. On a Transport Ship—Destination Unknown

87 *On the day after Christmas*: Dad only told Mom his exact sailing date later, when he was permitted to disclose it.
88 *the "V-mail" system*: An informative article about the V-mail system was published in the November–December 2008 issue of the WWII magazine *America in WWII*: "V-Mail: The GI's Lifeline," *America in WWII*, 4, no. 4, (2008): 40–43. Much of the information I include about the V-mail system is based on that article.
89 *"about the size of . . . 65 sacks of conventional mail"*: "V-Mail: The GI's Lifeline,"42.
89 *"By mid-1944 . . . slow voyage. . ."*: "V-Mail: The GI's Lifeline,"42.
89 *By war's end*: When the war with Japan ended, the planes had more room for regular mail, and so on November 1, 1945, the V-mail system was disbanded. "V-Mail: The GI's Lifeline,"43. Dad had stopped using V-mails in early June 1945, not long after V-E Day. By then, the regular airmail system was functioning well again. He enjoyed being able to write multipage letters to Mom and sometimes enclosed other items for her to read, such as cartoons and articles from the GI newspaper and magazine. The one exception I found was a V-mail he wrote to Mom in September 1945 when he was attending a course in Oberammergau. Since he was away from his base then, he probably used it because it was all he had on hand.

Chapter 8. The "British Isles"

95 *On January 7, 1945*: Although Dad wrote January 5, 1945, on his first letter after he had landed, he seems to have lost track of time, because he had written the same date on his previous letter, which he wrote before landing. On his discharge and separation document, the processing clerk wrote January 7, 1945, as the date of his arrival in Europe, so that is the date I used.

95 *"England"*: In 1998, I spoke with Dad about this period of time. He told me his unit was first sent to Bournemouth, a resort town in Dorset, where they practiced with their guns, and after that to Aldermaston in Berkshire County. The British gave the U.S. an airfield there to use as an Army Air Force base until after V-E Day in June 1945, "RAF Aldermaston," *Wikipedia*, http://en.wikipedia.org/wiki/RAF_Aldermaston.

95 *"somewhere in the British Isles"*: In an interview with Dad in the late 1990s, he told me he had been stationed in Paisley, Scotland, during this time.

96 *transport wounded soldiers*: In the same interview noted above, Dad told me he had helped load wounded soldiers onto the *Queen Elizabeth* and *Queen Mary* ships to be sent home.

97 *somewhere in Scotland*: As noted above, he was in Paisley, Scotland.

98 *advances on the eastern front*: Willmott, Messenger, and Cross, *World War II*, 258. The authors, in pages 242–247, also provide a brief but vivid description of the Soviets' "Advance into Poland," including a good timeline of their drive in "Operation Bagration," which had begun on June 23, 1944, in Byelorussia. "By the end of July, the Red Army had reached the Vistula River and Warsaw" and then "it advanced in the north through the Baltic States, and in the south through the Ukraine into southern Poland, Romania, Bulgaria, Yugoslavia, and Hungary." Willmott, Messenger, and Cross, *World War II*, 242.

99 *to purchase the handkerchiefs as a gift for Mom*: Mom saved those beautiful linen hankies, as well as the little box in which they were wrapped, for the rest of her life. My sisters and I often looked at them when we were growing up, and my sister Jonni still has them.

Chapter 9. France, the Remagen Front, a Passover Seder in Germany

105 *Dad's unit was shipped to France*: Brigadier General E. W. Timberlake, "Commendation on Performance of Duty in the Rhine and Central German Campaigns" (Germany, May 10, 1945), typed communication addressed to Lieutenant Colonel Joseph G. Howe, Commanding Officer, 581st AAA AW Bn. This document was forwarded to Howe by Colonel R. H. Myrah,

CAC Commanding Officer. Lt. Col. Howe in turn distributed it to his "Officers and Men."

The commendation contains a "narrative" section that outlines the movements and various combat missions of the 581st and helped to fill in the many blanks in Dad's correspondence. Because of censorship, he had not been able to write about much of this but could only vaguely allude to his location and combat-related activities. Unfortunately, I never asked him about this part of his journey. There is a gap in the letters he wrote to Mom from March 4 to March 9, 1945, when he was in rapid transit to the front.

105 *Just two days earlier*: Willmott, Messenger, and Cross, *World War II*, 270. See also Ken Hechler, *The Bridge at Remagen* (NY: Presidio, 2005), for an excellent account of the Remagen campaign and its importance in the final defeat of Nazi Germany. A more recent book that includes an exciting recounting of the battle is Atkinson, *Guns at Last Light*, 542–55.

105 *specially trained swimmers*: These swimmers were spotted and captured before they could set off their explosives, mainly because the Americans used blindingly powerful searchlights which "were mounted on tanks and were used for the first time at Remagen." Hechler, *Bridge at Remagen*, 190–91. See also Atkinson, *Guns at Last Light*, 555.

105 *Hitler told Field Marshal Albert Kesselring*: Hechler, *Bridge at Remagen*, 231.

105 *The bridge's crossing*: Hechler, *Bridge at Remagen*, 232.

106 *landed at Le Havre:* Timberlake commendation, 1.

107 *As General Eisenhower wrote*: Eisenhower quote accessed from Hechler, *Bridge at Remagen*, v.

107 *the Allies knew*: Hechler, *Bridge at Remagen*, v.

110 *Brigadier General Timberlake's*: Timberlake commendation, 1.

111 *He packed most*: When my siblings and I were children, we often looked at this box and its contents, and my sister Jonni still has these treasured heirlooms.

113 *"Allied invasion" money*: "Allied Military Currency," *Wikipedia*, https://en.wikipedia.org/wiki/Allied_Military_Currency. See also Walter Rundell, "Currency Control by the United States Army in World War II: Foundation for Failure," *Pacific Historical Review*, 30, no. 4 (1961).

114 *To reduce the quantities*: Kurt Greenbaum, "The Postmaster's Order Regulating How Soldiers Got Packages," *Well, Happy and Safe* website, http://www.igreenbaum.com/2013/10/29/the-postmasters-order-regulating-how-soldiers-got-packages/.

114 *U.S. Post Office*: Greenbaum, "Wartime Postmaster Details the Work of Mail Delivery in WWII," *Well, Happy and Safe* website, https://igreenbaum.com/2012/04/02/wartime-postmaster-details-the-work-of-mail-delivery-in-wwii. Details about the mail system in this paragraph are based on information from Greenbaum's post.

117 *the Ruhr . . . another transportation hub*: Willmott, Messenger, and Cross, *World War II*, 272–73.
118 *Brigadier General Timberlake's*: Timberlake commendation, 1.
118 *provisional trucking company*: Timberlake commendation, 1.
119 *Their battalion's record*: Timberlake commendation, 2.
119 *"Rock of Remagen"*: Timberlake refers to the 581st this way in a booklet published by the Information and Education unit about the Ministerial Collecting Center (MCC), where Dad's unit was later stationed, *The 581st Antiaircraft-Artillery-Battalion Looks at the Ministerial Collecting Center*, 1. See chapter 13 and accompanying notes for further discussion of the origin and role of the MCC.

Chapter 10. Death of Roosevelt, Moving Through the Countryside

122 *On April 13 . . . entering Leipzig*: For a general timeline of events, I relied on "World War II Chronology," http://members.aol.com/vetcenter1/ww-2dates.htm, 1–21. These particular events are listed on 19. This timeline was excerpted from *Compton's Interactive Encyclopedia* (Compton's NewMedia, Inc., 1995).
125 *the U.S. had rejected Heinrich Himmler's*: "World War II Chronology," 20.
125 *American and Soviet patrols met near Torgau*: "World War II Chronology," 20.
125 *San Francisco Conference*: "World War II Chronology."
127 *On April 28 . . . until May 2*: "World War II Chronology."
127 *Hitler committed suicide*: Willmott, Messenger, and Cross, *World War II*, 279.
127 *reported on May 1 . . . Rangoon, Burma*: "World War II Chronology," 20.
127 *On May 4*: "World War II Chronology," 20.
127 *U.S. Sixth Army*: "World War II Chronology," 20.
127 *closing in fast*: It actually took until May 9 for the Soviet forces to occupy Prague, and the last German troops in Czechoslovakia did not surrender to the Soviets until May 11. Willmott, Messenger, and Cross, *World War II*, 272.

Chapter 11. V-E Day in Occupied Germany

130 On *May 7 . . . at Reims*: "World War II Chronology," 20.
130 *On May 8 . . . in Berlin*: "World War II Chronology," 20.
134 *Adjusted Service Rating*: Earl F. Ziemke, *The U.S. Army in the Occupation of Germany 1944–1946* (Washington, D.C.: Center of Military History United States Army, 1985), 328–29.
134 *Himmler's April 22 offer*: "The Defeat of Hitler," *The History Place* website, http://www.historyplace.com/worldwar2/defeat/downfall-hitler.htm. See also Russell Hart and Stephen Hart, *The Second World War: Northwest*

Europe 1944–1945, vol. 6, *Essential Histories* (London: Osprey, 2002), 84. All quotes in this section are from the same source.

135 *"until they find the body"*: Willmott, Messenger, and Cross, *World War II*, 279. Hitler had ordered that his body and that of Eva Braun, his longtime mistress he married days earlier, should be burned after they committed suicide. The Germans carried the bodies from the underground bunker, placed them into a shell crater, burned them, then buried them. The bodies were apparently discovered by Russian soldiers on May 5, but the full story of what happened to the bodies of Hitler and Braun was not revealed by the Russians' FSB intelligence services until May 2015, when it was described as part of the seventieth anniversary of V-E Day and of Hitler's suicide. "What Really Happened to Hitler's Body?" *Virtual Jerusalem* website, http://virtualjerusalem.com/news.php?Itemid+16724. According to the article, Russian intelligence services were expected to release documents that provided "details of what happened to Hitler's body between 1945 and its unceremonious disposal in the 1970s." The Russian information was being made public to show he "died in Berlin and we have the papers to prove it" and to dispel conspiracy theories that Hitler and Braun "secretly escaped to South America."

When Russian officials discovered the partially burned bodies, captured Nazi officers told them that Hitler and Braun had committed suicide five days earlier and their bodies had been burned by officers. The Russians conducted a forensic analysis to confirm their identities and determine cause of death, but Stalin did not reveal this information to the West, according to the *Virtual Jerusalem* article, which described how the bodies were buried at Rathenow and one year later moved to Magdeburg in East Germany. "Hitler's skull was kept behind and is currently on the third floor of the State Archives of the Russian Federation," the article reports. In Magdeburg, the bodies were buried again and moved again and in May 1970, according to the article, "soldiers dug up the bodies, burned them to ashes, and then unceremoniously dumped them into the Ehle River."

Recently, a team of French pathologists were allowed to examine what were purported to be Hitler's jawbone and teeth in the Russian State Archive and concluded that the teeth were his, according to a May 2018 article on the *Smithsonian.com* website, disputing an earlier claim by an American archaeologist and bone specialist that the skull was that of a woman under age 40. The teeth seemed "to match X-rays taken of Hitler in 1944 and descriptions provided to the Soviets by Hitler's dentist and his dental assistant." Jason Daley, "Hitler's Teeth Confirm He Died in 1945," *Smithsonian.com* website, https://www.smithsonianmag.com/smart-news/hitlers-teeth-confirm-he-died-1945-180969133, 2. The same article states that it was then Soviet Premier Yuri Andropov who ordered Hitler's remains "to be thrown in the Biederitz River to prevent a burial site from becoming a place of pilgrimage for fascists."

135 *"hung upside down . . . into the gutter,"*: "The Defeat of Hitler."
141 *very costly affair*: The battle on Okinawa ended up being the most costly of the Pacific war. American casualties totaled 49,151, including 12,520 killed or missing. Phillips Payson O'Brien, *How the War Was Won: Air-Sea Power and Allied Victory in World War II* (Cambridge, United Kingdom: Cambridge University Press, 2015), 453–54.

Chapter 12. Occupied Germany, Visit to Holland

145 *nonfraternization policy*: For a detailed, and amusing, account of the eventual disintegration and demise of the Army's nonfraternization policy, see Ziemke, *U.S. Army in the Occupation of Germany*, 321–27. All information about the policy in this section comes from Ziemke's work.
147 *In Our Time:* This film was released in 1944 and set in 1939 Poland just before and after the Nazis invaded. It was a romantic drama starring Ida Lupino and Paul Henreid, *"In Our Time* (1944 film)," *Wikipedia*, https://en.wikipedia.org/wiki/In_Our_Time_(1944_film).
148 *they can give all of Germany to Russia*: At the time, the Cold War had not yet taken full effect, and Dad did not realize the "Iron Curtain" would soon be a reality.
152 *We hit Shanks*: Camp Shanks was located in Orangeburg, part of New York's Hudson Valley, and was the embarkation point for 1.3 million soldiers during the war, "Camp Shanks WW II Museum," *I Love NY* website, https://www.iloveny.com/listing/camp-shanks-ww-ii-museum/1529/. The GIs being shipped to Europe were prepared and equipped there; units were put on "alert" to let them know they would be shipping out within twelve hours, http://www.75thdivisiondad.com. They would travel by train to the docks at Weehawken, New Jersey, where they would be ferried out to waiting troop ships.
153 *"Komm Zurück"*: The song's title can be translated as "Come Back." It was very popular during the war and was a translation of the French song *"J'attendrai"* ("I Will Wait"), written by Louis Poterat and recorded by Rina Ketty in 1938. The French version is a translation of an Italian song from 1933, "Tornerai," composed by Dino Olivieri with lyrics by Nino Rastelli and "inspired from the humming chorus of Puccini's opera, *Madame Butterfly.*" *"J'attendrai" Wikipedia*, https://en.wikipedia.org/wiki/J%27attendrai.
154 *he again asked Mom*: Although I don't have any of Mom's responses to Dad's request to join him in Germany, given that she was willing to follow him to the South, I assume she would have gone to Europe, too, if it had been at all possible.
155 *George Washington*: The USAT *George Washington* had been recommissioned by the Navy in 1941 after having been used for passenger service and then

"laid up in the Patuxent River in Maryland in 1931." But her coal-burning engines did not provide the speed necessary to protect her against submarines, "SS *George Washington*," *Wikipedia*, http://en.wikipedia.org/wiki/SS_George_Washington. All information about the *George Washington* is taken from this source. After taking over the ship under the Lend-Lease arrangement, Great Britain had found that her boilers could not "maintain sufficient steam pressure to drive her otherwise serviceable engines." However, because of the great need for ships during the war, the ship was converted to an oil burner system by April 1943.

After completing an around-the-world voyage in December 1943, the *George Washington* was used in January 1944 to transport troops to the United Kingdom and the Mediterranean, making stops at Le Havre, Southampton, and Liverpool. The *George Washington* had transported Dad and his unit in late December 1944. They had landed in England, probably in Southampton, because that was one of the ship's regular stops. From there, he spent a short time in Bournemouth and Aldermaston before being sent to Paisley, Scotland.

156 *Valkenburg Recreation Center*: *Valkenburg Recreation Center* was an Army pamphlet given to the GIs who spent time there on passes. The pamphlet was the source for information about the center and the town in this chapter.

157 *to use their resources*: "World Wars," *Encyclopedia Britannica*, 15th ed., Vol. 29 (Chicago: Encyclopedia Britannica, Inc., 1998), 1023.

157 *close to famine*: "Netherlands," *Encyclopedia Britannica*, Vol. 24, 895.

CHAPTER 13. GUARDING THE MCC NEAR HELSA

165 *Fabrik Hessisch Lichtenau*: *The 581st Antiaircraft-Artillery-Battalion Looks at the Ministerial Collecting Center*, 20 (hereafter referred to as MCC booklet). Shortly after Dad's unit arrived at the MCC, he received this booklet published by the Army's Information and Education section explaining why the center had been set up and the role the 581st battalion would play in its operation. The booklet was written and arranged for Lt. Col. Robert G. Smith, Jr., Commander of the 581st AAA AW Bn. Mbl., by Captain Eugene F. Grewe. On the title page is a photo of Brig. Gen. E. W. Timberlake, Commander of the 49th AAA Brigade, and a commendation by him to the 581st, "Rock of Remagen." It says, "The 'Forty-Niners' are both happy and proud to have served with this outstanding battalion in the greatest military campaigns of history."

165 *complex of 800 buildings*: MCC booklet, 20.

166 *new responsibility*: MCC booklet, 24.

167 *Geneva Convention rules*: "The Geneva Convention 27 Jul 1929," *World War II Database*, http://ww2db.com/doc.php?q=329. The rules adopted in 1929

were in effect during WWII. They have been amended several times since, including in 1949.

167 *important files:* MCC booklet, 17.

167 *"came upon trucks":* MCC booklet, 19.

168 *"Goldcup":* MCC booklet, 19.

168 *Seventh Army:* MCC booklet, 20.

168 *"all places where trouble":* MCC booklet, 24–25.

168 *"may strike you . . .":* MCC booklet, 31.

168 *"submit to the temptation":* MCC booklet, 31.

169 *Isn't it better:* MCC booklet, 31.

174 *People on Our Side:* Edgar Snow was a left-wing journalist whose book *People on Our Side* was published in 1944. The *Saturday Evening Post* had sent him to India, China, and Russia in 1942 to report on those countries, "Edgar Snow," *Wikipedia,* http://www.wikipedia.org/wiki/Edgar_Snow.

174 *Forever Amber:* This was a popular romance novel by Kathleen Winsor, published in 1944, *"Forever Amber,"* *Wikipedia,* http://en.wikipedia.org/wiki/Forever_Amber_(novel).

174 *Dad was reading:* See note above. In his letter, Dad refers to the section in *People on Our Side* about India. Snow supported those who demanded that India be guaranteed independence from Great Britain, which Churchill opposed, in exchange for defending the country against a possible invasion from Japan. See review by Skydog at https://www.amazon.com/People-our-side-Edgar-Snow/dp/B00005WLIJ/customerReviews. Despite Dad's seeming left-wing views during the war, once the Cold War began in earnest, he turned sharply against the Communist parties in the Soviet Union and in the U.S. When I was living at home, I remember him always being a registered Republican voter.

175 *The TVA:* The Tennessee Valley Authority (TVA) was created in 1933 as part of the New Deal under President Roosevelt. Its purpose was "to improve navigability on the Tennessee River, provide for flood control, plan reforestation and the improvement of marginal farmlands, assist in industrial and agricultural development." "TVA: Electricity for All. The Origins of the Tennessee Valley Authority," *New Deal* Network, accessed at *VCU Libraries Social Welfare History Project* website, https://social welfare.library.vcu.edu/eras/great-depression/Tennessee-valley-authority-electricity. The river runs through seven states, including "some of the most disadvantaged areas of the South," according to the article. The TVA's mandate was "to improve 'the economic and social well-being of the people living in said river basin.'" Dad saw it as a good example of how government could help people. Today, it is the largest public power utility and one of the country's largest producers of electricity. "Tennessee Valley Authority," *Wikipedia,* http://en.wikipedia.org/wiki/Tennessee_Valley_Authority.

179 *"transition to civilian life":* Ziemke, *U.S. Army in the Occupation of Germany,* 330.

NOTES

180 *"Slopopolitan Opera Association"*: Program for performance of *Carmen (A Boilesk Voishin)*, produced by Special Services 253d Infantry.
180 *Those duties*: Ziemke gives a comprehensive overview of how the Army prepared for and implemented the post-V-E Day governance of Germany. He considers June 1946 the transition point at which civilian authorities assumed much of the control over reconstructing postwar Germany, although "Army-administered government would continue in Germany for another three years, the occupation for nine years, and the U.S. military presence for a generation or more," *U.S. Army in the Occupation of Germany*, 443.
182 *Agricultural Adjustment Administration*: The "AAA" was created in 1938 as part of the New Deal. The agency grew out of the Soil Conservation and Domestic Allotment Act of 1936, and it paid farmers to conserve and build soil. It was the foundation for the farm subsidies that exist today and replaced one that had been created in 1933 but had been struck down by the Supreme Court as unconstitutional. "Agricultural Adjustment Acts of 1933 and 1938 (AAA)," *Intellectual Takeout* website, "Agricultural Adjustment Administration," *Encyclopedia Britannica*, 15th ed. (1998), vol. 1, 155.
182 *some of his cousins*: Dad's cousin Marty Ellman and his wife, Ann, ran a poultry farm for several years in upstate New York, but they did not include Dad in their enterprise. Aunt Shirley told me Marty's father had loaned them money to purchase the farm, and she thought they left the business partly due to disputes with him. Marty's son, Eric, later told me that his parents sold the farm after the dispute and purchased and ran one by themselves in another town in upstate New York.
186 *Hitler Youth*: "Indoctrinating Youth," *United States Holocaust Memorial Museum* website, https://encyclopedia.ushmm.org/content/en/article/indoctrinating-youth.
186 *not rushing the trials*: Actually, the trials were delayed because it took time to gather evidence, find and depose witnesses, determine judicial jurisdiction over which bodies would try which defendants, and make other legal decisions. See Ziemke, *The U.S. Army in the Occupation of Germany*, 390–395.

CHAPTER 14. HIROSHIMA, NAGASAKI, VICTORY OVER JAPAN

195 *On August 10*: "World War II Chronology," 21.
198 *emperor's radio broadcast*: Willmott, Messenger, and Cross, *World War II*, 292–93. All information in this paragraph is from this source.
198 *On August 15*: "World War II Chronology," 21.
199 *Volga-Stalingrad area*: The city had been called Yekaterinoslav when Dad's father lived there. It was renamed Dnepropetrovsk by the Soviets and is now in Ukraine. The Ukrainians have renamed the city Dnipro.
200 *one addressed to me*: Unfortunately, I did not see Dad's letter to me until after he had passed away.

203 *not until August 28*: Willmott, Messenger, and Cross, *World War II*, 293.

203 *Edgar Snow's book*: *People on Our Side* was published in 1944. See note in chapter 13 about Snow, who had previously written about China, including Mao Tse-tung and the Communist Party. This book focused on "their role in the fight against fascism." "Edgar Snow," *Wikipedia*, http://www.wikipedia.org/wiki/Edgar_Snow, 2.

203 *On August 19*: Willmott, Messenger, and Cross, *World War II*, 292.

204 *Lieutenant General Jonathan Wainwright*: Martin Gilbert, *The Second World War: A Complete History* (London: Phoenix, 2009), 721.

204 *"haggard and emaciated"*: Gilbert, *The Second World War*, 721–22.

204 *captured by the Japanese*: Wilmott, Messenger, and Cross, *World War II*, 120–21.

206 *The Railway Mail Service*: The RMS had been established in 1862 as a more efficient, faster way to move mail, and the system grew along with the development of the railroads. The service was hampered during World War II by the demands for raw materials (including those the post office used), changes in train lines, and loss of personnel due to men being called into military service. In addition to mail, parcels were also being delivered by trains, so the railroad companies started to use separate cars for cargo, mail, and passengers, and blackout curtains on the mail cars allowed clerks to sort mail during the night. Miriam Pysno and Katherine Fetter, "Railway Mail Service. History of the Service: The Creation, 1832–1864," *Smithsonian National Postal Museum* website, https://postalmuseum.si.edu.

A few years after the war, the RMS was renamed the Postal Transportation System to reflect the agency's increasing use of airplanes and trucks. The last mail run on the railroad was on June 30, 1977, "as the last RPO car rolled into Washington, D.C.'s Union Station from New York City," Pysno and Fetter, "History of the Service: The Final Run, 1960s-1977," https://postalmuseum.si.edu.

206 *"every possible assistance"*: Senator Wagner's letter to Dad dated May 28, 1945.

208 *which encouraged Dad*: However, Marty Ellman and his wife ended up running a poultry farm without Dad, as noted in chapter 13.

209 *The Yank article*: "GI Farm Loan," *Yank: The Army Weekly* (August 26, 1945), no page numbers. This article is the source of all relevant information in this section.

211 *just vote for the*: The American Labor Party (ALP) was a New York-based, independent, pro-labor party that had been founded by former dissidents from the Socialist Party. Its primary purpose was to help promote Roosevelt's victory in the 1936 election. It was supported by several labor unions but lost much of its support to the Liberal Party of New York in the 1950s. After several election losses of its candidates, it was dissolved in 1956. "American Labor Party," *Wikipedia*, https://en.wikipedia.org/wiki/American_Labor_Party.

I was surprised to read about Dad's somewhat left-of-center views during the war, because I only remembered him voting Republican. I don't know when this dramatic shift occurred, although I guess it might have been during the Cold War when he—along with many others in the country—became disillusioned with and suspicious of the Soviet Union.

Chapter 15. Waiting It Out at Fifty-Eight Points

218 *"Occupational Troop Basis"*: Ziemke, *The U.S. Army in the Occupation of Germany*, 334–35.

218 *In Japan:* Richard Frank, Lecture at National World War II Museum's "International Conference on World War II" (New Orleans, Louisiana, 2016). See also "Victors against the Defeated: The Occupation of Japan," *Macrohistory: Worldhistory*, http://www.fsmitha.com/h2/ch23set-4.htm.

220 *wait for about five years*: Despite Dad's pessimism at the time he wrote this, my parents were able to purchase their first property before Dad was home a year, in late 1946 or early 1947. I assume it was because of the GI Bill, which set low-interest mortgages and allowed veterans to purchase a home with government loan guarantees, and a loan from a private lender. See M. Greenberg, "The GI Bill of Rights," in U.S. Department of State publication *Historians on America*, accessed at http://lipdigital.usembassy.gov/st/english/publication/ 2008/04,6-8. They purchased property with two buildings and two apartments in each. Our family occupied one unit and rented out the others, which helped my parents pay off the mortgage and the private loan. See Epilogue for more details.

220 *He just wanted a house*: Unfortunately, Dad's view of what he needed to be happy was not altogether shared by Mom, especially regarding financial matters. However, after he returned home, they did accomplish what he had hoped for in 1945—except for owning a farm. See Epilogue for details.

Chapter 16. Oberammergau, I & E School

224 *Passion Play*: Overwhelmed by the scenery in Oberammergau and his chance to see the city and location of its famous *Passion Play*, Dad did not comment on the anti-Semitic aspect of the event. Prior to the 2010 performance, the play's script was rewritten to make it less offensive to Jews and more historically accurate. But a group from the Anti-Defamation League in New York attended a preview and concluded that the play "continues to transmit hostile stereotypes of Jews and Judaism." S. Spano, "In the Alps, a Saving Grace," *Los Angeles Times*, June 6, 2010, L4. This article gives a good historical background of the play, as well as a description of the 2010 performance, which the author of the article attended.

225 *Garmisch-Partenkirchen*: For some historical background on the games, see

"Photos Reveal Anti-Semitism of 1936 Games," *Jewish Journal*, March 4–10, 2011, 13, 32. The article reviews an exhibition mounted in Garmisch-Partenkirchen by the town to educate current generations about those Winter Games. They had not been merely a sporting event but a "cover for a brutal dictatorship that oppressed political opponents and that harassed, humiliated, and disenfranchised Germany's Jews. That is 'the dark side of the medal.'" The exhibit was also timely, because in 2011 Munich was a contender for the 2018 Winter Olympics. "The mayor and others stress[ed] that the 2018 process affords the opportunity for reflection, perhaps even healing." "Photos Reveal," 32. However, the IOC chose Pyeongchang, South Korea, as the site of the 2018 Winter Olympics.

226 *was run by*: "681 9th Army Information and Education Special School," *NATO School Oberammergau* website, http://www.natoschool.nato.int/Organization/History/1933–1953.

226 *one of the methods*: Ziemke, *The U.S. Army in the Occupation of Germany*, 330.

227 *General Patton*: "George S. Patton," *Wikipedia*, http://.en.wikipedia.org/wiki/General_Patton#Postwar, 18. Unless otherwise noted, information about General Patton is taken from this source.

228 *civilians would starve*: Jonathan W. Jordan, *Brothers, Rivals, Victors: Eisenhower, Patton, Bradley, and the Partnership that Drove the Allied Conquest in Europe* (New York: New American Library, 2012), 534.

228 *a history of the war*: Although Patton accepted this position because he loved history, he soon lost interest in the task and began to travel. He had planned to leave this post and Europe when he was scheduled to begin his Christmas leave on December 10. For more detail about this part of Patton's life and career, see Jordan, *Brothers, Rivals, Victors*, 533–41.

228 *Patton had actually slapped*: Jordan, *Brothers, Rivals, Victors*, 226, 235–55, 266–70.

Chapter 17. "Till the End of Time," October 1945

231 *"Till the End of Time"* (chapter title): This is the title of a popular 1945 love song written by Buddy Kaye and composed by Ted Mossman. Although a number of artists recorded it, Perry Como had the biggest hit, reaching number one on the charts in August 1945, "Till the End of Time (song)," *Wikipedia*, https://en.wikipedia.org/wiki/Till_the_End_of_Time_(song), 1. That recording is probably the one Dad referred to in his October letter.

231 *Potsdam Conference*: "Potsdam Conference," *Wikipedia*, http://en.wikipedia.org/wiki/Potsdam_Conference. The Allies were represented by U.S. President Harry Truman, Soviet leader Joseph Stalin, and British Prime Minister Winston Churchill, who was replaced by Clement Attlee after U.K. election results became known during the conference.

235 *Category IV . . . it was a unit*: Ziemke, *The U.S. Army in the Occupation of Germany*, 329.

237 *Dad was surprised that they were able to put up*: Dad's sister Shirley told me that Marty's father had been a partner on that farm, but they left later because of disputes with him. Their son, Eric Ellman, confirmed Shirley's account, but said afterwards they purchased and ran a farm themselves in another town in upstate New York for many years.

238 *"Russian Partner"*: *Yank*, August 31, 1945, cover page.

240 *Pierre Laval*: "Pierre Laval," *Wikipedia*, http://en.wikipedia.org/wiki/Pierre_laval.

240 *Robert Ley*: For a brief summary of Robert Ley's background and role in the war, see "Robert Ley," *Wikipedia*, http://en.wikipedia.org/wiki/Robert_Ley.

241 *Otto Abetz*: "Otto Abetz," http://en.wikipedia.org/wiki/otto_Abetz. Abetz was sentenced by a French court in 1949 to twenty years in prison for his crimes but was released in 1954 after having served only a few years of his full term. He died in a car crash in May 1958. Although there has been speculation this might have been a planned revenge, it has not been proven.

241 *Francisco Franco*: "Francisco Franco," *Wikipedia*, https://en.wikipedia.org/?title=Francisco_Franco, 1. Fortunately for Spanish democracy, before Franco died at age 83, he named King Juan Carlos I to succeed him, and the king returned Spain to democracy.

241 *Tennessee Valley Authority*: See chapter 13.

Chapter 18. Pass to Paris, Farewell 581st, November 1945

248 *He also bought her*: I think Dad also bought Mom a small box of sample-size bottles of French perfume and souvenir French handkerchiefs in addition to the bottles of perfume and Swiss handkerchiefs he wrote about. I remember my sisters and I looking at these keepsakes when we were growing up and assuming they were mementos from the war. Mom saved them for her entire life.

251 *Alfried Krupp*: "Alfried Krupp von Bohlen und Halbach," *Wikipedia*, http://en.wikipedia.org/wiki/Alfried_Krupp_von_Bohlen_und_Halbach. In the Nuremberg war crimes trials, Alfried was tried and convicted of employing slave labor during the war, but his father was not tried due to ill health. He was sentenced to twelve years in prison and forfeiture of the company's property. However, he had served only three years when the American High Commissioner for Germany, John McCloy, had him pardoned and reversed the forfeiture of the company's property. According to articles in *The New Encyclopedia Britannica*, the company had also plundered property and plants in all of the countries Germany had occupied. Although Krupp had been ordered to sell about 75 percent of the value of its holdings, there were no buyers, and by the early 1960s, the company had regained its enormous value. However, Alfried's only son, Arndt, renounced his succession rights in 1966 in exchange for an annual stipend. After Alfried's death in

1967, the company "became a corporation wholly owned by a foundation called Alfried Krupp von Bohlen und Halbach-Stiftung." "Krupp GmbH" and "Krupp von Bohlen und Halbach, Alfried," *New Encyclopedia Britannica*, Vol. 7, 14–15.

253 *wooden box*: The wooden box and its contents always intrigued us when we were children. Dad told us some of the items had been made in underground factories in Germany.

CHAPTER 19. "PROCESSING," IN LIMBO, DEATH OF PATTON, DECEMBER 1945

265 *Again, he advised Mom*: His advice to Mom about not writing was wise. A letter she wrote to him on December 1 was forwarded from the 581st to the 84th Division and then returned to her in Jamaica at the end of the month.

269 *Based on other GIs' experiences*: See, for example, Roger A. Howard, *Call to Duty: A Personal Memoir of World War II*, edited and published by Pamela Howard Keagan (Indiana: AuthorHouse, 2010), 145. See also Porter Joyner and Martha Lanning Hughes, *Love & Kisses, Porter: 646 Letters Home from World War II* (Xlibris, 2010), 204

271 *asked my pediatrician*: I cannot confirm the exact sequence of events regarding this issue because Mom had passed away by the time I wrote this chapter. But she had told me many times that my illness had allowed Dad to come home early on an emergency furlough.

271 *On December 13*: Letter from American Red Cross, Central Chapter of Queens, dated December 13, 1945. Signed by Ruth L. Freeman, Supervisor, Communications.

274 *General Patton*: For a detailed account of Patton's accident and his last days, see Ladislas Farago, *The Last Days of Patton* (New York: McGraw-Hill, 1981). Chapters 18–23 recount the accident, the days leading up to his death, his final moments, his death, and the burial ceremony at the American Military Cemetery at Hamm in Luxembourg. For a brief account, see "George S. Patton," *Wikipedia*, http://en.wikipedia.org/wiki/General_Patton#Postwar, 18–19.

274 *Patton died*: Patton's wife, Bea, who had flown from the States to be with him, decided to have him buried alongside his men of the Third Army in the American Military Cemetery in Luxembourg, after the Army told her they had not returned any of the others home to be buried. She is quoted as saying, "I know George would want to lie beside the men of his Army who have fallen." His wife chose the cemetery in Luxembourg because that country was the site of the Battle of the Bulge, where her husband "had met some of the stiffest opposition and his Army had sustained the greatest casualties." Farago, *The Last Days*, 301. See also Alan Axelrod, *Patton: A Biography* (New

York: Palgrave Macmillan, 2006) for a more recent and concise treatment of Patton's life, including an analysis of his legacy and impact on the Army today. The controversies surrounding his accident and death continue. See, for example, *Killing Patton*, Bill O'Reilly and Martin Dugard (New York: Holt, 2014), which made the *New York Times* nonfiction bestseller list.

275 *where Patton's body lay in state:* Farago, *The Last Days*, 302.

Chapter 20. Emergency Furlough, Home!

277 *December 22*: Special Orders, Number 314, issued from Head Quarters 84th Infantry Division, APO 84, U.S. Army, 22 December 1945. The authorizing cable had been sent on December 19, 1945, and was received by Headquarters on December 22, effective December 23.

278 *Frank Greco*: The letter dated February 27, 1946, also told Dad that after his departure the 581st had been assigned to the trucking detail for the MCC, which Frank described as "hell." When the MCC's mission was completed, all of the documents were moved by train to Berlin, and the unit was transferred to Camp Herzog in Hessisch Lichtenau, which had been set up by the Germans to house German and foreign workers during the war. Depending on their number of points, the men were then dispersed to different divisions for processing and shipment home. As of late February, Greco's group of forty-six-pointers were in the 141st Division in Geislingen, about forty miles from Stuttgart, awaiting processing. The information that Frank conveyed to Dad about what happened to the MCC and its staff was later confirmed by receipt of documents from the Eisenhower Library in Abilene, Kansas, that I discovered had possession of them. In the "Operations Report," dated February 16, 1946, the Commanding Officer, Major Walter M. Barclay, reported that "during the month of January and early February" the unit provided security guards to "accompany each of the eight (8) trains which transported the MINISTERIAL COLLECTION CENTER documents and personnel to its new location in Berlin." It also noted that on February 5, 1946, the unit was relieved of its security mission of guarding the MCC.

Greco also enclosed notes from several others, including "Chocolate," "Phil. (Eddie)," and "Wick the Kid." He described the hilarious ways the men passed the time while in transit and waiting, which usually involved teasing Wick and "Frick." They especially enjoyed playing the spelling game of "Ghost" and made sure that Wick, who had a very poor education, got stuck with the most difficult words of all.

Wick's note to Dad was particularly touching. He recalled how they loved to sing the popular song "Bell Bottom Trousers," which was playing on the radio as he was writing. He said he would always remember "those days on the Hill, our snacks at Midnight and Guard [*sic*]." Reflecting the typical GI skepticism about official notices, he described as "a lot of Propaganda" a notice he had recently seen posted on the bulletin board that indicated the unit was starting to process.

278 *According to his official record*: Enlisted Record and Report of Separation, Honorable Discharge.

278 *Dad was officially separated*: Enlisted Record; Army of the United States Separation Qualification Record; Army of the United States Honorable Discharge.

279 *active service*: Enlisted Record and Report of Separation.

Epilogue

284 *He filed a disability claim:* Letter from Veterans Administration, April 25, 1946. The letter disallowed Dad's claim of impaired hearing and back injury, finding the injuries had not been "incurred in service in line of duty, or one that has been aggravated thereby, to a 10% or more degree." File number ADJ-C-9 942 877.

285 *letters of appreciation*: Two examples of customers who praised Dad's work are found in a letter from Mrs. Gladys Hopp, dated December 1967, and another from Solomon S. Dobin, n.d.

288 *Aunt Shirley read a poem*: See Appendix, "D-Day, 60th Anniversary, Thousand Oaks, CA."

289 *to deliver an American flag*: The flag was mounted in a beautiful triangular frame and prominently displayed in my sister Jonni's home in Tampa. She is currently in the process of moving and sent me this precious heirloom for safekeeping.

APPENDIX

D-Day, 60th Anniversary, Thousand Oaks, CA

For Abraham Martin Klapper (1915–2004)
T5, Battery A, 581st AAA, AW Bn,
49th AAA Brigade, First Army

Over two thousand miles between us now,
I sit in a suburban community park
on a green hillside surrounded by gardens
listening to a band play '40s tunes,
watching 80 plus year-olds standing at attention,
if they can still stand,
when the song of their branch of the service plays.
Everyone applauds them—
some wipe away tears.

The music makes me remember you, Dad,
jitterbugging with your kid sister Shirley,
throwing her over your back, never dropping her,
she always trusting you not to.
Now, at 89, in a nursing home in Florida,
unable to stand, let alone walk,
sometimes barely remembering Mom's name,

hardly able to hear my voice
over long distance lines,
all you say when I call is, "I can't hear you,
when are you coming?"
forgetting where I live,
"Can you get me out of here?"

On my bureau for the past 20 years
has been that '44 furlough shot
of you in your Army uniform,
smiling confidently, hat cocked to the side,
tie knotted smartly under the collar
of your khaki shirt,
antiaircraft command patch on your sleeve.
Handsome, broad shouldered,
you hold seven-month-old me,
wearing a wide-brimmed bonnet
and a baby-teeth grin,
in your muscular arms.
My 23-year-old, dark-haired, brown-eyed mother
holds onto your wrist as if she'll never let go.

Only a few years ago did you tell me
you'd been on the front lines
in an antiaircraft machine gun crew
defending the bridge at Remagen,
where the U.S. Army first crossed the Rhine.
In Germany, you became your unit's translator,
because the Yiddish you grew up with
was close enough to do the job.
In the countryside, when you entered homes
to search for weapons or enemy soldiers,
you said the inhabitants always sputtered,
"Me *nichts* Nazi,"

but when you saw a copy of *Mein Kampf*
in one house,
the residents refused to destroy it,
until you tore it up.

No lover of the military, you joined to fight
the Germans who were killing us there
so you wouldn't have to fight them here.
When you left Fort Dix after your discharge,
you refused to salute the last officer you saw,
but, today, Dad, it's my turn
to salute you!

—Bonnie Goldenberg
© 2004, 2020, 2022

SELECTED BIBLIOGRAPHY

WITH THE EXCEPTION OF a few important sources, this selected bibliography does not repeat the many internet sites or other articles I cited in the chapter notes and references. As the body of work on World War II seems endless, I have included here only material that provided relevant background to the events my father was writing about and those works I frequently consulted while writing this book. I have also included a few privately published and primary source documents.

Atkinson, Rick. *The Guns at Last Light: The War in Western Europe, 1944–1945*. New York: Henry Holt, 2013.
Axelrod, Alan. *Patton: A Biography*. New York: Palgrave Macmillan, 2006.
Beevor, Antony. *Ardennes 1944: Hitler's Last Gamble*. London: Viking, 2015.
___. *The Fall of Berlin 1945*. New York: Penguin, 2003.
___. *The Second World War*. New York: Little, Brown, 2012.
___. *Stalingrad*. London: Viking, 1998.
Bishop, Chris, and David Jordan. *The Rise and Fall of the Third Reich: An Illustrated History; Germany's Victories and Defeat 1939–1945*. London: Amber Books, 2005.
Citino, Robert. *The Wehrmacht's Last Stand: The German Campaigns of 1944–1945*. Kansas: University Press of Kansas, 2017.
Craig, William. *Enemy at the Gates: The Battle for Stalingrad*. Old Saybrook, CT: Konecky & Konecky, 1973.
D'Este, Carlo. *Patton: A Genius for War*. New York: HarperCollins, 1995.

Farago, Ladislas. *The Last Days of Patton*. New York: McGraw-Hill, 1981.

"Fort Stewart," *Wikipedia*, accessed September 16, 2011, http://en.wikipedia.org/wiki/Fort_Stewart#Anti-Aircraft_Artillery_Center.

Forty, George. *US Army Handbook 1939–1945*. New York: Barnes & Noble, 1995.

Fritzsche, Peter. *An Iron Wind: Europe Under Hitler*. New York: Basic Books, 2016.

Gilbert, Martin. *The Second World War: A Complete History*. London: Phoenix, 2009.

Grewe, Captain Eugene F. *The 581st Antiaircraft-Artillery-Battalion Looks at the Ministerial Collecting Center*. Written and arranged for Lt. Col. Robert G. Smith, Jr., Commanding the 581st AAA AW Bn. Mbl. Published by [U.S. Army] Information and Education, n.d.

Hart, Russell, and Stephen Hart. *Essential Histories: The Second World War (6); Northwest Europe 1944–1945*. Oxford: Osprey, 2002.

Hastings, Max. *Overlord: D-Day and the Battle for Normandy*. New York: Simon & Schuster, 1984.

Havers, Robin. *Essential Histories: The Second World War (2); Europe 1939–1943*. Oxford: Osprey, 2002.

Hechler, Ken. *The Bridge at Remagen*. New York: Presidio, 2005.

Hirshson, Stanley P. *General Patton: A Soldier's Life*. New York: HarperCollins, 2002.

Jones, Michael. *After Hitler: The Last Ten Days of World War II in Europe*. New York: New American Library, 2015.

Jordan, Jonathan W. *Brothers–Rivals–Victors: Eisenhower, Patton, Bradley, and the Partnership that Drove the Allied Conquest in Europe*. New York: New American Library, 2012.

Klapper, Martin. *From Four to Forty and Then Some*. Boulder, CO: Privately published memoir, 2012.

Michler, Manfred. *Die verhexte Brücke: Die Warheit über den Brückenkopf von Remagen*. Koblenz: Volker Thehos, 1992. Booklet purchased at Das Friedensmuseum Brücke von Remagen in 2004.

Miller, Donald L. *The Story of World War II: Revised, Expanded, and Updated from the Original Text by Henry Steele Commager*. New York: Simon & Schuster, 2006.

Moore, Deborah Dash. *GI Jews: How World War II Changed a Generation*. Cambridge, MA: Belknap, 2004.

National WASP WWII Museum. *Women Pilots of World War II*. Sweetwater, TX: Pamphlet published by Museum, n.d.

Norris, David A. "V-Mail: The GIs' Lifeline." *America in WWII*, December 2008, 40–43.

O'Brien, Phillips Payson. *How the War Was Won: Air-Sea Power and Allied Victory in World War II*. Cambridge, UK: Cambridge University Press, 2015.

Schwartz, Dianne, and Alte Schiller. *The Ancestry of the PHAIR Family Circle*. Privately published, October 1965. Retyped and footnotes added, September 1988. Footnotes updated and expanded, August 1991, by Harold Shultz and Nora Mandel.

Skylighters. Website of the 225th AAA Searchlight Battalion, accessed November 6, 2013, http://www.skylighters.org/longisland/upton.html.

Sladek, Karen. *Lucky Stars and Gold Bars: A World War II Odyssey*. Seattle: Penlyric Press, 2003.

Steinman, Louise. *The Souvenir: A Daughter Discovers Her Father's War*. New York: Plume, Penguin, 2002.

Swanston, Alexander, and Malcolm Swanston. *The Historical Atlas of World War II*. New York: Chartwell Books, 2010.

Timberlake, Brigadier General E. W. "Commendation on Performance in the Rhine, and Central German Campaigns." Addressed to Lt. Col. Joseph G. Howe, Commanding Officer, 581st AAA AW Bn, APO 230, U.S. Army, May 10, 1945.

Weinberg, Gerhard L. *A World at Arms: A Global History of World War II*. 2nd ed. New York: Cambridge University Press, 2005.

Weinberg, Gerhard L. *World War II: A Very Short Introduction*. Oxford: Oxford University Press, 2014.

White, Osmar. *Conquerors' Road*. Cambridge: Cambridge University Press, 2003.

Willmott, H. P., Charles Messenger, and Robin Cross. *World War II*. New York: DK Publishing, 2009.

Zerlin, Leonard. *World War II Memories*. Simi Valley, CA: Privately published, 1996.

Ziemke, Earl F. *Stalingrad to Berlin: The German Defeat in the East*. Washington, DC: Center of Military History United States Army, 1968.

Ziemke, Earl F. *The U.S. Army in the Occupation of Germany: 1944–1946*. Washington, DC: Center of Military History United States Army, 1985.

ACKNOWLEDGMENTS

I COULD NOT HAVE WRITTEN this book without the help of my sisters, Dr. Jonni Klapper and Havela Drucker. They have supported the project from the beginning, when I first received those shopping bags of letters from our mother. Jonni spent many hours on the phone with me, answering questions about details I did not know or remember. I am especially grateful to her for "rescuing" important memorabilia from my parents' garage when Mom was moving to a condo after Dad had been placed in an assisted living facility.

Dad's late youngest sister, Shirley Shultz, and Mom's late brother, Aaron Schein, provided valuable firsthand accounts of certain important incidents in my parents' story that were not described in their letters, documents, or other miscellaneous papers. I am so grateful for their contributions.

My husband, Merrill, listened patiently to my ideas and trepidations for many years, as I first began to organize the letters and then write. He was the impetus for our trip to Germany and visit to the bridge at Remagen that I describe in the Epilogue, and he shares my avid interest in World War II history. My son, Samuel, currently completing his doctoral thesis in political science, has always been an enthusiastic believer in his mother. Thanks for being by my side all this time.

Our family thanks our father's buddies from the 581st for their physical and emotional support when he was with them in Camp Stewart, Georgia, and then in England, Scotland, in transit to and in battle in Germany, and during the postwar occupation. Their sense of duty and loyalty to one another helped ensure Dad's survival and successful return home.

The Witty Women Writers group (the WWWs) from the Ventura County Writers Club listened to me read several chapters of this book while it was still in draft form. Cathryn Andresen, Kathleen Auth, Pat Caloia, Sheli Ellsworth, Carol Fogel, Lee Wade, and Claudette Young were my first audience. I knew I could trust their sympathetic ears and expect their encouragement, which they always gave me. They helped me believe this book would become a reality and not just a dream.

My cousin Harold Shultz and his wife, Nora Mandel, who has always embraced the PHAIR family as her own, have kept our family history alive and up-to-date not only by continually revising our original records but also by putting it online for all its members to share. Nora hosts the PHAIR website and posts news about us throughout the year. The group still holds annual meetings most years, although our numbers have diminished over time due to the passing of the older generations, lack of interest by some of the younger members, and geographical distance. Now that I live so far from most of the others, I especially appreciate Harold and Nora's efforts to keep me close to this strong, enduring family that always meant so much to my Dad.

Norm Klapper, son of my father's close first cousin, Martin Klapper, who also served in the U.S. Army, kindly gave me a copy of his father's memoir, *From Four to Forty and Then Some,* which included some important family history and photos. I especially appreciate Norm's permission to use two pictures that I found especially moving because they were taken just after my father returned from the war at the family seder he and my mother attended and at a PHAIR family circle meeting that spring.

The work of two authors, one of whom I personally met, was especially important to me because their books encouraged me to continue with mine. I met Karen Sladek and her late father, Lyle Sladek, a World War II veteran, when she spoke about her book, *Lucky Stars and Gold Bars: A World War II Odyssey,* at the Thousand Oaks library. Sladek's book is also based on her father's wartime letters, which recount his stateside training and flying over the "hump" in the China-Burma-India theater while working as a cryptographer. He, too, was stationed postwar in a variety of locations, including the Mediterranean and Europe, before finally being discharged in June 1946. His frustration at the many delays in being discharged after the war and at the inequalities in application of the point system mirrored my father's experience and feelings.

Louise Steinman's book *The Souvenir: A Daughter Discovers Her Father's War* grew out of her father's letters from the Pacific that she found while clearing out her parents' condo after their deaths. Like Karen Sladek's book, it provided a guide and inspiration that I could also write a book with the material I had been so fortunate to receive.

Jan Skutch and Julia Muller of the *Savannah Morning News* were kind enough to search for an updated URL for an article Jan wrote in April 2009 about the Housing Authority of Savannah, which I mentioned in my chapter about the Cherokee Homes, where my mother, grandmother, uncle, and I lived for a few months while visiting my father at Camp Stewart. I was excited to discover that Jan was still at the newspaper and want to thank him for taking the time to respond to my query. He made this part of my parents' story come even more alive to me.

I am grateful to Michelle Kopfer, an archives technician at the Dwight D. Eisenhower Presidential Library in Abilene, Kansas, for so promptly answering my request for information about the 581st that I discovered was stored in its library. She sent me copies of an "After Action Report" from June 1945 and an "Operations Report" from February 1946, after Dad had left to return home. The latter tracked what happened to the unit after the records and staff of the MCC were sent to Berlin, confirming what his friend Frank Greco had written to him in his letter that month. It was moving to see these official documents describing his unit's activities, which were only declassified in 1960.

Susan Leon was the first professional editor to review my manuscript and give it an overall evaluation. I appreciate her critique, suggestions, and advice about how to craft it into a better product.

When it was time to search for a copy editor, I was lucky to find Tammy Ditmore, who turned out to be even more than that. Her detailed, thoughtful work made me feel that I had a partner on this journey and was no longer flying solo. It's been a pleasure working with her.

Now to thank those who helped with the final production process to turn my raw manuscript into a book. The first step was to scan the many photos I wanted to include, some of which were very old and in poor shape, and for some of those I did not even have the originals. So I was fortunate to find Mitch Plessner of Plessner Digital & Archive, an experienced digital photographer and archivist, who was so careful with my treasured photos and worked so diligently to produce the best-quality scans possible. Thank you, Mitch, for your excellent work.

To coordinate the many production experts necessary to produce a book, I am so grateful to have found Marla Markman, my project manager. Her team included Karen Axelton, an experienced copywriter whose skills I admire, and who helped me craft the title of this book, my bio, and the back-cover book summary. The proofreading job fell to Cindy Doty and Wyn Hilty, whose diligent work I appreciate so much. Many thanks to Glen Edelstein, the talented artist who designed the book cover and interior design, and to Peri Gabriel who polished the final interior design and book cover. Kelly Cleary designed the beautiful logo for Sunset Hills Press reflecting the southern California landscape where I live. Thanks to Richard Sheppard who designed the specially tailored map illustrating my father's Army service in continental Europe, including Germany, patiently redrawing it several times to include the many elements I had requested. Last, but not least, thanks to Anne Fifer for creating the index for the book.

Thanks to Adanna Moriarty for designing my beautiful website, and the Authors Guild community whose members graciously shared their accumulated wisdom when responding to my requests for advice about social media and other publicity issues.

I have dedicated this book to my parents, and I want to thank them again for giving me this treasure. I am especially grateful to my mother for having saved my father's letters for so many years. They both seemed to know when they were writing to each other that they were witnesses to history, and that their personal letters would also be important to others in the future.

INDEX

A

AAA (Agricultural Adjustment Administration), 182, 315
AAA (antiaircraft artillery), 80
Abetz, Otto, 241, 319
acting sergeant, 23–24, 27–28
Adjusted Service Rating, 134
affordable housing. *see* Cherokee Homes
African-American soldiers, 43, 176–79
AGCT (Army General Classification Test), 14
AGF (Army Ground Forces) exam, 65
Agricultural Adjustment Administration (AAA), 182, 315
"Allied invasion" money, 113
Allies, 43, 46–47, 66, 96, 107, 112, 121, 122, 127, 135, 305
allotments, 31, 236–37
ALP (American Labor Party), 211, 316–17
America in WWII (article), 89
American and British culture, 95–96
American Labor Party (ALP), 211, 316–17
antiaircraft artillery (AAA), 80
anti-British rhetoric, 177–78, 235
antilabor sentiment, 233–34
anti-Semitism, 182
Antwerp, Belgium, 78
Ardennes Forest, 83

Army Directory Service, 114
Army Emergency Relief, 16, 25
Army General Classification Test (AGCT), 14
Army Ground Forces (AGF) Exam, 65
Army, segregation, 43, 176, 303-04
athletics, 155
atomic bombs, 193–95
AWOL soldiers, 29–31

B

basic training, 16–24
The Battle for Russia (sic: The Battle of Russia) (film), 48–49, 304
Battle of the Bulge, 83, 96, 306
Battle of the Hürtgen Forest, 83
Bavaria, 221–22, 228
Bayswater, Queens, 285–86
Belgium, 83
Belzec concentration camp, 77
Berlin, Germany, 46–47, 124, 127, 130, 288
bicycles, 250–51
bivouac, 28, 32, 61, 65–67, 135
black American soldiers, 43, 176–79
black market, 180, 207, 227
Board of Health, 31, 59
Boynton Beach, Florida, 288–91
bris (circumcision), 19
Britain, 174–75, 177–78
bull sessions, 233, 257, 268
buzz bombs, 80

C

Camp Führen, Germany, 166
Camp Herbert Tareyton, Le Havre, France, 277
Camp Herzog, Germany, 165
Camp Kilmer, New Jersey, 278–79
Camp Shanks, New York, 82, 312
Camp Stewart, Georgia, 41–52, 63–69, 75–83
Camp Teichhof, Germany, 165
Camp Upton, New York, 9, 13–15, 302
censorship, 80–84, 89, 96, 110, 124–25, 136, 202–3
chapel, 20–21
Cherokee Homes, 55–61
China, 203
Churchill, Winston, 43
CIC (Counter Intelligence Corps), 183–84
civilian jobs overseas, 232
classification examinations, 14
combat stress, 228
Congress, 217–21, 235, 254, 269
cooperative farming, 181–82, 208–11
corporal rank, 242
Counter Intelligence Corps (CIC), 183–84
Cross, Robin, 198
Crusade in Europe (Eisenhower), 107

D

D-Day, 65–66, 147
"D-Day, 60th Anniversary, Thousand Oaks, CA" (Klapper), 323
Delray Beach, Florida, 286
demobilization program, 202, 219. *see also* redeployment
discharge, basis for, 134–37
draft, 8–9, 180, 218–19, 232, 254

E

education program, 179
82nd Airborne, 270
84th Infantry Division, 258–59, 265–75
Eisenhower, Dwight D., 105, 107, 122, 134, 228
Ellman, Marty (Abe's cousin), 8, 208, 237, 315
emergency home furloughs, 243, 255, 271, 277–79
England, 95–101, 308
epidemics, 173–74
ETO (European Theater of Operations), 127, 244
Europa (German liner), 198
European Theater of Operations (ETO), 127, 244

F

Fabrik Hessisch Lichtenau, 165
farming, 181–82, 208–11
Farm Security Administration (FSA), 209
Far Rockaway, New York, 5–6, 24–25, 283–85
FHA loans, 269
Fifteenth Army, 228
First Army, 116–19, 125
The 581st Antiaircraft-Artillery-Battalion Looks at the Ministerial Collecting Center (booklet), 166–69, 313
581st antiaircraft unit, 105–8, 116–19, 166–69
Florida years, 286
Fort Dix, New Jersey, 268–69, 278–79

INDEX

Fort Eustis, Virginia, 15–34
Fort Meade, Maryland, 30
49th AAA Brigade, 168
France, 83, 105–6
Franco, Francisco, 241, 319
French and Russian refugees, 125–26
FSA (Farm Security Administration), 209
furloughs, 30, 59–61, 179, 227, 243, 247–49, 255, 271, 277–79
Fürstenhagen, Germany, 165, 288

G

Galicia, 301
Galitzianer, 6, 301
Garmisch-Partenkirchen, Germany, 225, 318
Geneva Convention, 167, 313–14
George Washington (ship), 155, 312–13
German Ministries and the Ministerial personnel, 168
German POWs, 118, 124, 185, 200
Germany
    after V-E Day, 179–81
    black market, 207
    civilians in, 110, 121–23, 132–33, 138–39, 145–48, 150–51, 153–55, 159–61, 165, 177, 182–86, 242, 249–53, 258
    death of Patton, 274–75
    Klapper in, 107-277
    mopping up, 126–28
    moving through, 122–26
    Potsdam Conference, 231–32
    readiness date preparation, 265–69
    rebuilding, 168–72
    redeployment delay, 269–73
    relations with, 182–86
    Seventh Army in, 149–61

V-E Day, 127–28, 129–31
GI Bill of Rights, 269, 283–84, 317
GI farm loan, 209
Goldcup operation ("Operation Goldcup"), 167–68
Great Britain, 235
Greco, Frankie, 136, 238, 278, 321
guard duty, 27–28, 207

H

Heidelberg, Germany, 223, 265–75
Helsa, Germany, 174–76, 184–85, 204–5, 227, 253–58
Hessisch Lichtenau, Germany, 258–59
Himmler, Heinrich, 125, 134–35
Hirohito (Emperor), 198
Hiroshima, Japan, 193–94
The History Place, 135
Hitler, Adolf, 105, 127, 135, 186, 311
Holland, 156–59
homebound units, 256
Housing Authority of Savannah, 55
Howe, Joseph, 56
Hunter Army Airfield, 60, 305

I

I & E (Information and Education) school, 221–22, 226–27
immigrant benevolent organizations, 76
immunizations, 14–15
India, 314
infiltration course, 28
inflation, 220
Information and Education (I & E) school, 221–22, 226–27
In Our Time (film), 147, 312
Italy, 29–30

J

Jamaica, Queens, 64, 80, 125, 136, 211–12, 257, 279
Janowska concentration camp, 284
Japan, 78, 112, 134, 141, 147, 172–73, 193–98, 203–5, 232
Jesup, Georgia, 67
Jewish co-op movement, 210
Jewish-style food, 20-21, 31
Jewish Welfare Board, 42, 44, 50
Jews, 2-3, 6, 19, 76–77, 112, 199, 238, 301

K

Kassel, Germany, 117, 165, 179–80, 249–53, 287–88
Kesselring, Albert, 105
Klapper, Abraham
    after his discharge, 283–84
    anticipating furloughs, 59–61
    basic training, 16–24
    birth of daughter, 24–28
    at Camp Stewart, 41–52, 63–69, 75–83
    at Camp Upton, 13–15
    carpentry business of, 284–85
    censorship, 81–84
    corporal rank, 242–44
    courtship, 5–9
    current affairs discussed by, 240–41
    D-Day invasion, 65–66
    84th Infantry Division, 258–59
    emergency home furlough, 277–79
    in England, 95–101
    farming future, 181–82, 208–11
    final visits to, 287–88
    in the First Army, 116–19
    Florida years, 286
    in France, 105–8, 247–49
    friends and comrades of, 237–40
    funeral for, 288–89
    German civilians, 110, 121–23, 132–33, 138–39, 145–48, 150–51, 153–55, 159–61, 165, 177, 182–86, 242, 249–53, 258
    in Germany, 107–277
    guard duty, 138, 145, 155, 166–7, 179, 207
    headstone for, 291
    in Holland, 156–59
    I & E School, 221–22, 226–27
    as interpreter, 108, 121–23, 139, 147–48, 154, 160, 169–70, 184, 251
    issues on the home front, 236–37
    Japan's surrender, 193–98
    lectures, 227, 231–34
    letter to Bonnie, 200–202
    letter-writing campaign, 217–21
    living conditions in Kassel, Germany, 249–53
    looking forward to civilian life, 131–34, 196–97, 211–12, 257–58
    maneuvers and memories, 28–34
    under military rule, 149–53
    mopping up, 126–28
    moving through Germany, 122–26
    Nazi operations, 199–200
    New Year, 90–92
    as orientation man, 151, 174–76
    in Paris, France, 247–49
    and Patton, 227–28, 274–75, 277
    point system, 134–37

against prejudice, 176–79
preparing for peacetime, 206–8
readiness date preparation, 265–69
rebuilding Germany, 168–72
recreational programs, 137–41
redeployment, 172–74, 234–36, 253–57, 269–73
Remagen bridge battle, 105–07, 202–3
in Scotland, 95–100
Seventh Army, 149–61
Thanksgiving 1943, 47–49
touring German towns, 221–25
on a transport ship, 87–88
V-E Day, 129–31
V-mail system, 88–90, 307
waiting for discharge, 215–17
Klapper, Bonnie Sue (Abe's daughter), 24–28, 67–69, 200–202, 323–25
Klapper, Ceil (Abe's aunt), 8, 301
Klapper, Lillian Schein (Abe's wife)
after Abe's discharge, 283–84
anticipating furloughs, 59–61
in Bayswater, Queens, 285–86
birth of daughter, 24–28
Cherokee Homes, 55–61
courtship, 5–9
death of, 289–91
emergency home furlough request, 243, 255, 271, 277–79
farming future, 208
finding work, 57–59
Florida years, 286
to Georgia, 50–52
issues on the home front, 236–37
in Jamaica, Queens, 64, 80
letters from, 29–30, 46, 95–96, 97–98, 122, 124–26

letter-writing campaign, 218
redeployment, 172–74, 254–55
relatives murdered by Nazis, 76–77
Thanksgiving 1943, 47–49
Victory gardens, 16–17, 302–3
Klapper, Louis (Abe's father), 7, 236–37
Klapper, Matthew Charles "Chuckie" (Abe's son), 285–86
Klapper, Miriam ("Mierke") (Abe's mother), 7
Klapper, Shirley (Abe's sister), 5–9, 115, 127
Klapper, Sylvia (Abe's sister), 5, 8
Klinefelter, Robert, 216–17
"Komm Zurück" ("Come Back") (song), 153, 312
Krupp, Alfried, 251–52, 319–20
Kuril Islands, 204

L

labor strikes, 233–35
landsleit organization, 76
Laval, Pierre, 240, 319
lectures, 227, 231–34
Lederle (pharmaceutical company), 59
Le Havre, France, 105–8, 277–78
letter-writing campaign, 217–21
Ley, Robert, 240, 319
life insurance, 269–70
living conditions in Kassel, Germany, 249–53
loans, 209, 269
London, England, 101
Long Island, New York, 67, 75
longshoremen's strike, 234–35
looting, 180–81
Ludendorff Bridge, 105–07, 287
Lützelsachsen, Germany, 266

Luxembourg, 83
Lwów, Poland, 76–77

M

MacArthur, Douglas, 204
MacEvoy Shipbuilding Corporation, 55
Manchuria, 203–4
maneuvers and firing range practice, 32–33
Manila, Philippines, 204
Mannheim, Germany, 223, 274
Marseille, France, 268
Maryland, 30
Mauldin, Bill, 211
MCC (Ministerial Collecting Center), 165–86, 287–88, 321
MCC booklet. *see The 581st Antiaircraft-Artillery-Battalion Looks At The Ministerial Collecting Center* (booklet)
McCray, Leo, 285
Mead, James (New York Senator), 218
Mein Kampf, 184, 325
Memorial Day, 141
Messenger, Charles, 198
militarism, 219
Ministerial Collecting Center (MCC), 165–86, 287–88, 321
Missouri Valley Authority (MVA), 241
Montgomery, Bernard Law (British Field Marshal), 127
Mussolini, Benito, 17, 127, 135
MVA (Missouri Valley Authority), 241

N

Nagasaki, Japan, 195
Nazis, 76–78, 112, 147–49, 150, 157, 159, 167–68, 199–200
"negro detachments," 43
New Brunswick, New Jersey, 278
Newport News, Virginia, 15–34
New York Port of Embarkation Army Post Office, 114
New York Post Office's Postal Concentration Center, 114
Niederweidbach, Germany, 136
Ninth Army, 131
nonfraternization policy, 145–46, 150, 175–76, 312
Normandy, 147, 257–58
Nuremberg Trials, 251–52, 319–20

O

Oberammergau, Germany, 222, 224–25
Occupational Troop Basis, 218
occupation forces, 196, 203, 205, 208, 218, 232, 235, 254
Officer Candidate School (OCS), 15, 27
Orangeburg, New York, 268
organized religion, 31
orientation lectures, 80–81, 95
orientation men, 151, 174–76
overseas mail and shipments, 114, 309

P

Pacific, 134, 141, 172–73. *See also* Japan
Paisley, Scotland, 95–100
parades, 77
Paris, France, 247–49
Passion Play, 222, 224, 317–18

Passover, 112
Patton, George S., 117, 227–28, 274–75, 318, 320–21
Peace Museum Bridge at Remagen, 287
peacetime, 206–8
peacetime draft, 232
Pearson, Drew, 228
People on Our Side (Snow), 174–75, 203, 314, 316
PHAIR Family Circle, 293, 303
Philippines, 78, 204, 306
Pidyon ha-Ben, 19
POE (Port of Embarkation), 83, 172
point system, 207, 216, 219, 235–36, 243–44
Pompano Beach, Florida, 286
Port of Embarkation (POE), 83, 172
Port Wentworth, 55–61
Potsdam Conference, 231–32, 318–19
prejudice, 176–79
PTSD, 228

Q

Queen Mary and *Elizabeth* (ships), 140, 308

R

race relations in the South, 43
Railway Mail Service (RMS), 206, 257, 316
Rangoon, Burma, 127
readiness date preparation, 265–69
recreational programs, 137–41
Red Cross, 13, 15, 19, 90, 96, 97, 99, 225, 243, 271
redeployment
    appealing to Congress, 217–21
    concrete news about, 255–57
    delay in, 235–36, 271–73
    labor strikes, 233
    packed and ready to go, 258–59
    point system, 207, 216, 219, 235–36, 243–44
    predictions, 243–44
    readiness date preparation, 265–69
    redeploymentitis, 253–55
    rumors of, 172–74, 234–36
reenlistment, 257
Reidsville, Georgia, 67
Reims, France, 130
Remagen, Germany, 105–07, 115, 118–19, 202–3
Remagen bridge battle, 105–07, 202–3
replacement troops, 256
Rhine River, 105–07
RMS (Railway Mail Service), 206, 257, 316
Rockaway Beach, New York, 80
Rockland County, New York, 82
Roosevelt, Franklin D. (President), 17, 121, 126
Rosh Hashanah, 31
Ruhr industrial region, 117
Russian relations, 97–98, 171–72, 177–78, 238–40
Russo-Japanese relations, 80, 172–73, 193–205

S

sanitation standards, 173–74
Savannah, Georgia, 41–52, 55–61, 63–69, 75–83
Schein, Aaron (Lillian's brother), 50, 56, 289
Schein, Lillian. *See* Klapper, Lillian Schein

Schein, Marcus (Lillian's father), 6, 25
Schein, Sophie (Lillian's mother), 6
Scotland, 95–100, 139–40
Seckenheim, Germany, 223
2nd Armored Group, 270
seder, 112
segregation, 43, 176–77, 303–04
Seventh Army, 149–61, 168, 172
70th Infantry Division, 170–71
sex hygiene, 14, 146, 272–73
Shanks, Orangeburg, New York, 268
681st Ninth Army, 226
Sixth Army, 127
Snow, Edgar, 174–75, 203, 314, 316
Soviet Union, 97–98, 122–28, 171–72, 177–78, 193–98, 203–4, 233, 238–40, 306
Spain, 241
special services units, 180
Stalin, Joseph, 46–47, 304
Stars and Stripes (newspaper), 66, 141, 145, 151, 178, 193, 253
St. Lawrence Seaway project, 241
Switzerland, 221, 227

T

T5 (technical corporal, technician fifth grade), 56
Tennessee Valley Authority (TVA), 241, 314
Third Army, 228
359th Infantry landing in Normandy, 257–58
Timberlake, E. W., 106–7, 110, 118–19, 168
transport ship, 87–88
Truman, Harry, 181, 303–4
TVA (Tennessee Valley Authority), 241, 314

U

uniforms, 14
United Nations, 125, 127
United Service Organizations (USO), 21, 42, 66, 154–55, 179–80
University Center in England, 209–10
unveiling ceremony, 290–91
The U.S. Army in the Occupation of Germany (Ziemke), 146, 179, 315
U.S. labor market, 254
USO (United Service Organizations), 21, 42, 66, 154–55, 179–80
U.S. Post Office, 114

V

VA (Veterans Administration), 209–10, 269, 284
Valkenburg, Netherlands, 177
Valkenburg Recreation Center, 156–59, 313
V-E Day, 129–31
venereal diseases, 13–14, 146, 272–73
Veterans Administration (VA), 209–10, 269, 284
Victory gardens, 16–17, 302–3
V-mail system, 88–90, 307
Volga-Stalingrad area, 199, 315

W

WAC (Women's Army Corps), 21, 146
Wagner, Robert F., 206, 218, 257
Wainwright, Jonathan (Lieutenant General), 204
Walden, New York, 227, 237
war crimes, 186, 240–41, 251–52

wartime housing projects, 64
wartime rationing and restrictions, 206–7
western front, 83, 98
Wickersham "Wick," 237–38, 321
Willmott, H. P., 198
Witzenhausen, Germany, 251
Women's Army Corps (WAC), 21, 146
World War II (Willmott, Messenger, and Cross), 198
WW2 US Medical Research Centre, 14

Y

Yank (magazine), 66, 209, 238
Yiddish, 7, 31, 108
Yom Kippur fast, 31
Your Hit Parade (music program), 243

Z

Ziemke, Earl F., 146, 179, 315

ABOUT THE AUTHOR

PHOTO BY MERRILL GOLDENBERG

BONNIE GOLDENBERG'S JOURNEY INTO World War II history began when she was given a treasure trove of letters her parents had exchanged during her father's service in a U.S. Army antiaircraft battalion from 1943 until 1945. Those letters became the foundation of this book.

Goldenberg is a poet whose works have been published in a variety of literary journals and anthologies. Before leaving her professional career to focus on raising her son, she was a labor attorney in New York and Washington, D.C., and a writer and editor for a legal publishing house in New York City.

In addition to writing, Goldenberg is the business administrator of her husband's biopharma startup. She and her husband live in Thousand Oaks, California.

www.ingramcontent.com/pod-product-compliance
Lightning Source LLC
Chambersburg PA
CBHW072045110526
44590CB00018B/3039